The Au
Kosher Dining Guide Series

The Authoritative

New York City

Bela Flom & Company
New York City

ISBN Number 0-9656896-2-X
Library of Congress Cataloging Pending

5759 / 1999 EDITION

Benjamin J. Flom, Editor

Published by:
Bela Flom & Company
P.O. Box 350201
Brooklyn, New York 11235-0201

Telephone: (718) 332-8547
Facsimile: (718) 769-5240
E-mail: mail@diningkosher.com

Cover art, title page, advertisements by Bela Flom
Computer graphics by Benjamin J. Flom

Printed in the U. S. A. By:
Moriah Offset Corp.
115 Empire Blvd. Brooklyn, N.Y. 11225, Tel: (718) 693-3800

Dedicated to my father
Moshe Schertz, זכרונו לברכה,
and my mother, Mina,
who together instilled within me a love of knowledge, and
whose devotion to Yiddishkeit will always remain an inspiring
example by which to live.

Table of Contents

Brooklyn

Southern Brooklyn

Flatbush & Midwood

Kings Highway

Western Brooklyn

Northern Brooklyn

Queens

South & Central Queens

Central Queens

North Eastern Queens

Staten Island

Northern Central Staten Island

Manhattan

Lower Manhattan

Midtown Manhattan

Villages & Vicinity

Upper West Side

Upper East Side

Bronx

Long Island

Westchester

Introduction

This new 5759/1999 edition of *The Authoritative New York City Kosher Dining Guide* is without doubt our best effort yet. The scope of coverage has been further increased and many new value-enhancing features have been added.

Thirty-three restaurants have closed in the past year, while fifty-five restaurants have been added. This large turnover rate reflects the dynamic nature of the current New York City kosher restaurant scene. Westchester, covered by The Guide for the first time this year, accounts for thirteen of these additions. What this means is that our consumers now have the benefit of authoritative kosher dining information for the whole New York City Metro region!

We are also happy to expand the restaurant discount program, initiated last year. As an extra special bonus to our readers, we have included the *Kosher Privilege Card* with the book. We expect that the card will make taking advantage of the discounts and Restaurant of the Month Club Specials that much easier and more convenient. Additional discounts may be added during the upcoming year, possibly going into areas beyond dining. Be sure to check our web site or our newsletter the *Kosher Dining Times* for the latest information. While some would consider a program of this caliber to be a great product in itself, we offer the card to our readers at no extra cost in the hope that we can encourage diners to eat out more frequently. Ultimately we hope to raise the stands of kosher restaurants on the whole and at the same time, to encourage even more restaurants of a higher caliber to open. This would not only increase support for our community, but would also, extend the dining choices available for everyone to enjoy.

Our internet site, www.diningkosher.com, is another innovation introduced last year. This web site allows us to provide *Guide* users with updated restaurant information between printed editions. This ongoing support to our readers sets *The Authoritative Kosher Dining Guides* apart from not only kosher guides, but all dining guides published. Our diners get the most relevant, up-to-date information anywhere. With thousands of visitors a month, our web site promises to evolve into an independent center of entertainment news that will focus on events that will be of interest to Jewish consumers. This unique integration of electronic and printed media is quite an exciting innovation, whose benefits we are just beginning to exploit.

A Word of Thanks

To Benjamin Joseph Flom for not only editing *The Guide,* but for his tireless work in web site design, marketing, book distribution, billing, designing many ads and countless other business related help, my heart felt thanks and appreciation. He also, designed and produced many of the pages with computer graphics in the guide. To my husband Bernard for proofreading and assisting with editorial duties.

A special recognition is also forthcoming to my brother, Rabbi Dr. Chaim E. Schertz of the well known Orthodox Congregation Kesher Israel in Harrisburg, Pennsylvania. A renowned Torah and Talmudic scholar, he is always there to answer my questions with exceptional expertise.

Bela Flom

Our Intent

The goal of the Kosher Dining Guide is to provide the kosher eating public with the most comprehensive, relevant, and current source of kosher restaurant information possible. The particular needs of the kosher eating community are met by not only listing the restaurants; but by identifying the authority certifying each restaurant, noting claimed certification details, and providing contact information for the kashrus supervisors so any further information can easily be gotten. The information should be useful, honest, truthful, unbiased, and unencumbered, to enable a prospective diner to intelligently discern those restaurants that will best suit his or her needs.

To eliminate any confusion behind a restaurant's claim of kashrus, we include all restaurants that are labeled or present themselves as kosher. We do not discriminate against Reform, Conservative, or Orthodox standards or those claiming kashrus via New York State certification. While recognizing that the degree of strictness varies by hashgacha, we do not attempt to judge or suggest that one group's parameters are necessarily superior to those of another. **Defining what is or is not kosher, and what is an acceptable level of strictness in kashrus observance, should be done by an individual with the help of his or her Rabbi.** For the Orthodox, we elaborate on stringent and lenient aspects of the kosher certification as represented by the certifier.

We recognize that a restaurant not being closed during the Sabbath may be enough for some to distrust its kashrus. Without assessing the merit of such a position, but out of respect to those who do live by it, we clearly identify those restaurants whose **hours of business** include the Sabbath as, **"RESTAURANT IS OPEN 7 DAYS A WEEK."** This is done in two areas on the page: once by the hashgacha, and once by the hours of business. It is noted twice to insure that this fact is not possibly overlooked by a concerned party and to avoid any possible ambiguity as to whether an establishment is opened or closed. **In this designation we do not take into account any considerations other than the hours of business for a particular establishment.** We do not in any way imply by this designation that the restaurant, and/or those individuals involved with the operation of the restaurant, the owners, the managers, the employees, the mashgiach, or the hechsher organization, are not Shommer Shabbos. **One should not feel on the basis of anything contained within this publication, that such a designation indicates a lower level of observance of, or vigilance to, the laws of Kashrus.** We cannot, would not, and do not represent such a point of view, as our guide does not take a position on such issues.

It should also be noted at this time, that **even by some orthodox standards, legitimate halachic arguments can be made for allowing certain kosher restaurants to remain open on Shabbos under very specific and strict conditions.**

Although we identify a restaurant's kosher supervision, and have to the extent possible verified that the supervision in fact certifies the restaurant, **we do not in any way certify that a place is kosher, or guarantee any level of kashrus or any aspect of kashrus for any restaurant.** Diners with questions about the kashrus of a particular restaurant should directly contact the restaurant or its certifying rabbi or organization. Information for this is included in the book.

Our restaurant reviews are personal, stem from our experiences with these restaurants, and reflect our demanding and discriminating standards. We acknowledge that every restaurant can have a bad day, and so we offer our reviews as only one factor for you to consider when making your dining decisions. Our reviews will always remain objective and will never be influenced by offers of free meals, discounts, advertising, or any other consideration.

Every reasonable effort has been made by us to locate all the kosher establishments within NYC, Long Island, and Westchester right up to the date of publication. Factual information is obtained directly from the restaurants and appears in the guide faithfully, without any prejudice or malice on our part. Incorrect or changed information that comes to our attention will appear corrected in future printings, and will be immediately posted as corrections on our web site. We may have unknowingly omitted a kosher restaurant. Exclusion from our guide does not imply that a restaurant is not kosher. Overlooked restaurants, as they become known to us, and new restaurants which may have opened after our publication date, will appear in upcoming editions. No kosher restaurant is deliberately excluded from our guide. **We feel it is our** obligation to report on every restaurant that presents itself as kosher.

What is State Certification?

New York State has a statute addressing anything within the state that is sold and represented as kosher. To ensure truth in kosher advertising, these guidelines, which are "in accordance with Orthodox Hebrew religious requirements," were established in 1879, by NY State and are under the jurisdiction of the Board of Agriculture and Markets, Dept. of Kosher Law Enforcement. Any restaurant wishing to affix the word kosher (or parve) to its name or advertise itself as being kosher (or parve), must adhere to these guidelines or face stiff penalties and public exposure. Within these criteria is the requirement that the restaurant must submit to inspections by state agents, whose duty it is to report any kashrus transgressions they may witness as defined by state law. Inspections may take place 4-6 times per year depending on the restaurant's location: the more remote the location the fewer number of visits it receives.

Some restaurants within *The Guide* maintain that they adhere strictly to the kosher laws and guidelines as set forth by New York State, but do not have any rabbinic hechsher. We make note of this fact and refer to them as having no hechsher.

The Guide recognizes that some individuals could **incorrectly** assume that the Guide is validating the kashrus of all the restaurants within its covers or that it may question others. It must be stressed, again, that this is not the case.

Restaurant Discounts

Many restaurants have volunteered to offer dining incentives (see bottom of each restaurant page) to those who show the current year's edition or the new "Kosher Privilege Card." The discount or other offer may be used repeatedly through November 30, 1999 unless otherwise noted. If additional discounts are added during the year, they will be posted on our web site or in our monthly newsletter, the *Kosher Dining Times*.

IN ALL CASES, DISCOUNTS ARE AVAILABLE <u>ONLY</u> TO DINERS WHO PHYSICALLY PRODUCE *THE AUTHORITATIVE NEW YORK CITY KOSHER DINING GUIDE* (CURRENT EDITION) OR THE CURRENT *KOSHER PRIVILEGE CARD*. AS A COURTESY, PLEASE DO THIS BEFORE BILLING, SO THE CHARGES DO NOT HAVE TO BE COMPUTED TWICE. NO INCENTIVES WILL BE EXTENDED TO DINERS WHO CANNOT SHOW THE GUIDE OR THE CARD. IN MOST CASES, DISCOUNTS IN THE GUIDE CANNOT BE APPLIED TO OR BE COMBINED WITH ANY OTHER DISCOUNTS OR SPECIALS OFFERED BY THE RESTAURANT. <u>PLEASE NOTE: TAX AND GRATUITIES ARE NEVER INCLUDED IN ADVERTISED PRICES, SPECIALS, OR DISCOUNTS.</u>

Restaurants will be reminded about their discount offers, and will instructed to make sure all their employees are informed of them. This year restaurants will receive "Kosher Privilege Card" decals for display in their windows or doors to be placed next to the charge cards they accept. Look for these decals and patronize those restaurants that display them. We do not anticipate any problems. However, should any arise, we wish to apologize in advance for any inconvenience you may experience. We ask diners to contact us if they are unable to receive a discount that has been printed in *The Guide*. In every case, restaurant management has signed an agreement with us to honor their offer(s).

A GUIDE TO THE GUIDE

The **Quick Reference Symbols** give you pertinent information at a glance. With them you can quickly decide which restaurants are suitable at that moment, and which are not (e.g. a dairy restaurant when you can only eat meat, or an expensive restaurant when you are short of funds).

Handicap Information: The handicap symbol in this book indicates that the main dining area and bathrooms are on street level or at most one step above street level. **It does not necessarily mean that a restaurant has a handicap ramp or bathroom facilities or stalls**. This is done to allow disabled diners to have the greatest number of restaurant choices at their disposal. Readers should refer to comments on the restaurant page for further clarifications as to what they can expect. However, severely handicapped individuals and wheelchair bound diners should call the restaurant in advance to verify a restaurant's specific handicap accommodations.

Hechsher: This identifies the individual, or organization, which certifies the establishment is Kosher. In parentheses are any stringencies or leniencies that further describe the certification of that particular restaurant. The Hashgacha Directory has contact information to allow you to direct any kashrus queries to the proper supervising authority. Our Intent has further information.

Address: Establishments are arranged by location. Primarily they are divided into neighborhoods, ordered firstly from southernmost to northernmost and then from westernmost to easternmost. An alphabetical index of restaurants is included in the back of the book. This will help you find an eatery if you already know the name, or inform you if a restaurant of a certain name exists.

Price Ranges: Prices are listed from the lowest priced item to the highest, most prices fall toward the middle. The ranges are a gauge for how much you can expect to spend at a given restaurant. We did not feel it necessary to give all the prices, for evaluation. Unless otherwise noted "Drinks" are non alcoholic.

Ambiance (Decor): Informs you of proper attire, degree of formality, and the atmosphere, if any, you can expect.

Comments: Reviews to help guide your choices.

Hours: The hours listed reflect, those in effect at the time we went to print. Hours, however, are subject to change. If you are pushing the limit of a restaurant's closing time, it would be wise to call ahead to make sure that they will be open, and will serve you when you plan to arrive.

The Restaurant Of The Month Club

The Restaurant of the Month Club has evolved into a month long celebration of fine dining at New York City's best kosher restaurants. Each month our diners are offered a Prix Fixe meal, often at substantial savings, at different restaurants throughout the city. This offer is exclusive to Guide purchasers with the *Kosher Privilege Card* or latest guide edition. In the past sophisticated kosher diners looked with horror at the state of kosher eateries and with the meager selection of fine kosher available to choose from -- but no longer! Today the quality and the variety of options have increased and with the club, experiencing these has been made easier.

All are welcomed to take advantage of these fabulous meals, gourmands and novices alike. Announcements of Club Specials are often appear in our newspaper ads, our newsletter, the *Kosher Dining Times*, and are posted on our web site, **www.diningkosher.com.** Check these sources regularly for all types of upcoming events. If you would like more information about our club activities, you can also call, fax, mail or e-mail us.

The Authoritative
New York City Kosher Dining Page
On the Web
www.diningkosher.com

Updated **Kosher** **Dining** **Guide** **Information** :

In our pursuit to ensure that readers have the most current, up-to-date dining information at their disposal, *The Authoritative New York City Kosher Dining Guide* has created a web site. We are acutely aware of the fact that the restaurant industry is highly volatile, with establishments constantly opening and closing. Our response to this situation, www.diningkosher.com, will keep readers informed about restaurant closings, changes in hechsher, and any other changes taking place during the course of the year, between printed editions of *The Guide*.

Updates on the site are organized by the page numbers in the book, followed by the name of the restaurant, and then the specific changes to the printed material. Links at the top of the page allow one to narrow a search to a specific area.

The updates are posted regularly, as we become aware of changes that occur. Readers are encouraged to contact us with any information that they are privy to, and that has not already been posted. This will allow us to share it with all guide users.

Readers who do not have access to the internet, but would like to receive by mail our newsletter, the *Kosher Dining Times,* which also has the updated material, should contact us. The *Kosher Dining Times* is available for the nominal fee of $8.95 to cover printing and mailing costs.

Articles about Dining Out and Cuisine :

Periodically we will post articles about matters relevant to Kosher diners, as issues present themselves. This can include items ranging from the latest in kashrus and hashgacha information, to information about new wine vintages, to new kosher trends or fads popping up in restaurants. Article submissions from outside sources will be considered, so if you have something to say about kosher dining or kashrus in general, and offer some proof of expertise in the field you're addressing, we will consider publishing the article on our site.

Our Bulletin Board :

Readers are invited to post their comments. We welcome feedback on *The Guide*, descriptions of any restaurants, details of any dining experiences, questions about kosher dining, or anything else of relevance on your mind. Receive replies to your postings from all over the world, and respond to others' comments. We hope you take advantage of this opportunity to sound off and let us know what you are thinking. We look forward to hearing from you. Tell the world!

Final Note

Trying out a new restaurant is always an adventure. You must be open minded and receptive to new experiences to fully appreciate the special features of each one. There may be times when you come away not completely satisfied, but that is part of trying new things. This restaurant guide attempts to lessen the number of unsuccessful dining excursions and to insure, at the very least, that the surprise element is at a minimum.

In response to questions of why we do not use a rating system, we're not enamored with rating designations because they don't really say much about a restaurant. We feel they are inherently unfair to the restaurants and would only serve as a distraction, rather than a resource. Many restaurants would suffer as people would only notice the ratings and fail to read the reasoning behind them. All restaurants have both good and bad aspects, which would be obscured by a simple rating. Conversely, we also want to avoid lionizing restaurants that may be good overall, but may have certain deficiencies that should be recognized. All restaurants have good and bad days, and even individual dishes are subject to a host of variables each time they are prepared. Because of its brevity, a rating system has inherent limitations that preclude it from being useful. A symbol simply cannot embody everything that needs to be said.

Also, a reader's discretion may differ from ours. He or she may not agree that our criticisms are deficiencies, or regard our accolades as noteworthy. We feel a more fair system is to require everyone to fully read our views. This should best enable readers to formulate their own informed opinions.

We have done our best to make this guide helpful, and hope that you find it easy and enjoyable to use.

So, what are you waiting for?................. Eat and enjoy!

Gravesend
Sheepshead Bay
Flatlands

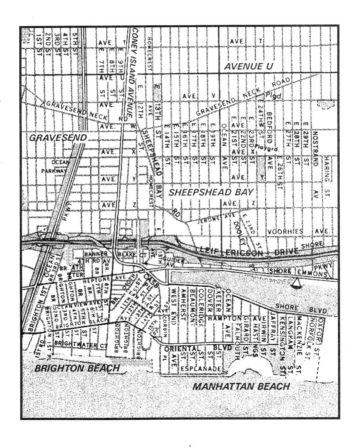

Borough: Brooklyn
Section: Gravesend

The Authoritative New York City Kosher Dining Guide

Restaurant: Fuji Hana   *Phone Number:* (718) 336-3888
                            Fax: (718) 376-5556
Address: 512 Avenue U (bet. E. 5ᵗʰ St. - Ocean Pkwy.)

Hechsher: Vaad Harabbanim of Flatbush (Glatt Kosher)

Proprietor/Manager: Mr. Izzy Gindi

Type(s) of Food: Meat - Japanese

Price Range:	*Lunch*	*Dinner*	*Take out*
Entrées:	$4.95-$13.95	$6.95-$22.95	Same - Delivery Available
Desserts:	$3.95-$4.95	*Special Bento Box Lunch:* $10.95	
Drinks:	$1.50-$3.00	$3.50-$4.50/gl (Wine) $3.50 (Beer)	

Food Specialties: Sushi, Sashimi, Special Boats, Teriyaki, Tempura, Noodle Entrées

Description: All entrées served with Green Salad or Miso soup, rice and Green Tea. Food is modified to taste. Children's portions are available. Kosher saki. Complete sushi, Sashimi and Maki selections. The Bento Box Lunch includes salad, miso soup and entrée with white rice.

Comments: For the uninitiated, this can be an opportunity to explore exciting new cuisine that is attractively displayed and served in generous portions. This time we ordered and can recommend the fresh House Salad, Noodle Soup, Sushi, and the generous Chicken Ramen. The combination of Chicken & Beef Teriyaki was flavorful, although the beef slices in the dish inexplicably ran the gamut from being very delicious to being dry. The Ice Cream Tempura would be better without as much oil. The sushi was fine. All in all, a reasonably satisfying meal.

Ambiance (Decor): The interior is elegant, attractive, and serene with crème colored walls that serve as canvases for murals of Japanese landscapes. The pleasurable setting is tastefully appointed for semi or informal dining. Spacious L-shaped room, seats 100 and tends to be noisy with nothing in the room to absorb sounds. Sushi bar. Full Bar.

Service: Competent and attentive

General Comments: A pleasant family restaurant, that is popular with singles on Thursday nights. Arrive early in the evening for the best service and for food at its optimum.

Hours: Sun-Thurs: 12pm-11pm   **Friday Closed**   Sat: 1 hr aft Shabbos till ? Call

Credit Cards Accepted: MC, Visa, Diners Club, Carte Blanche

Restaurant Discount:

Borough: Brooklyn
Section: Sheepshead Bay

The Authoritative New York City Kosher Dining Guide

Restaurant: Jay and Lloyd's Kosher Deli and Family Restaurant
Phone Number: (718) 891-5298
Fax: None
Address: 2718 Avenue U (bet. E. 27ᵗʰ St. - E. 28ᵗʰ St.)

Hechsher: NO HECHSHER - RESTAURANT IS OPEN 7 DAYS A WEEK

Proprietor/Manager: Jay and Lloyd

Type(s) of Food: Meat - Deli, Jewish American

Price Range:　*Lunch* (11am-3pm)　*Dinner*　*Take out*
　Entrées: $5.95-$7.95(Special)　$8.95-16.25　Same -Delivery Available
　Desserts: $1.95-$2.50　*Sandwiches:* $5.25-$8.95, $5.95-$11.95 (Hot Open)
　Drinks: $ .75-2.50, $2-$2.50 (Beer) *Kid's Menu:* $4.95-$5.95
　　Lite Menu: $7.95-$12.95　*Complete Dinner:* $5.25 + Entrée

Food Specialties: Steak Tidbits, Roast Chinese Style Veal, BBQ Steak Tidbits

Description: They have a Vegetarian/Lite Menu (14 choices, some with poultry), Dinner Specials, Daily Lunch Specials (11 choices, e.g. Hot Open Sandwich with French fries and beverage $7.95, or Vegetarian Lasagna with garlic bread), and From Our Char-Broiler (Jumbo Rib Steak smothered in onions or Tender Baby Lamb Chops w/ Mint Jelly). The food is homemade, and baking is done on premises. All deli is Hebrew National. The Kid's Menu includes fountain soda, fries, and an onion ring.

Comments: A restaurant catering to families. Their motto: "Let us feed you with…warmth, kindness and deli in your belly!" The Kid's Menu, for diners under 10, doubles as a game sheet.

Ambiance (Decor): The dining area is set apart from the take-out counter reducing congestion and increasing diner comfort. The spacious mid-sized room has a clean, well-kept appearance. Laminated tables and tile floor offer a childproof environment.

Service: Standard

General Comments: A family restaurant that goes out of its way to make dining here a fun experience for even the smallest member of the family with games and toy giveaways.

Hours: Sun-Sat: 10am-10pm - RESTAURANT IS OPEN 7 DAYS A WEEK

Credit Cards Accepted: MC, Visa, AmEx

Restaurant Discount:

Borough: Brooklyn
Section: Sheepshead Bay

The Authoritative New York City Kosher Dining Guide

Restaurant: Tokyo of Brooklyn   *Phone Number:* (718) 891-6221
                                     Fax: None
Address: 2954 Avenue U (bet. Nostrand Ave. - Haring St.)

Hechsher: Rabbi Elbaz (Glatt Kosher, Mashgiach Temidi)

Proprietor/Manager: Roger

Type(s) of Food: Meat - Japanese

Price Range: *Lunch*   *Dinner*   *Take Out*
  Entrées: Closed $18.95-$26.95 $11.95-$23.95 Delivery Available
  Desserts: $ 2.95-$5.75   *Children's Dinner:* $11-$12.95
  Drinks: $2.00-$2.50 $3 (Beer), $2.95-$2.50 (Mixed Drinks), $3/gl (Wine)

Food Specialties: Hibachi Dinners & Combinations, Sushi & Sashimi, Tempura

   Description: Hibachi Dinners include soup, house salad with ginger dressing,
      hibachi vegetables, steamed rice and green tea. The entrée offerings list
      chicken, sirloin steak, tuna, sole, salmon, faux shrimp, and duck. Sushi
      & Sashimi Rolls $2-$5.25/ea. Full bar.

   Comments: Introducing kosher Hibachi and its characteristic cooking
      calisthenics featured at one's table. Of the appetizers, Chicken Negimaki
      or the Tempura are very good. Clear soup, with its mushrooms and
      scallions was agreeable and the best choice. The "Filet Mignon" &
      Chicken Combo were cooked to perfection. **Note:** Do not order the meat
      well done, as it will come out too dry. You can also ask the chef to vary
      the vegetable sides. The sushi is okay.

Ambiance (Decor): The traditional Japanese theme is played in a dimly lit room with
   black walls, latticed ceiling, red carpeted floor and wood latticed room dividers.
   The 8 hibachi tables with their integrated cook tops seat either 8 or 4 in the
   main dining area. The full bar area off the entry has banquette seating and 5
   small wood bar tables for 2. The rear sushi bar seats 25. Lower level restrooms.

Service: Accommodating

General Comments: The experience is what makes the trip!

Hours: Sun-Thurs: 3pm-12pm   **Friday Closed**   **Sat:** 1 hr after Shabbos till 1am

Credit Cards Accepted: MC, Visa, AmEx, Discover, Diners Club

Restaurant Discount: 15% Off

4

Borough: Brooklyn
Section: Flatlands

The Authoritative New York City Kosher Dining Guide

Restaurant: Mill Basin Kosher Deli & Fine Art Gallery *Phone Number:* (718) 241-4910 *Fax:* (718) 241-4389
Address: 5823 Avenue T (bet. E. 58ᵗʰ St. - E. 59ᵗʰ St.)

Hechsher: Rabbi Leonard Bronstein - RESTAURANT IS OPEN 7 DAYS A WEEK

Proprietor/Manager: Mark Schachner

Type(s) of Food: Meat - Deli

Price Range:

	Lunch	Dinner	Take out
Entrées:	$10.95-$17.95	Same	Same - (Free local Delivery)
Desserts:	$2.50-$2.95	*Sandwiches:* $5.75-$11.25 (Combo)	
Drinks:	$1.10-$1.50, $2.25-$4 (Beer), $3.50-$3.75/gl, $13-$18/btl (Wine)		

Food Specialties: Sandwiches, Broiled Prime Rib, Brisket, London Broil

> *Description:* Deli menu with the main focus on sandwiches of every variety such as: Chinese Style Roast Veal (on garlic bread with duck sauce), Chickwich (half roast chicken), Sweet & Spice Delight (white turkey breast & pastrami with Russian dressing and cole slaw) and the Guyisha Special (an overstuffed club sandwich of turkey, roast beef, hard salami, lettuce, tomato, onion & mayo). All sandwiches are served with homemade cole slaw and pickles.

> *Comments:* Extensive sandwich selection.

Ambiance (Decor): This is an old fashioned deli with a twist: it doubles as an art gallery. Original artworks, which are for sale, are displayed around the room for your enjoyment while you eat. Exhibits change every three months and feature original art by artists such as Erté and Chagal. There is even a "museum gift shop" that sells posters, etc. Seating for 120 people. The backdrop is set in warm tones of beige, coffee and orange, rust. Informal.

Service: Standard

General Comments: Now you can satiate your stomach and soul at the same time.

Hours: **Sun-Sat:** 9am-9pm - RESTAURANT IS OPEN 7 DAYS A WEEK

Credit Cards Accepted: MC, Visa

Restaurant Discount: 10% Off In Dining Room Checks Only
Not To Be Combined With Any Other Discounts or Coupons

Borough: Brooklyn
Section: Southern Brooklyn Pizzerias

The Authoritative New York City Kosher Dining Guide

Flatlands:

Dagan Pizza   *Tel:* (718) 209-0636
1560 Ralph Avenue
Vaad Harabbanim of Flatbush

Kings Highway
& Vicinity
Bensonhurst

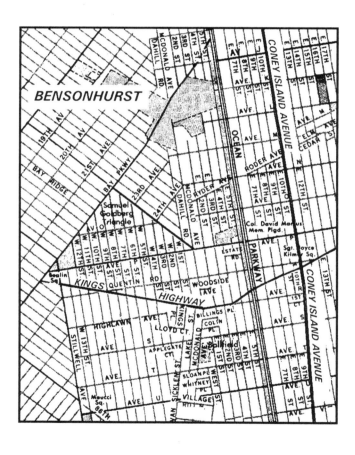

Borough: Brooklyn
Section: Kings Highway

The Authoritative New York City Kosher Dining Guide

Restaurant: Lou's Delicatessen

Phone Number: (718) 627-3180
Fax: (718) 376-2213

Address: 514 Kings Highway (bet. E. 2nd St. - E. 3rd St.)

Hechsher: Rabbi Israel Steinberg

Proprietor/Manager: Louie & Ruth

Type(s) of Food: Meat - Delicatessen

Price Range:

	Lunch	Dinner	Take out
Entrées:	$10.95-$19.95	Same	Free Delivery ($40 min.)
Desserts:	$1.50-$2.25	Sandwiches: $5.50-$9.95, $12.50 (Hot Open)	
Drinks:	$ .75-$1.50, $2.95-$3.50 (Beer)	Combos: $9.75-$9.95	

Food Specialties: Deli Sandwiches, Steaks, Prime Cut Roast Beef, Lamb Chops

Description: A traditional deli menu based on sandwiches and the obligatory entrées, such as Hungarian Goulash, Stuffed Derma, Stuffed Cabbage, Braised Fresh Brisket, Boiled Chicken in a Pot and Prime Cut Roast Beef (in natural gravy). However, Entrée Specials meander somewhat to include a few non-traditional items like Pepper steak, Chow Mein or Veggie Burgers. Eggs & omelets offer breakfast possibilities.

Comments: The Corned Beef is very lean and the Pastrami slightly less so. Quality is top notch, as is the flavor. Deli is among the best in the city.

Ambiance (Decor): Mirrors cover the walls and visually enlarge the dining room. In spite of all the reflection, however, the room remains comfortably lighted. The standard set-up begins with the display/service counter running along the left wall and tables alongside the right. Additional tables are in the back. Casual.

Service: Friendly, old fashioned hospitality.

General Comments: 40 years in the business, in what may be the oldest continuously owned and operated mom and pop deli in New York City. Lou knows all his customers (sometimes several generations) and personally welcomes everyone into his establishment. Bragging rights that have been earned: "We're not the best because we're the oldest, we're the oldest because we're the best!"

Hours: **Sun-Thurs:** 9:30am-9:30pm **Fri:** 9am-2 hrs before Shabbos **Sat. Closed**

Credit Cards Not Accepted: CASH ONLY!

Restaurant Discount:

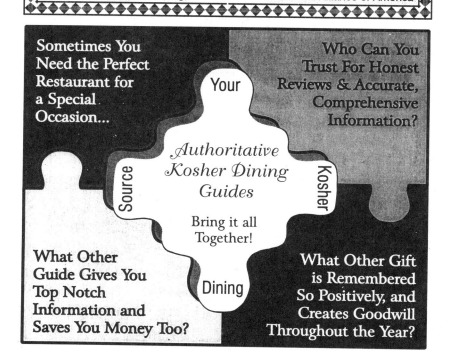

Borough: Brooklyn
Section: Kings Highway

The Authoritative New York City Kosher Dining Guide

Restaurant: Carmel (Name expected to change)   *Phone Numbers:* (718) 339-0172
                                                                   (718) 339-9553
Address: 523 Kings Highway (bet. E. 2ⁿᵈ - E. 3ʳᵈ St.)   *Fax:* (718) 645-6866

Hechsher: Vaad Harabbanim of Flatbush (Glatt Kosher)

Proprietor/Manager:

Type(s) of Food: Meat - Israeli, Middle Eastern

Price Range: *Lunch*   *Dinner*   *Take out*
   Entrées: $11.00-$15.00   Same   Same-Delivery Available
   Desserts: $1.75-$3.00   *Breakfast:* $5.50
   Drinks: $ .75-$1.50 $2.00 (Malt Beer)

Food Specialties: Grilled Steaks, Fish, Shish Kebob, Salads

> *Description:* The steaks and the various kabobs are generally of good quality
> and come with two side dishes from a selection of: super fresh salad,
> rice, beans, fries, okra and vegetable cous-cous. The soups have a
> homemade flavor and are freshly made; vegetable is a personal favorite.
> The fish portions are large, the quality is good and the flavor usually
> does not disappoint. Carefully prepared, the food is neither overcooked
> nor dry. Both whole fish and fish fillets are available. Daily specials.

> *Comments:* The grilled foods are well prepared, as is the falafel, chummus,
> and techina. Portions are large and filling.

Ambiance (Decor): The feeling of an outdoor cafe is suggested by a decorative
awning overhanging the service counter in the rear and tables covered by cloths
and topped with glass arrayed in front (seats 70). Though now a Middle Eastern
theme, a new motif is planned for later this year. The anticipated
metamorphosis will add space for entertainment. For family and informal
entertaining.

Service: Usually competent and friendly

General Comments: A fixture on this corner for many years, the restaurant continues
to reinvent itself. Expect changes in the name, management, and menu.

Hours: **Sun-Thurs:** 11am-12am **Fri:** 11am-3pm
   Sat: Opens 1 hr after Shabbos till 1am

Credit Cards Accepted: MC, Visa

Restaurant Discount: 10% Off (Discount will remain valid under new name)

Borough: Brooklyn
Section: Kings Highway

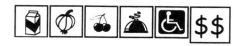

The Authoritative New York City Kosher Dining Guide

Restaurant: Bon Ami (Name expected to change) **Phone Number:** (718) 645-5700
Fax: None
Address: 523 Kings Highway (cor. E. 3rd St.)

Hechsher: Kehila, Vaad Harabbanim of Flatbush (Pas Yisroel, Cholov Yisroel)

Proprietor/Manager: Mayer

Type(s) of Food: Dairy, Vegetarian – Italian, Eclectic

Price Range:	**Lunch**	**Dinner**	**Take out**
Entrées:	$10.95-$17.95	Same	Same - Delivery Available
Desserts:	$3.95-$6.95	**Breakfast:** $10.50/Adult, $7.50/Child	
Drinks:	$ .95-$2.95	**Salads:** $4.50-$9.50	**Sandwiches:** $6.75-$9.50

Food Specialties: Salads, Pasta, Fettuccine Alfredo, Forcaccia, Pizza, Fish

> **Description:** A nouveau cuisine menu is planned and experimented with. It leans heavily on Italian, but will also incorporate a potpourri of international dishes that are slated to change periodically. Most impressive is the selection of salads, 13 currently (e.g. nicoise, portobella, hummus w/pine nuts & olives, Caesar, mesculun, etc.). Pasta "Diva" combines fusili curls with chunks of salmon in a cream sauce. Fish choices include salmon, tuna & St. Peters (whole fish). Entrée-like sandwiches offer grilled cheese bruschette, grilled vegetables & marinated grilled tuna. $15 Min./person.

> **Comments:** Something refreshingly different to look forward to!

Ambiance (Decor): The simple café decor of Bon Ami (50 seats) will soon give way to a more romantic setting. The lighting will get dimmer, table settings will become more formal and there will be music in the air. On weekends, the music will be live. Envisioned is an injection of sophistication and a new adult attitude during designated childfree hours for relaxed & stress free dining.

Service: Standard

General Comments: Promises of exotic ingredients & flavor combinations in a stress free environment, it sounds almost too good to hope for. RSVP suggested.

Hours: **Sun-Thurs:** 10am-12pm **Fri:** 10am till 2 hrs before Shabbos
Sat: Opens 1 hr after Shabbos till 2am

Credit Cards Accepted: MC, Visa, AmEx

Restaurant Discount: 10% Off (Discount will remain valid after name change.)

Borough: Brooklyn
Section: Kings Highway

The Authoritative New York City Kosher Dining Guide

Restaurant: Jerusalem Steak House Phone Number: (718) 336-5115
                                    Fax: None

Address: 533 Kings Highway (bet. E. 3rd St. - E. 4th St.)

Hechsher: Vaad Harabbanim of Flatbush (Glatt Kosher)

Proprietor/Manager: Yossi, Menachem

Type(s) of Food: Meat - Middle Eastern, American

Price Range: Lunch   Dinner   Take out
    Entrées: $12.00-$17.00   Same   Same - Delivery Available
    Desserts: $1.50-$3.00
    Drinks: $1.25-$1.75   Breakfast: $5.50-$6.00

Food Specialties: Grills, Kabobs, Fresh Fish, Salads, Shawarma

> Description: This is an Israeli Steakia serving grills and kabobs (including beef, lamb, chicken, and fish). The salads span the Middle East (e.g. Babaganoush, Turkish, Moroccan, Israeli, Taboulli) and come regular or small. St. Peters, the only fish selection specified, is served either fried or grilled. Entrées come with two side dishes chosen from among: rice, okra, beans, cous-cous, fries and salad. Soups include Yemenite, bean, vegetable and soup of the day.

> Comments: The preparation & presentation is competent. The overall quality of the food is acceptable, but I personally prefer a more restrained application of spices. The St. Peters is served whole on a large platter brimming with sides. Its texture is fine, but its flavor is nondescript. The salads, however, are worth mentioning for their freshness. Lg. portions.

Ambiance (Decor): Although it fails to create an exciting atmosphere, this modern, medium sized restaurant is well suited for family dining. Casual.

Service: Israeli waitress

General Comments: The restaurant has its devotees, but I am not personally dazzled.

Hours: Sun-Thurs: 11am- Midnight Fri: 11am- 3 hrs before Shabbos
       Sat: Opens 1 hr after Shabbos till 12:30am

Credit Cards Not Accepted: CASH or CHECK ONLY!

Restaurant Discount:

Borough: Brooklyn
Section: Kings Highway

The Authoritative New York City Kosher Dining Guide

Restaurant: Back To Nature

Phone Number: (718) 339-0273
Fax: None

Address: 535 Kings Highway (bet. E. 3rd St. - E. 4th St.)

Hechsher: Vaad Harabbanim of Flatbush

Proprietor/Manager: David Shamah

Type(s) of Food: Dairy, Vegetarian - Eclectic

Price Range:

	Lunch	Dinner	Take out
Entrées:	$7.95-$16.95	Same	Same
Desserts:	$1.75, $2.50-$5.00		Delivery Available
Drinks:	$ .90-$3.00	**Sandwiches:** $3.95-$5.95	

Food Specialties: Cakes, Pastries, Stuffed Baked Potatoes, Salmon Teriyaki

Description: Wide variety of vegetarian dishes, various Tofu items and Stuffed Baked Potatoes are featured. There's even vegetarian pizza! Fresh fish entrées, such as Salmon Teriyaki are here as well. An extensive selection of teas, coffee, espresso, cappuccino, cakes, and frozen yogurts are featured as are fresh squeezed vegetable and fruit juices. Their stated goal is to offer food that is "wholesome, flavorful from the freshest ingredients available." No artificial ingredients or additives are used and diet restrictions are accommodated.

Comments: The focus is on good tasting, attractively presented cuisine emphasizing natural food rather than "health food."

Ambiance (Decor): Newly decorated, with café atmosphere. Its modern interior is airy, clean and conducive to lengthy conversations over a cup of coffee and/or a tofu dessert. Informal.

Service: Standard

General Comments: A menu that meanders all over the place, but has a common thread: light tasting dishes. The food is generally well prepared, but be very specific about how well done you wish to have your order cooked.

Hours: **Sun-Thurs:** 11:30am-9:45pm **Fri:** 11am-2 hrs before Shabbos
Sat: (Winter Only) Opens 1½ hrs after Shabbos

Credit Cards Accepted: MC, Visa, AmEx

Restaurant Discount:

Borough: Brooklyn
Section: Kings Highway

The Authoritative New York City Kosher Dining Guide

Restaurant: David's Restaurant

Phone Number: (718) 998-8600
Fax: None

Address: 539 Kings Highway (bet. E. 3rd St. - E. 4th St.)

Hechsher: Rabbi Benjamin Seruyah, Hananiah Elbaz

Proprietor/Manager: David and Rob Suad

Type(s) of Food: Meat - Middle Eastern

Price Range:

	Lunch	*Dinner*	*Take out*
Entrées:	$11.00-$15.00	Same	Same
Desserts:	$1.75-$2.50		Delivery Available
Drinks:	$1.00-$1.50		

Food Specialties: Stuffed Chicken, Shish Kebob, Steaks, Salads, Falafel, Soups

> *Description:* Standard Middle Eastern fare. The Stuffed Chicken (filled with rice and meat), stuffed eggplant, zucchini, artichoke, and grape leaves are popular dishes. Daily Specials. Generous portions.

> *Comments:* The salads are particularly good, especially the chummus, techina, falafel and taboulli. At times the cooked dishes and daily specials can be overcooked. Generally, expect reasonably good food, with few surprises.

Ambiance (Decor): As is apparently typical of the Israeli steakia genre, this small and narrow restaurant is short on atmosphere. The bright fluorescent lights don't help in creating any sort of mood. Also typical are the white tablecloths topped with glass. A relaxed and unassuming environment for informal dining.

Service: In off hours very helpful and accommodating. Mealtimes coincide with a bustling take-out business. During these chaotic periods service is competent.

General Comments: A popular fixture in the neighborhood for decades and still going strong. Their durability speaks volumes. A good option for informal family dining. Large parties should call ahead!

Hours: **Sun-Thurs:** 10am-12am **Fri:** 10am-2 hrs before Shabbos
Sat: Opens 1 hr after Shabbos till 12:30am

Credit Cards Accepted: MC, Visa, AmEx, Discover, Carte Blanche, Diners Club

Restaurant Discount: 15% Off

Borough: Brooklyn
Section: Kings Highway

The Authoritative New York City Kosher Dining Guide

Restaurant: Think Sweet Café

Address: 546 King Highway (bet. E. 3rd - E. 4th St.)

Phone Number: (718) 645 3473
Fax: None

Hechsher: Rabbi Dovid Katz

Proprietor/Manager: Mordechai

Type(s) of Food: Dairy - American

Price Range:	Lunch	Dinner	Take Out
Entrées:	None	Same	Same – Local Free Delivery
Desserts:	$ .50-$2.50	**Sandwiches:** $1.50-$6.00	
Drinks:	$ .70-$2.50	**Omelets:** $3.50-$5.00	

Food Specialties: Omelets, Sandwiches, Cakes, Coffees, Salads

Description: This is a sandwich shop menu that is quite limited. Omelets, made to your order, are the only hot choices. Sandwiches, on bagel, bread, or Middle Eastern flat bread, make up the bulk of what is served. Salads include egg, tuna, Israeli, etc. As the name of the shop implies assorted cakes are the establishment's raison d'être. Coffees include espresso and cappuccino.

Comments: A miniature menu for a miniature establishment. Light fare for casual dining.

Ambiance (Décor): The very small interior accommodates only two tables (8 seats total) and 6 stools at a window counter. Nothing fancy or even particularly distinctive here. There are no restrooms.

Service: Self-serve

General Comments: This is a place to consider for a quick snack, breakfast, lunch and light supper.

Hours: **Sun-Thurs:** 8am-10pm   **Fri:** 8am-1½ hrs before Shabbos
Sat: 1½ hrs after Shabbos till 11pm

Credit Cards Not Accepted: CASH ONLY!

Restaurant Discount:

Borough: Brooklyn
Section: Kings Highway

Restaurant: T For 2 Café

Phone Number: (718) 998-0020
Fax: None

Address: 547 Kings Highway (cor. E. 4ᵗʰ St.)

Hechsher: RabbiYisroel P. Gornish (Cholov Yisroel)

Proprietor/Manager:

Type(s) of Food: Dairy – Italian, Sushi

Price Range: *Lunch*   *Dinner*   *Take Out*
   Entrées: $10-$15 (Sushi-$8-$15) $19-$22 (Sushi-$11-$27.50)   None
   Desserts: $3.95-$4.95   *Dinner Specials:* $19.95
   Drinks: $1.25-$4.25 (Cappucino, Café Latté)   Liquor License pending.

Food Specialties: Fresh Fish, Pastas, Soups, Salads, Sushi, Sashimi

   Description: Two separate menus: one for Sushi and the other Italian. Focus is
      on fresh fish and pasta. The expanded fish selection is the centerpiece of
      the Dinner Special. The tempting, salads include: Caesar, Mixed House,
      Lowfat Health, and Fresh Mozzarella & Tomato.

   Comments: Fresh & Smoked Mozzarella appetizer and the Broiled Filet of
      Sole Almondine entrée are personal favorites. For dessert, the Chocolate
      Mousse Cake is light, not too sweet and delicious. Without doubt, the
      quality of the sushi rates with the best. The Onion Soup is not gratinee,
      but topped with a French pastry crust. Spaghettini Fungi is a pasta must.

Ambiance (Decor): Upscale, sophisticated in mahogany and white, compact, formal.
      Subdued lighting emanates from art deco lamps. Tablecloths, fresh flowers, and
      candles, create a pleasant and romantic backdrop for a thoroughly pleasurable
      dining experience. The sushi bar by the entry blends in harmoniously. Seats 50.

Service: Formal, but friendly and accommodating.

General Comments: A delightful respite from the mundane: uncommonly good food
      in an unusually attractive setting, overseen by an ebullient & gracious
      proprietor. $20 min.order/person and 15% gratuity is added to the bill.

Hours: **Sun-Thurs:** Lunch: 12pm-3pm   Dinner: 5pm-10:30pm   **Friday Closed**
      Sat: Opens 1 hr after Shabbos till 12am

Credit Cards Accepted: MC, Visa, AmEx, Discover

Restaurant Discount: 10% Off

Borough: Brooklyn
Section: Kings Highway

The Authoritative New York City Kosher Dining Guide

Restaurant: Bella Luna *Phone Number:* (718) 376-2999
  Fax: None

Address: 557 Kings Highway (bet. E. 4th - E. 5th St.)

Hechsher: Rabbi Yisroel P. Gornish

Proprietor/Manager: Abe Salama, Danny Ben-Baruch

Type(s) of Food: Dairy - Italian

Price Range: *Lunch*   *Dinner*   *Take Out*
Entrées: $13.95-$14.95 (Fish), $9.95-$13.95 (Pasta)   Same
Desserts: $4.00   *Daily Specials*   Delivery Available
Drinks: $1.50-$3.00, $4/gl (Wine), $3/gl (Beer) *Kid's Portions:* ½ Price

Food Specialties: Linguine funghi, Ravioli salmone affumicato, Sogliola di limone

> *Description:* Two menus: one standard, and one that changes monthly. The standard entrées are limited to fresh fish (sole, cod or salmon), pasta and pizza. 5 salads (including Tri colori, Spinaci, Cesare, Mescalina, and Arugula), 6 appetizers, 5 pizzas and 6 desserts round off the standard menu. Forcoccia served. Accoutrements change daily.

> *Comments:* Everything is very fresh and served in satisfying portions. The pasta is homemade. Not gourmet yet, but given a chance to evolve, who an tell? For dessert: the Tiramisu....definitely!

Ambiance (Decor): Airy, casual, and pleasantly decorated. Chagal prints on the yellow-orange walls. Hunter green tablecloths topped with glass, wood chairs (74), ceramic tile floor, high intensity ambient lighting (soft lighting), and pasta filled glass canisters provide color accents and character. Informal.

Service: Accommodating and responsive

General Comments: Chef Luigi Postiglione, of the Culinary Institute of Naples, with 15 years of experience behind him, brings an authentic and creative vent to his culinary repertoire via the two menus. The restaurant is already quite busy.

Hours: **Sun-Wed:** 11am-11pm **Thurs:** 11am-1am **Friday Closed**
  Sat: 1 hr after Shabbos till 2am

Credit Cards Not Accepted: CASH ONLY!

Restaurant Discount:

Borough: Brooklyn
Section: Kings Highway

The Authoritative New York City Kosher Dining Guide

Restaurant: Mabat   *Phone Number:* (718) 339-3300

       Fax: None

Address: 1809 East 7th Street (bet. Quentin Rd. - Kings Hwy.)

Hechsher: Vaad Harabbanim of Flatbush

Proprietor/Manager: Yoram and Jaybe Levy

Type(s) of Food: Meat - Israeli Steak House

Price Range:	*Lunch*	*Dinner*	*Take out*
Entrées:	$10.00-$15.00	Same	Same - Delivery Available
Desserts:	$3.25		
Drinks:	$1.50-$2.00	($2.50 Imported Beer)	

Food Specialties: Salads, Steaks, Kabobs, Chicken Wings, BBQ

> *Description:* Carnivore's delight. Meats are usually of excellent quality and are seared to perfection. Salads are always very fresh and there is a nice variety. Order what you like, it is very hard to go wrong.

> *Comments:* You will eat well here. Unlike certain other places, if there is a line, do <u>wait</u>. You'll be glad you did. Pita and condiments are generously restocked at your table, as necessary.

Ambiance (Decor): Modern, black and stainless interior with a decidedly relaxed sophistication reminiscent of East Village cafés. Very small with nine tables of four. Not for claustrophobes, can feel crowded when they're busy. Some of the wooden chairs and tables rock and are not particularly comfortable.

Service: The young Israeli waitresses are very nice and accommodating. Menus have recently been introduced, but most patrons are faithful, repeat customers who don't need them. The waitresses guide the uninitiated through the menu and cheerfully provide samples to taste if one is unfamiliar with a dish.

General Comments: This restaurant has been a family favorite for some time. Call with party over six to see if/when group can be accommodated. The only real down side here is that everything is sold à la carte, including all side dishes.

Hours: **Sun-Thurs:** 12pm-12:30am   **Friday Closed**
     Sat: 1hr after Shabbos-12:30am

Credit Cards Not Accepted: CASH ONLY!

Restaurant Discount:

Borough: Brooklyn
Section: Kings Highway

The Authoritative New York City Kosher Dining Guide

Restaurant: Pita Elite

Phone Number: (718) 376-0666
Fax: None

Address: 1723-25 East 8th Street (bet. Quentin Rd. - Kings Hwy.)

Hechsher: Rabbi Yisroel P. Gornish (Glatt Kosher)

Proprietor/Manager:

Type(s) of Food: Meat – Middle Eastern

Price Range:	*Lunch*	*Dinner*	*Take Out*
Entrées:	$5.75-$7.75	Same	Same – Free Local Delivery
Desserts:	$3.00	*Pita Sandwiches:* $3.00-$7.00	
Drinks:	$1.00-1.50	*Soups:* $2.75	*Open Salad Bar*

Food Specialties: Shawarma, Falafel, Steak, Soups, Salads, Shish Kebobs

> *Description:* The short, but to the point, menu is displayed above the service counter. Pita sandwiches or platters served with fries form its core. Homemade soups are freshly made, as are the salads. Homemade Baklava is the sole dessert offered. An interesting departure from this Middle Eastern menu is the addition of "Thai Chicken." An oddity, perhaps, but it has proven to be quite popular, nevertheless. The salad bar is limited in scope offering Israeli salad, fried eggplant and sours.

> *Comments:* The food is fresh and surprisingly good. We sampled most everything and were not disappointed. The Baklava was a special surprise. It was delicious and not overly sweet.

Ambiance (Decor): A fast food eatery that is short on decor. 38 seats inside and during warm weather a few tables outside. A service counter takes up the back wall. The lighting is bright. Childproof surfaces make it a family option. Casual.

Service: Self-serve

General Comments: When decor is not important, a satisfying option, especially during the early morning hours.

Hours: **Sun-Thurs:** 9:30am-3am   **Fri:** 9:30am till 1 hr before Shabbos
Sat: 1 hr after Shabbos till 3am

Credit Cards Accepted: MC, Visa, AmEx, Discover, Diners Club

Restaurant Discount: 10% Off

Borough: Brooklyn
Section: Kings Highway

The Authoritative New York City Kosher Dining Guide

Restaurant: Nathan's

Phone Number: (718) 627-5252
Fax: (718) 627-3275

Address: 817 Kings Highway (bet. E. 8th St. - E. 9th St.)

Hechsher: OU, Kehilah (Glatt Kosher)

Proprietor/Manager:

Type(s) of Food: Meat - Deli

Price Range:

	Lunch	Dinner	Take Out
Entrées:	$5.99-$10.29	Same	Same – Delivery Available
Desserts: None	*Deli Sandwiches:* $6.99-$8.25 (Add $3 for L,T & Slaw)		
Drinks: $ .79-$2.29	*Burgers:* $1.29-$5.99	*Franks:* $2.25-$2.89	

Food Specialties: Franks, Burgers, Fried Chicken & Nuggets, Deli, Philly Steak

Description: Naturally, there are the Hot Dogs served in a variety of ways: w/ sauce, w/ onions, w/ Chili, and as nuggets. Burgers come in an assortment of sizes. Combo Meals are served with fries and a medium fountain drink and also come in various sizes. Also on the menu: knishes, soup, pretzels, and 2 salads (Garden & Chicken). The deli selection offers corned beef, pastrami, roast beef, and turkey.

Comments: A menu for kids of all ages.

Ambiance (Decor): Not just another stamped out Nathan's, this one features a wall mural of the Kotel, along with the fast food chain's package of colorful interior and child proof surfaces. A kosher first is the integrated play area for the children. Need I say casual? It's a safe bet that the 74 seats will be sought after by the younger set.

Service: Self-serve

General Comments: For those unfamiliar, Nathan's is a hot dog chain originating from Coney Island. Called "Nathan's Famous" for around a hundred years this is their first entrée into the American kosher market after having recently opened a few restaurants in Israel.

Hours: **Sun-Thurs:** 11am-1am **Fri:** 11am-2pm **Sat:** 1 hr aft Shabbos till 1-2am

Credit Cards Accepted: MC, Visa, AmEx

Restaurant Discount:

Borough: Brooklyn
Section: Kings Highway

The Authoritative New York City Kosher Dining Guide

Restaurant: Bamboo Garden *Phone Number:* (718) 375-8501
  Fax: (718) 375-8503
Address: 904 Kings Highway (bet. E. 9th St. - E. 10th St.)

Hechsher: Rabbi Yisroel P. Gornish (Glatt Kosher, Mashgiach Temidi)

Proprietor/Manager: Lazar

Type(s) of Food: Meat, Vegetarian - Chinese

Price Range: *Lunch*(11am-3:30pm) *Dinner* *Take out*
  Entrees $5.50-$6.95 $8.95-$18.95 Same - Free Local Delivery
  Desserts: $2.50-$4.50 *Diet Menu:* $ *Kid's Menu:* $6.95
  Drinks: $1.00 *Tuesday Night Smorgasbord:* $14.95 (6pm-10:30pm)

Food Specialties: Lucky Castle, Duck w/ Honey Walnuts, Green Jade Steak

> *Description:* The menu offers a healthy dose of the traditional favorites and some intriguing less familiar ones such as: Sea Bass w/ Garlic & Black Bean Sauce, Sizzling Mushroom Steak, West Lake Chicken, and Har Har Chicken w/ Sausage. Entrées include chicken, beef, duck, fish, and vegetarian selections, as well as Diet, American, and Kids choices ($4.95-$5.50). 12 soups and 12 appetizers. The Lunch Special: soup, entrée, and rice (fried or white). Altogether, a well stocked menu.

> *Comments:* Under new management again, and this time the change is significant. The Tuesday smorgasbord is among the best around, offering variety & good quality. I especially enjoyed the Chicken with Peanuts, which was laden with the nuts. The Wonton soup is very satisfying. In general, the food appears to be fresh and well prepared.

Ambiance (Decor): The interior was conceived with a neutral palette: beige walls, brown trim and black with beige carpeting. The booths lining the walls provide orange accents. Faux Windows suggestive of shoji screens line the walls in a repetitive pattern emitting deffuse fluorescent light. Tables and booths.

Service: Standard

General Comments: New ownership, same location, almost new name, new prices, different menu, new approach? Apparently so. Off to a fine start. Worth a try!

Hours: **Sun-Thurs:** 11am-11pm (Last seating 10:30pm)
  Sat: 1 hr after Shabbos till 12pm

Credit Cards Accepted: MC, Visa

Restaurant Discount:

Borough: Brooklyn
Section: Kings Highway

The Authoritative New York City Kosher Dining Guide

Restaurant: Mama's Restaurant   *Phone Number:* (718) 382-7200
                                                    Fax: None
Address: 906 Kings Highway (bet. E. 9th St. - E. 10th St.)

Hechsher: Vaad Harabbanim of Flatbush (Glatt Kosher)

Proprietor/Manager:

Type(s) of Food: Meat - Middle Eastern

Price Range:	*Lunch*	*Dinner*	*Take out*
Entrées:	$3.50-$7.50	Same	Same
Desserts:	None		Delivery Available
Drinks:	$1.00 -$1.50	*All-You-Can-Eat Salad Bar*	

Food Specialties: Falafel, Shawarma, Salads, Shish Kebob, Steaks

> *Description:* A typical Israeli Shwarma fast food menu with no surprises. The salad bar offers falafel, Israeli salad, fried eggplant and mostly pickled items. Shwarma is the piece de resistance, while various kebobs and grills offer other entrée options.

> *Comments:* With an order, one gets unlimited trips to the salad bar, which is always full, and includes all the falafel you can eat. What there is appears to be fresh.

Ambiance (Decor): A service counter in the back of the room is the focal point. The decor is unremarkable and the bright fluorescent lighting destroys any chance at creating atmosphere. Laminate tables, wooden chairs, and disposable utensils are indicative of the general tone. Child friendly environment. Casual.

Service: Self-serve

General Comments: Economical prices and the all-you-can-eat salad bar make this restaurant a favorite with singles, especially students.

Hours: **Sun-Thurs:** 11am-11pm (Closings May Vary)   **Fri:** 11am-3pm
         Sat: 1 hr after Shabbos till ? (Hours Vary)

*Credit Cards **Not** Accepted:* CASH ONLY!

Restaurant Discount:

Borough: Brooklyn
Section: Kings Highway

The Authoritative New York City Kosher Dining Guide

Restaurant: Fontana Bella a.k.a. Sea Dolphin   *Phone Number:* (718) 627-3904
Fax: None
Address: 2086 Coney Island Ave. (bet. Ave. R - Kings Hwy.)

Hechsher: Rabbi Yisroel P. Gornish, (Cholov Yisroel, Pas Yisroel)

Proprietor/Manager: Danny Goshen

Type(s) of Food: Dairy - Italian

Price Range:

	Lunch	*Dinner*	*Take out*
Entrées:	$12.00-$18.00	$18.00-$22.00	Same
Desserts:	$4.50-$5.00		
Drinks:	$3.50		

Food Specialties: Hand made pasta, fish dishes, Middle Eastern Salads

Description: A hybrid menu of two separate restaurants, joined together: Fontana Bella's strictly Italian fare and Sea Dolphin's numerous fish specialties. The latter also offers a number of cold Middle Eastern appetizers like Babaganoush, Chummus, etc. Everything is à la carte.

Comments: Most noteworthy is the sophisticated use of spices and the variety of sauces. Fish preparation is top rate: flavorful & moist. The French Onion Soup is particularly good, brimming with onions & not at all too salty. Portobello Mushrooms & Vegetable Misto are terrific appetizers.

Ambiance (Decor): Every inch of wall space is covered with something: from amateurish paintings, to a collection of unrelated photos, to all kinds of decorative nik-naks. This visual smorgasbord of completely unrelated items, oddly blends together in the dimly lit room creating a rich tapestry. The tables are formally set with white tablecloths, napkins, candles and plastic flower arrangements displayed in an assortment of novel vases further contribute to the room's eclectic texture. Potted plastic plants and trees complete the picture. The clutter is somewhat garish, but the decorative naiveté exudes simple honesty and a degree of warmth and character. The room has an intimate feel, which is conducive to quiet conversation. Formal, but diners come attired as they wish.

Service: Formal service that is friendly, attentive, and accommodating

General Comments: A visual and gastronomical feast! A good date possibility.

Hours: **Mon-Thurs:** 12pm-11pm   **Friday Closed**
Sat: Opens 1 hr after Shabbos till business stops   **Sun:** 12pm-11pm

Credit Cards Accepted: MC, Visa, AmEx

Restaurant Discount: 10% Off Mondays & Tuesdays For Dinner Only

Borough: Brooklyn
Section: Kings Highway

The Authoritative New York City Kosher Dining Guide

Restaurant: Reliable Kosher Combo

Phone Number: (718) 339-0054
Fax: None

Address: 1218 King Highway (bet. E. 12th - E. 13th St.)

Hechsher: Rabbi Zvi Josephy (Cholov Yisroel)

Proprietor/Manager: Zion

Type(s) of Food: Dairy - American

Price Range: **Lunch** **Dinner** **Take Out**
Entrées: None Same Same – Local Free Delivery
Desserts: $ .75-$2.00 **Sandwiches:** $2.75-$5.00
Drinks: $1.00-$2.75 **Soups:** $3.25 **Salad Platters:** $6.00

Food Specialties: Pizza, Baked Goods, Health Breads, Sandwiches, Coffees, Salads

Description: A sandwich shop/coffeehouse/bakery/pizzeria menu that is restricted to sandwiches, soups, salads, and pizza. Sandwiches are served on their self-baked selection of breads such as whole wheat, semolina, 8 grain, croissants, and bagels. Spreads include tuna salad, lox, egg salad, and a variety of cheeses. Four soups to warm your heart and tummy include vegetable, minestrone, mushroom & barley and lentil. Coffees include espresso and cappuccino. The three salads served are Israeli, Caesar, and mesculun.

Comments: We haven't tried the pizza yet, but the brownies and the "light" napoleons are truly memorable, perhaps the best I've had anywhere.

Ambiance (Decor): Newly renovated, it has a European ambiance. This 19 seat eatery has wood chairs and tables and a large glass display case towards the back that shows off the cakes and cookies that are baked on premises. Casual.

Service: Self-serve

General Comments: For those with a sweet tooth, this is nirvana. To assuage that guilt, you can order something healthful first. This pâtisserie on Kings Highway has hours that are epitome of convenience.

Hours: **Sun-Thurs:** Open 24 hours **Fri:** Closes 1 hr before Shabbos
Sat: 1 hr after Shabbos

Credit Cards _Not Accepted:_ CASH ONLY!

Restaurant Discount:

Borough: Brooklyn
Section: Kings Highway

The Authoritative New York City Kosher Dining Guide

Restaurant: Adelman's   *Phone Number:* (718) 336-4915
                                  Fax: (718) 336-9027

Address: 1906 Kings Highway (bet. E. 19th St. - Ocean Ave.)

Hechsher: Rabbi Leonard Bronstein - RESTAURANT IS OPEN 7 DAYS A WEEK

Proprietor/Manager:

Type(s) of Food: Meat - Deli

Price Range: *Lunch*   *Dinner*   *Take out*
   Entrées: $ 4.95-$7.75 $10.25-$15.50 $9.25-$14.50 Free Local Delivery
   Desserts: $1.50-$1.80   *Sandwiches:* $5-$7.95 (Reg.), $9.50-$9.95 (Hot)
   Drinks: $ .75-$1.90   *Daily Specials:* $7.25-$10.95 *Dinner:* $9.95-$11.50

Food Specialties: Deli, Prime Rib Steak, Roast Turkey, Brisket, Burgers

> *Description:* A deli menu with some embellishments including: the Italian
> Kitchen (3 choices e.g. Chicken Cacciatore), the Chinese Kitchen (3
> choices e.g. Hot Oriental Beef on Garlic Bread), and the Fish of the Day.
> There is a well stocked all-you-can-eat salad bar with a nice selection of
> salads and condiments ($2.00 sharing charge). The Lunch (11am-3pm)
> and Dinner Specials include entrée vegetable, potato, cup of soup, and
> coffee or tea.

> *Comments:* "I'd go out of my way for Adelman's Pastrami…" " Adelman's
> won me over with food and service"- Arthur Schwartz, Daily News.

Ambiance (Decor): Newly renovated, the restaurant now sparkles in red and white.
Looks bright, clean, fresh and well maintained. Televisions tuned to sporting
events help to create "the sports deli." Informal.

Service: Standard

General Comments: The original store was located in Borough Park. They moved to
the present location 15 years ago. Although not under the same ownership, this
restaurant has been in business for a total of 50 years and has a loyal following.

Hours: **Mon-Sun:** 8am-9:30pm - RESTAURANT IS OPEN 7 DAYS A WEEK

Credit Cards Accepted: MC, Visa, AmEx

Restaurant Discount: 10% Off

26

Borough: Brooklyn
Section: Kings Highway

The Authoritative New York City Kosher Dining Guide

Restaurant: Essen Delicatessen

Phone Number: (718) 677-3600
Fax: None

Address: 2817-2819 Nostand Avenue (bet. Kings Hwy. - Ave. P)

Hechsher: Kehilah (Glatt Kosher)

Proprietor/Manager:

Type(s) of Food: Meat – Deli

Price Range:	*Lunch*	*Dinner*	*Take Out*
Entrées:	$11.00-$18.00	Same	Same- Free Local Del. ($10 Min)
Desserts:	NONE	*Deli Sandwiches:* $5.75-$8.75, $10.95 (Steak)	
Drinks:	$ .95-$1.25	*Specials*	5 ft. Heroes

Food Specialties: Sandwiches, Steaks, Kebobs, Lamb Chops, Burgers, BBQ Wings

Description: Although only two weeks old, the menu has already been drastically modified. The intriguing Arroz Con Pollo, Chinese chicken & beef stir fry, Italian specialties and other eclectic dishes have been cut out of the regular menu. Remaining are the deli sandwiches, grills, vegetarian dishes, soups, salads and specialty items like Borekas, Knockwurst, Stuffed Cabbage or Peppers, and Veal Sausage (w/ green peppers). Deli sandwiches and entrées become meals with an addition charge of $2.80-$3.50. These specials include a choice of soup or salad & fries or mashed potatoes.

Comments: We're told that the cut dishes were removed because customers objected to waiting the 15 min. required to prepare them (talk about society's need for instant gratification!) However, expect these dishes to reappear as weekly specials.

Ambiance (Decor): A cozy bistro-type setting that is both casual and congenial. Its stucco ceiling, tile-work, & lattice work are Mediterranean inspired. A large painting of Jerusalem commands attention. Tablecloths & glass. Seats 45.

Service: Standard

General Comments: Open just two weeks and already establishing a following.

Hours: **Sun-Thurs:** 10am-10pm **Fri:** 10am-1 hr before Shabbos **Saturday Closed**

Credit Cards Accepted: MC, Visa, AmEx

Restaurant Discount: 10% Off

Borough: Brooklyn
Section: Kings Highway

The Authoritative New York City Kosher Dining Guide

Restaurant: Pita Corner   *Phone Number:* (718) 627-3373
                                                           Fax: None

Address: 419 Avenue P (cor. E. 2nd St.)

Hechsher: Rabbi Yisroel Gornish (Glatt Kosher)

Proprietor/Manager: Sylvia

Type(s) of Food: Meat – Middle Eastern

Price Range: *Lunch*   *Dinner*   *Take Out*
   Entrées: $2.75-$5.00   Same   Same – Delivery Available
   Desserts: None at present time. *Free Salad Bar w/ Entrée*
   Drinks: $1.00-$1.25

Food Specialties: Shawarma, Falafel, Chummus, Babaganoush, Soups, Salads, Fries

   Description: A sparse fast food menu that will no doubt develop over time.
      Soups (2) change and are made fresh daily. The all-you-can-eat salad
      bar varies from day to day and has a nice selection that includes falafel,
      Babaganoush, bean, Israeli, Turkish, red cabbage, mushroom and
      pepper, chummus, techina and assorted condiments. Salad as the main
      dish: small ($2) and large ($5). Diners choose between pita sandwiches
      and platters. At this time there are no desserts, but fresh fruit is planned.

   Comments: Makes up in quality what it lacks in quantity. Salads are very fresh
      and appetizing. The falafel is fresh and made just right.

Ambiance (Decor): Only 6 stools and a laminate, L-shape eating bar, which runs in
   front of the window and along an adjacent wall. The fluorescent lighting
   provides a bright setting, as do the white tiled floor and walls.

Service: Self-serve

General Comments: Open just three weeks at this writing. Hopefully, it will remain
   as bright and clean, as it is today. **Handicap Note:** Although the restroom is on
   street level, it is accessed through a narrow rear passageway and is itself
   narrow.

Hours: **Sun-Thurs:** 12pm-2am   **Fri:** 12pm-1 hr before Shabbos (Summer, Spring)
      Friday Closed (Winter) **Sat:** 1 hr after Shabbos till 2 am

Credit Cards Accepted: MC, Visa, AmEx

Restaurant Discount:

Borough: Brooklyn
Section: Bensonhurst

The Authoritative New York City Kosher Dining Guide

Restaurant: Empress Kosher Deli

Address: 2210 86th Street (Bay Pkwy. - Bay 3rd St.)

Phone Number: (718) 265-8002
Fax: (718) 372-7941

Hechsher: Rabbi Bronstein – RESTAURANT IS OPEN 7 DAYS A WEEK

Proprietor/Manager: Ellen Rubin

Type(s) of Food: Meat - Deli

Price Range: *Lunch* (11am-3pm)   *Dinner*   *Take Out*
Entrées: $6.95 (Special) $10.75-$17.95   Same – Delivery Available
Desserts: $1.85-$2.50   *Kid's Menu:* $6.75   *Sandwiches:* $6.25-$10.15
Drinks: $1.25-$1.50 *Early Bird Sp.Dinner:* $8.95/single, $15.95/couple

Food Specialties: Grilled Chicken, Triple Decker Combo Sandwich, Franks, Kebobs

Description: The menu is packed with choices that along with the requisite selection of Deli Sandwiches, includes fresh fish (Broiled Salmon Steak or Filet of Sole), Kebobs, BBQ Chicken, Salads, Philly Steak, BBQ Buffalo Wings, Char-Broiled Burgers, and an array of traditional cooked dishes. Not quite traditional are the Kosher BLT (Kosher Beef Bacon, Lettuce, Tomato & Mayo on Toast), Belgian Waffles, French Toast and assorted Egg Sandwiches and Omelets served with parve cream cheese, parve tofutti ice cream, or kosher Canadian "Bacon."

Comments: A deli with a difference! The liberal use of kosher substitutes for dairy products and for non-kosher items like bacon is intriguing.

Ambiance (Decor): From all appearances this is an old fashioned, traditional deli. Recently spruced up, it nevertheless evokes an old time Coney Island flavor. Eat in booths or on chairs (total 70 seats) at marble topped tables.

Service: Standard

General Comments: Viva la difference!

Hours: **Sun-Thurs:** 9am-9:30pm   **Fri-Sat:** 9am-10pm
RESTAURANT IS OPEN 7 DAYS A WEEK

Credit Cards Accepted: MC, Visa, AmEx

Restaurant Discount: 15% Off Dining-In Excluding Lunch & Dinner Specials

The Authoritative New York City Kosher Dining Guide

Pizzerias:

Taam Tov Eatery Ltd.　　　　　**Tel:** (718) 998-5200
509 Avenue P
Rabbi Yisroel Gornish
(Cholov Yisroel)

Kosher Hut Pizza　　　　　**Tel:** (718) 376-8996
709 Kings Highway
KEHEILA Kashrut

Reliable Kosher Combo　　　　　**Tel:** (718) 339-0054
1218 Kings Highway
Rabbi Zvi Josephy
(Cholov Yisroel)

Shalom's Pizza　　　　　**Tel:** (718) 339-7884
1621 Kings Highway
Vaad Harabbanim of Flatbush

Pizza Nosh　　　　　**Tel:** (718) 253-3200
2807 Nostrand Avenue
Vaad Harabbanim of Flatbush
(Cholov Yisroel)

Donut Shops:

Dunkin' Donuts　　　　　**Tel:** (718) 583-0915
2630 86th Street
כ-K

Flatbush
Midwood

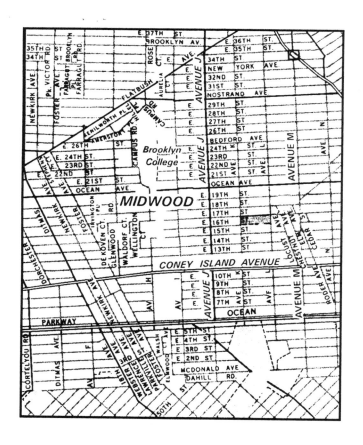

▰ ◉ ⌷ ▲ ♿ $$

The Authoritative New York City Kosher Dining Guide

Restaurant: Shang Chai

Address: 2189 Flatbush Avenue (cor. Ave. R)

Phone Number: (718) 377-6100
(718) 377-6101

Fax: None

Hechsher: Vaad Harabbanim of Flatbush

Proprietor/Manager: Alan Chan

Type(s) of Food: Meat - Chinese (Cantonese)

Price Range:

	Lunch	*Dinner*	*Take out*	
Entrées:	$10.00-$12.00	$13.00-$19.75	$12.50-$19.25	Free Local Del.
Desserts:	$2.50	*Smorgasbord:* $12.95 Thurs. 6pm-9pm		(Min. $20)
Drinks:	$1.50, $3.50-$4.50 (Mixed Drinks, glass of Wine)			

Food Specialties: Steak and Phoenix, Shang-Chai Delight, Lemon Chicken and Pungent Duck, Cantonese Duckling, Wor Shu Opp

Description: The menu features a nice selection which includes all the favorites and allows for American options as well. No MSG upon request, and they will spice to your taste. Á lá cárte and Special Family Dinners offered. Entrées come with lettuce, tomato and cucumber salad, rice, tea, parve ice cream and fortune cookies. Nice portions. The Thursday night smorgasbord offers a selection of meat (fewer and cheaper lately) and vegetarian dishes (vegetable sushi).

Comments: À la carte food is generally well prepared.

Ambiance (Decor): Redecorated several years ago in green marble, mauve, and black, with chrome trim. Recently extended, this restaurant now accommodates 180-190 seats. Divided into two large dining areas, one section (140 seats) is at times reserved for affairs. Seating at tables or booths.

Service: Generally good, owner attends to any concerns.

General Comments: We've eaten here for many years and usually leave satisfied. The spacious dining room is warm and inviting. At times, one can be drawn int the festive mood of an adjacent table's celebration. Large groups are easily accommodated, but reservations are a good idea at peak hours (even though they're not always held). Can be casual or more formal. Parking lot in front.

Hours: **Sun-Thurs:** 12pm-11pm   **Friday Closed**   **Sat:** 1 hr after Shabbos-2am

Credit Cards Accepted: MC, Visa, AmEx

Restaurant Discount:

Borough: Brooklyn
Section: Midwood

The Authoritative New York City Kosher Dining Guide

Restaurant: Zilli's Restaurant

Phone Number: (718) 998-8111
Fax: Same

Address: 1928 Coney Island Avenue (bet. Ave. O - Ave. P)

Hechsher: Kehila (Glatt Kosher)

Proprietor/Manager: Yoram

Type(s) of Food: Meat – Middle Eastern

Price Range:

	Lunch	*Dinner*	*Take Out*
Entrées:	$6.95-$9.95	$13.95-$28.95	$11.95-$14.95
Desserts:	$2.50-$4.00	*Daily Specials*	Free Local Delivery
Drinks:	$1.00-$2.00	*Sandwiches:* $7.00-$9.00	

Food Specialties: Shawarma, Salads, Steaks, Shish Kebobs, Sandwiches, Soups

Description: Shawarma is the piece de resistance: choices include chicken, turkey, veal and beef. The Shish Kebob selection is equally varied. Eggplant salad is another specialty. Free salad bar is included. Everything is freshly homemade daily. Soon the pita will be, as well.

Comments: Everything Middle Eastern that you'd want to order including steaks, chops, and kabobs. However, the menu and the recipes continue to change as Zilli's gets its sea legs. Look for intermittent specials.

Ambiance (Decor): Not your typical Shawarma eatery. The neutral cream color scheme permeates everything: the walls, the upholstered chair seats, the tablecloths, napkins, and even the tiled floors. This homogenous canvas is easy on the eyes and provides a quiet background ripe for future embellishment. Dining is at the rear of the restaurant, while a glass display counter in the front delineates the take-out area. Seating for 52 is in a casual-semi formal setting that invites family dining. An attempt to inject a little finesse into the Israeli steakia.

Service: Ironing out the kinks. Not there yet.

General Comments: Newly opened and still smoothing out the rough edges.

Hours: **Sun-Thurs:** 12pm-2am **Fri:** 12pm till 2 hrs before Shabbos (Summer Only)
Sat: 1 hr after Shabbos till about 2am at first, but eventually till 4am

Credit Cards Accepted: MC, Visa

Restaurant Discount: 20% Off

Borough: Brooklyn
Section: Midwood

The Authoritative New York City Kosher Dining Guide

Restaurant: Bissaleh Café & Restaurant   *Phone Number:* (718) 998-8811
                                            Fax: None

Address: 1922 Coney Island Avenue (bet. Ave. O - Ave. P)

Hechsher: Torah-K (Cholov Yisroel)

Proprietor/Manager: Sapir Gamliel

Type(s) of Food: Dairy - Israeli, Yemenite, Italian

Price Range:	Lunch	Dinner	Take out
Entrées:	Closed	$7.00-$15.00	Same – Delivery Available
Desserts:g		$3.75-$7.00	
Drinks:		$1.50-$4.00	

Food Specialties: Bissaleh, Malawah, Ftuts, Borekas, Pizza, Fish, Pasta, Salads

> *Description:* Bissaleh (sesame topped dough with different fillings), Malawah (served with tomato sauce, Bissaleh shug and hard-boiled egg), Ftuts (w/ shug & tomato sauce), Bissaleh Pizza (a small pie with your choice of toppings), Turkish, Greek, Yemenite and Israeli salads, and five different soups (incl. French Onion) are offered. Choice of 7 coffees.

> *Comments:* All sides are ordered separately. The soups are good. The French Onion Soup has a full-bodied flavor but I would prefer more cheese. The Mushroom Soup is full of mushrooms, has just enough cream, and the use of seasoning is measured. The Greek Salad (a small portion is enough for two moderately hungry people) no longer has the creamy feta cheese it used to have. Dessert is something to look forward to.

Ambiance (Decor): The café style dining room seats approx. 60. Stylized pictures of food, jars of beans and grains, and other food related items adorn the walls. Muted TV's allow diners to keep abreast of sports scores and the news.

Service: Friendly, laissez faire attitude, not always attentive

General Comments: Congenial place, with an unhurried pace. Often filled with smoking Israelis, who proliferate, especially after dinner - the peak hours.

Hours: **Sun-Thurs:** 5pm-5am **Friday Closed** **Sat:** 1 hr after Shabbos-5am

Credit Cards Not Accepted: CASH ONLY!

Restaurant Discount: 10% Off

Borough: Brooklyn
Section: Midwood

The Authoritative New York City Kosher Dining Guide

Restaurant: Benjy's BBQ & Grill

Phone Number: (718) 677-0820
Fax: (718) 677-3708

Address: 1620 Coney Island Avenue (Ave. L - Ave. M)

Hechsher: Kehilah (Glatt Kosher)

Proprietor/Manager: Benjy

Type(s) of Food: Meat - American

Price Range:

	Lunch	Dinner	Take Out
Entrées:	$11.95-$16.95	Same	Same - Free Local Delivery
Desserts:	$2.95-$3.95	**Deli Sandwiches:** $5.95-$6.95	
Drinks:	$1.00-$1.50	**Kid's Meals:** $4.95	

Food Specialties: Steaks, Burgers, Kebobs, Buffalo Wings, Grilled Chicken, Salads

Description: A steakhouse, burger and deli restaurant rolled into one. Along with the steaks, Buffalo Wings, Chilidogs and deli, there is a selection of pasta, salads, and soups. You can also order some cooked items besides the grills like Shepherds Pie, Chicken Franchaise, and Spaghetti & Meatballs. The burgers all come served on a bun with lettuce, tomatoes & onions. The Kid's Meals include an entrée and fries.

Comments: Kebobs aside, the food is essentially American. The menu is not huge, but it offers a nice selection.

Ambiance (Decor): Seating accommodates 55 in this newly opened restaurant. The color scheme of grays and green offsets the white tablecloths and glass on the tables. Mirrors line the walls, but the décor is generally noncommittal. Informal, but it strives for "class."

Service: Standard

General Comments: Stated intention of offering really good quality food at reasonable prices in a classy setting are encouraging.

Hours: **Sun-Thurs:** 11am-11pm **Friday Closed** **Sat:** 1 hr after Shabbos till ?

Credit Cards Accepted: MC, Visa, AmEx, Discover, Diners Club

Restaurant Discount: 10% Off

The Authoritative New York City Kosher Dining Guide

Restaurant: Bagel & Cheese

Phone Number: (718) 998-8778
Fax: None

Address: 1304 Avenue M (cor. E. 13th St.)

Hechsher: ARK (Cholov Yisroel, Pas Yisroel, Chemach Yashan)

Proprietor/Manager: Chaim

Type(s) of Food: Dairy - American

Price Range:

	Lunch	*Dinner*	*Take Out*
Entrées:	$4.99-$4.99	Same	Same – Delivery Avail. ($15 Min.)
Desserts:	$.69-1.00	*Sandwiches:* $1.00-$4.95	*Salads:* $3.99/lb.
Drinks:	$.80-$1.35	*Breakfast Menu:* $1.99-$2.99	

Food Specialties: Sandwiches, Eggplant Parmigian, Soups, Omelets, Pastas

> *Description:* A light café menu featuring bagels with assorted spreads, salads, soups, omelets, etc. Pasta staples include stuffed shells, baked ziti, and lasagna. Other pasta dishes change daily. Choose pancakes for breakfast, or order the Breakfast Special consisting of eggs, fries, bagel and coffee or tea. The eggplant parmigian is especially popular.

Comments: Not an extensive menu, but good for light meals and snacks.

Ambiance (Decor): An appetizing store with some tables up front. A glass display counter dominates the rear and serves diners, as well as, take-out orders. Not much attempt at creating a dining room setting. Bathroom is on basement level.

Service: Self-serve

General Comments: Note the late closing time for late night snacking and light after movie suppers.

Hours: **Sun-Thurs:** 6am-12:30am **Fri:** 6:30am-½ hr before Shabbos
Sat: 1 hr after Shabbos till 1am

Credit Cards Accepted: MC, Visa

Restaurant Discount:

Borough: Brooklyn
Section: Midwood

The Authoritative New York City Kosher Dining Guide

Restaurant: Glatt Kosher Number 1   *Phone Number:* (718) 375-1070
                                                                              Fax: None

Address: 1411 Avenue M (bet. E. 14th St. - E. 15th St.)

Hechsher: Rabbi Dovid Katz (Glatt Kosher)

Proprietor/Manager: Achmir

Type(s) of Food: Meat - Chinese

Price Range:	*Lunch (Special)*	*Dinner*	*Take out*
Entrées:	$5.00-$6.00	$7.00-$13.50 or	Same
Desserts:	None	*Dinner Special* $8.45	Free Delivery(5-10pm)
Drinks:	$ .85		Min.$15.00

Food Specialties: General Tso's Chicken, Orange Flavored Beef, Curry Chicken

Description: The Lunch Special offers 16 popular dishes, (e.g. Moo Goo Gai Pan, Sweet & Sour Chicken, Sesame Chicken and Beef & Broccoli), served with plain or fried rice. The Dinner Special adds another 12 dishes to that list, making a total of 28 dishes, which are served with soup and rice. All items are cooked without MSG and are made fresh. Special Diet Dishes are steamed instead of fried. Small portions.

Comments: The specials are quite reasonably priced and offer great value for your money. Alas, the food leaves much to be desired. The meat and chicken are over tenderized and come in scant quantities.

Ambiance (Decor): Stretching the definition to its limits, this "restaurant," comprised of two tables with chairs in front of the service counter, is more of a take-out business than a dining room. However, you can eat-in. At the same time you can watch the chef prepare the food, which is a performance in itself!

Service: Self-serve

General Comments: This is primarily a take out establishment, but a handy place to know of when shopping along Avenue M, for a quick bite, or when you feel like staying home and not cooking.

Hours: **Sun-Thurs:** 11am-11pm   **Friday Closed**
         Sat: 1 hr after Shabbos till 11pm

Credit Cards Not Accepted: CASH ONLY!

Restaurant Discount:

Borough: Brooklyn
Section: Midwood

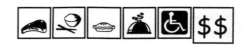

The Authoritative New York City Kosher Dining Guide

Restaurant: Yunkee

Phone Number: (718) 627-0072
Fax: (718) 645-6336

Address: 1426 Elm Avenue off Avenue M (bet. E. 14th St. - E. 15th St.)

Hechsher: ARK - Association for Reliable Kashruth (Glatt Kosher)

Proprietor/Manager: Yitzy Svei (manager)

Type(s) of Food: Meat – Chinese, American

Price Range:	*Lunch*	*Dinner*	*Take out*
Entrées:	$15.95-$19.95	Same	Same - Delivery Available
Desserts:	$2.75	*Monday Dinner Buffet Special:* $14.95	
Drinks:	$1.75-$1.95	*American Menu Entrées:* $13.95-$19.95	

Food Specialties: Crisp Chicken w/ Honey Walnuts, BBQ Back Ribs, Texas Burger

> *Description:* The Chinese menu is a comprehensive offering of chicken, duck, beef, veal, & lamb entrées. The Monday night all-you-can-eat buffet includes soup, unlimited trips to the buffet and salad bar, tea, and dessert from the rolling cart. The salad bar offers a nice variety daily. A few American dishes have always been offered, but that list has recently been expanded with items like Chicken Mesquite and Buffalo Wings joining the deli sandwiches & platters, Southern Fried Chicken, Broiled Rib Steak, etc.

> *Comments:* There is a very noticeable improvement in the food preparation. No longer is the food greasy, the meat is tender and of better quality, and the vegetables are fresh and not overdone. The salads are refreshing, while the rich desserts are sinful. I can't say I've ever seen anyone having deli.

Ambiance (Decor): Narrow and long, the main dining room, with its tables set close together, can feel crowded, especially at the height of mealtimes. A smaller adjacent room has similar characteristics. Carpeted floors, tablecloths, candles and flowers on the tables, give the dining room a warm, but somewhat formal look. The jade, orange and tan color scheme suggests an oriental theme. When not crowded, the restaurant is a pleasant, intimate setting for relaxed dining.

Service: Standard

General Comments: A restaurant with a loyal following, especially on Mondays.

Hours: **Sun-Thurs:** 5pm-11pm **Friday Closed**
    Sat: 1 hr after Shabbos till 12:30am (after Succos)

Credit Cards Accepted: MC, Visa, AmEx, Discover

Restaurant Discount:

38

Borough: Brooklyn
Section: Midwood

The Authoritative New York City Kosher Dining Guide

Restaurant: Chap-A-Nosh
Phone Number: (718) 627-0072
Fax: (718) 645-6336
Address: 1424 Elm Street off Avenue M (bet. E. 14th - E. 15th St.)

Hechsher: ARK - The Association for Reliable Kashruth (Glatt Kosher)

Proprietor/Manager: Yitzy Svei

Type(s) of Food: Meat - Chinese, American

Price Range: **Lunch**   **Dinner**   **Take out**
  Entrées: $13.00-$17.00   Same   Same - Delivery Available
  Desserts: $ .75   **Dinner Specials:** $8.95 & $10.95, $11.95
  Drinks: $0.95-$1.15 soda   **Summertime Bachelor Special:** $11.95

Food Specialties: Chinese Menu, American Menu, Deli Sandwiches, Texas Grill

  Description: The extensive Chinese menu has numerous beef, poultry, veal,
    lamb and vegetable selections. The much smaller American menu, has
    added grilled selections which include spicy Buffalo Wings, beef
    burgers, Pastrami burgers, grilled chicken with a Texan accent, BBQ
    beef back ribs, grilled Chicken w/ Mesquite sauce, spicy chicken
    nuggets and shoestring fries Cajun style.

  Comments: A unique hybrid menu: traditional Chinese (same kitchen as
    Yunkee) and an American fast food burger joint steakhouse. One of two
    places we know of where Lo Mein comes with fried rice.

Ambiance (Decor): Recently renovated in fresh green, white and honey colored
    wood, this fast food restaurant has been transformed into a visually delightful
    eatery. Childproof, with its tiled floor, molded benches and washable tables.
    With fanciful graphics of trees in the windows, the room has taken on a playful
    and lighthearted expression. Now more than ever, a family favorite. No doubt it
    is still noisy, but much more inviting. Styrofoam plates and plastic utensils.

Service: Self-serve

General Comments: Fast food for families with young children and singles.

Hours: Sun-Thurs: 12pm-11pm   **Friday Closed**   **Sat:** 1 hr aft Shabbos -12:30am

Credit Cards Accepted: MC, Visa, AmEx

Restaurant Discount:

Borough: Brooklyn
Section: Midwood

The Authoritative New York City Kosher Dining Guide

Restaurant: Shawarma Hamacabim

Phone Number: (718) 382-0410
Fax: None

Address: 1510 Elm Street off Avenue M (bet. E.15th St. - E.16th St.)

Hechsher: Vaad Harabbanim of Flatbush (Mashgiach Temidi)

Proprietor/Manager: Motti

Type(s) of Food: Meat - Middle Eastern

Price Range: *Lunch*   *Dinner*   *Take out*
   Entrées: $3.00-$7.00 (Pita), $6.00-$14.00 (Plate)   Same
   Desserts: $ None   Delivery Available
   Drinks: $1.00

Food Specialties: Shawarma, Shish Kabobs, Rib Steak, Soup Specials, Chicken

> *Description:* A fast food Shawarma eatery. The limited menu has the basics
> served either in a pita or on a platter. Both come with the free salad bar.
> Platters include a portion of fries. 3 freshly made soups change daily.
> Also offered are lamb burgers, Cornish hen, sweet breads, rib steak,
> chicken nuggets, baby lamb chops, fried chicken cutlet, falafel, beef and
> chicken kabobs. Grilled eggplant & squash are available at the salad bar.

> *Comments:* The portions are very small. Let them know that you're
> disappointed and they may add more without additional charge. The raw
> salads are fresh, but small paper plates and tongs that don't hold much,
> make you work for your supper! Insist on a larger plate to avoid having
> to make repeated trips to the salad bar.

Ambiance (Decor): A long Formica counter with stools dominates this year old fast
food stop. Tables in the back offer another seating option. All the cooking is
done behind the counter in full view of patrons. Faux light blue tiles cover the
walls, giving the fluorescent-lit room a bright appearance. Casual, child proof.

Service: Self-serve on plastic utensils and small paper plates.

General Comments:

Hours: **Sun-Thurs:** 11am-1am **Fri:** 11am till 2 hrs before Shabbos
   Sat: 1 hr after Shabbos till 3am

Credit Cards Not Accepted: CASH ONLY!

Restaurant Discount:

Borough: Brooklyn
Section: Midwood

The Authoritative New York City Kosher Dining Guide

Restaurant: Shalom Hunan

Phone Number: (718) 382-6000
Fax: (718) 382-7466

Address: 1619 Avenue M (cor. E. 16ᵗʰ St.)

Hechsher: Vaad Harabbanim of Flatbush (Glatt Kosher, Mashgiach Temidi)

Proprietor/Manager: Michael

Type(s) of Food: Meat - Chinese

Price Range: *Lunch*   *Dinner*   *Take out*
  Entrées: $8.50 or $10.00 $11.25-$18.50 $9.00-$18.00
  Dessert: $2.00-$2.50   Free Delivery >$25.00, in 2.5 miles
  Drinks: $1.25-$3.00, $12-$25/btl (Wine), $2.75-$3.50 (Beer), $5/gl (Mix)

Food Specialties: Sesame Chicken, Chicken with Garlic Sauce, Champagne Chicken

  Description: The fairly extensive menu has all the standard favorites, but also
    includes items not often seen: a Fish Category (incl. Sweet & Sour
    Crispy Fish, Hunan Crispy Fish or Lotus Fish), a Duck category (six
    offerings e.g. Bo-Lo Lichee Duck or Polynesian Duck), as well as a
    Light & Delicious Dieter's Selection (features steamed options without
    oil, MSG or corn starch). There are even two "American" choices which
    include Broiled Chai Rib Steak and the Oriental Frank. The Lunch
    Special comes with soup, egg roll and fried rice. Spices to your taste.

  Comments: Adequate portion size, sometimes well prepared, but á la carte
    only. Take out suffers greatly.

Ambiance (Decor): Chinese decor in muted colors, rear lit stained glass "windows"
  or screens make for a pleasant effect in the mid-sized room. Tablecloths,
  candles, and flowers on the tables contribute to the semi formal atmosphere.
  Dimmed lights create a more intimate setting. An additional basement level
  room is similarly appointed and is opened when warranted.

Service: Generally good service, however, not as prompt in their room downstairs

General Comments: It's worth a visit or two to taste some of their specialty dishes.

Hours: **Sun:** 12:30pm-10:30pm **Mon-Thurs:** 11:30am-10:30pm **Friday Closed**
  Sat: 1 hr after Shabbos-1am

Credit Cards Accepted: MC, Visa, AmEx

Restaurant Discount:

Borough: Brooklyn
Section: Midwood

The Authoritative New York City Kosher Dining Guide

Restaurant: Tov U'Maitiv

Phone Number: (718) 258-7991
Fax: None

Address: 2668 Nostrand Avenue (cor. Ave. M)

Hechsher: Rabbi Shlomo Mendelson (Glatt Kosher)

Proprietor/Manager:

Type(s) of Food: Meat - Deli, Jewish, American

Price Range:	Lunch	Dinner	Take out
Entrées:	$3.00-$10.00	Same	Same
Desserts:	None		
Drinks:	$ .85-$1.00		

Food Specialties: Roasts, Salads, Deli, BBQ Chicken, Southern Fried Chicken

> **Description:** Entrées such as Hungarian Goulash, Mussaka, Sweet & Sour Meatballs, and Stuffed Chicken are complemented by 9 different soups, extensive side dish selections, a large array of salads, as well as deli choices (sandwiches, by the pound or as entrée). Heimishe cooking.

> **Comments:** Home cooking on the fast food track without mass produced banality. A large portion of the business is take-out, so service is quick. The food looks fresh and appetizing.

Ambiance (Decor): Recently renovated, but the deli and take-out counter still dominates the room. Five tables provide seating for those who wish to eat in. No formalities or pretensions here. A place to sit and eat, but not a setting in which to entertain. Disposable plates and cutlery.

Service: Self-serve or they will accommodate

General Comments: A fine line separates this establishment from a take-out and restaurant. I did, however, observe several people dining here when I visited before dinner time.

Hours: **Sun-Thurs:** 9am-9pm   **Fri:** 9am- 2hrs before Shabbos
Saturday Closed

Credit Cards Not Accepted: CASH ONLY!

Restaurant Discount:

Borough: Brooklyn
Section: Midwood

The Authoritative New York City Kosher Dining Guide

Restaurant: Essex on Coney
Phone Number: (718) 253-1002
Fax: (718) 253-8322
Address: 1359 Coney Island Avenue (bet. Ave. J - Ave. K)

Hechsher: Vaad Harabbanim of Flatbush, also Kehilah - (Bodek Vegetables, Glatt Kosher, Chassidishe Shechita, Mashgiach Temidi)
Proprietor/Manager:

Type(s) of Food: Meat - Deli, Chinese

Price Range:

	Lunch	*Dinner*	*Take out*
Entrées:	$13.00-$19.95 (Deli)	Same	Same- Delivery Available
Chinese:	$7.95 (Lunch Special)	$12.95-$19.95	*Children's Menu:* $5.95
Desserts:	$2.75-$3.25	*Deli Sandwiches:* $5.50-$9.25	
Drinks:	$ .90-$1.25, $2.50/btl. (Lg. Soda) $4.00 (Pitcher Soda)		

Food Specialties: Deli Sandwiches, Spare Ribs, Veal & Lamb Chops, Rib Steak, Orange Duck, Dragon & Phoenix, Fong Wan Gay, King Kung Po

Description: A restaurant with a dual personality: one is a deli with a wide-ranging sandwich selection, (from Burgers, to Overstuffed Sandwiches, to Specialty Sandwiches and Hot Open Sandwiches), and categories like Diet Delights, Pasta, and Salad Platters. The other is a complete Chinese menu with a Lunch Special (w/ fried rice & soup), (11) Specialties, Combo platters (w/ rice & an egg roll) and a full regular menu.

Comments: The quality of the deli meat is ok, but it used to be better. The Chinese is disappointing. Although the vegetables are fresh and the meat appears to be of good quality, the seasoning lacks finesse. Both my soup & my entrée were returned because they were too salty. I ordered deli.

Ambiance (Decor): Nostalgia for Brooklyn in the 1920s & 1930s, particularly for Coney Island defines the setting in the fluorescent lit 1st room. The 2nd dining room more than doubles the capacity, but is nondescript & looking worn. The 3rd is used for overflow crowds or for parties.

Service: Standard

General Comments: Parking is usually hard to find.

Hours: **Sun-Thurs:** 11am-12am **Fri:** 11am-2pm **Sat:** 1½ hrs after Shabbos-12am

Credit Cards Accepted: MC, Visa, Diners Club

Restaurant Discount:

The Authoritative New York City Kosher Dining Guide

Restaurant: China Medhadrin Plus

Phone Number: (718) 677-5530
Fax: (718) 677-5536

Address: 1206 Avenue J (bet. E.12th St. - E.13th St.)

Hechsher: Kehilah (Glatt Kosher)

Proprietor/Manager:

Type(s) of Food: Meat - Chinese

Price Range: **Lunch** (12-3:30pm)   **Dinner**   **Take Out**
   Entrées: $ 10% Off $9.75-$10.95   Same - Free Local Delivery
   Desserts: None *Diet Dishes:* $7-$10   *Children's Special:* $1.50-$5
   Drinks: $ .85   *Lunch Special:* 10% Off (Noon-3:30pm)

Food Specialties: Orange Chicken, Kung Po Beef, Sesame Chicken, Curry Chicken

Description: Fast food establishment with concise menu. No virtuoso dishes, mostly basic fare. The Special Diet Dishes eliminate items like corn, corn starch, sugar and MSG. They could be served lightly sautéed, if preferred. Good sized portions. Some American appetizers like Fried Chicken Wings, BBQ Chicken Wings and French Fries are thrown in, as well. Chicken Nuggets, Hot Dog & Fries are some of the Children's Special dishes offered. Vegetarian selections ($6.75/ea) served with rice.

Comments: A basic "no-frills" Chinese menu.

Ambiance (Decor): This tiny, newly opened establishment is like its menu, unpretentious, basic and without frills. It accommodates 15-20 eat-in diners and has a strong emphasis on take-out.

Service: Self-serve

General Comments: A take-out establishment with seating for eating in.

Hours: **Sun-Thurs:** 11:30am-10:30pm **Fri:** 11:30am- 2 hrs before Shabbos
   Sat: 2 hrs after Shabbos till 11pm

Credit Cards Accepted: MC, Visa

Restaurant Discount:

Borough: Brooklyn
Section: Midwood

The Authoritative New York City Kosher Dining Guide

Restaurant: Bernie's Place   ***Phone Number:*** (718) 677-1515
                                                         Fax: (718) 677-9052

Address: 1217 Avenue J (bet. E. 12th St. - E. 13th St.)

Hechsher: Rabbi Yisroel P. Gornish (Cholov Yisroel, Kemach Yashan)

Proprietor/Manager: Still hosted by Bernie, but under new management.

Type(s) of Food: Dairy - Continental

Price Range: ***Lunch***   ***Dinner***   ***Take out***
    Entrées: $7.65-$10.00 (Spa) $9.95-$22.95   Same - Delivery Available
    Desserts: $ .50-$2.00 $3.50-$7.50   ***Early Bird Dinner:*** $16.95
    Drinks: $1.50-$4.00,   Beer & Wine Served   ***Dinner Special:*** $18

Food Specialties: Fresh Seafood, Eggplant Rollatini, Quiche, Pastas, Salads

> ***Description:*** A sophisticated menu that keeps evolving. The new Special Spa Lunch includes a soup, salad, sandwich and coffee or tea. Add $ .50 to include yogurt. To order a Salmon entrée instead of the sandwich add $2. The Early Bird Dinner (4:30pm-6:30pm) offers a selected special menu as does the Dinner Special menu. A la carte features: French Onion Soup, Seafood Chowder, Soup Of The Day and Gazpacho (a Mexican specialty served cold). Dishes run the gamut from potato crepes, to fresh salmon croquettes, to pizzetta margherita. Desserts are baked fresh daily on the premises and are complemented by an extensive beverage selection, including café mocha, cappuccino, café latté, shakes, freshly squeezed juices, teas, etc.

> ***Comments:*** Fine cuisine finally arrives in Brooklyn with cosmopolitan flair, and attractive presentation. Impressively generous portions.

Ambiance (Decor): During the day, the wood tables are uncovered and the restaurant takes on a café atmosphere. At night, the tablecloths and fresh flowers come out to set a more formal and elegant, yet comfortable tone. (56 seats).

Service: Gracious, responsive, formal service and superbly hosted by Bernie

General Comments: Classical music completes a tranquil and upscale setting. For business or pleasure, a refreshing change of pace on Ave. J.

Hours: Sun-Thurs: 11:30am-11pm   **Friday Closed**
       Sat: 2 hrs aft Shabbos till 12pm

Credit Cards Accepted: MC, Visa, AmEx

Restaurant Discount: 10% Off excluding Spa Lunch Or Any Other Specials

Borough: Brooklyn
Section: Midwood

The Authoritative New York City Kosher Dining Guide

Restaurant: Kosher Delight

Phone Number: (718) 377-6873
Fax: (718) 253-6189

Address: 1223 Avenue J (cor. E. 13ᵗʰ St.)

Hechsher: Rabbi Samuel David Beck, Vaad Harabbanim of Flatbush - (Glatt Kosher)

Proprietor/Manager: Shmuel Shapiro, Manager

Type(s) of Food: Meat - Deli, Chinese

Price Range:

	Lunch	*Dinner*	*Take out*
Entrées:	$8.00-$16.50	Same	Same – Local Delivery Available
Desserts:	$1.50-$1.95	*Chinese Entrées:* $10.95-$15.95	
Drinks:	$ .60-$1.30	*Sandwiches:* $5.50-$8.25	*Hero:* $20.95/ft.

Food Specialties: Burgers, Grill, Kebobs, Fried Chicken, Deli, Chinese Menu, Ribs

> *Description:* The fast food chain store menu of burgers and fries has been extended to include Chinese and deli. Chinese dishes are made fresh to order w/o MSG. Hero by the Foot has been added to the deli sandwich selections. Fried chicken is sold by the piece in various box sizes, buckets, etc. Soups and salads are also offered.

> *Comments:* The food tends to be greasy, but it has its devotees. Portions are scant and everything is à la carte.

Ambiance (Decor): The first floor restaurant has plastic everything, with trays to eat on. Tends to be hot, smoky, and crowded during meal hours. A favorite for families with small children, and consequently it can be noisy and chaotic. Sometimes long lines wind through the store, especially during meal times. Fast food restaurant. This branch has opened a second floor dining room, that has regular tables and chairs (not the molded plastic ones downstairs) and is more of an adult dining room. Large glass windows overlook Ave. J.

Service: Self-serve, long lines and bustle make getting service and food difficult

General Comments: The mystique of fast food: the chicken lacks meat, the burgers are small and unspectacular, the food in general is prepared in a haphazard manner, and there is no health consciousness in sight, but people love it!

Hours: **Sun-Thurs:** 11am-11pm **Fri:** 11am-4pm **Sat:** 1 hr after Shabbos till 2am

Credit Cards Accepted: MC, Visa, Discover

Restaurant Discount:

Borough: Brooklyn
Section: Midwood

The Authoritative New York City Kosher Dining Guide

Restaurant: Jerusalem Steak House II   *Phone Number:* (718) 258-8899
Fax: None

Address: 1319 Avenue J (bet. E.13th - E.14th St.)

Hechsher: Kehilah (Glatt Kosher)

Proprietor/Manager: Yossi, Menachem

Type(s) of Food: Meat - Middle Eastern

Price Range:	Lunch	Dinner	Take out
Entrées:	$12.00-$18.00	Same	Same - Delivery Available
Desserts:	$1.75-$3.00		
Drinks:	$1.25-$1.75	*Breakfast:* $5.50-$6.00	

Food Specialties: Grills, Shish Kebobs, Shawarma, Rib Steak, Fish, Soups, Salads

> *Description:* The usual Middle Eastern steak house menu featuring beef, lamb, chicken, and koufta kebobs, as well as Steaks, Lamb Chops. Cooked dishes include Marinated Chicken, Shnitzel, Chicken Liver and Sweet Breads. All main dishes include 2 sides. Ten Middle Eastern salads (e.g. Babaganoush, Tabouli and Chummus) and four soups (e.g. Yemenite, Bean and Vegetable) are also served.

> *Comments:* This is the same menu offered at the original Jerusalem Steak House restaurant on Kings Highway.

Ambiance (Decor): A virtual twin of the Kings Highway restaurant. Brightly lit and basic in conception. Typical of its genre, with white tablecloths and glass covering the tables.

Service: Standard

General Comments: Open since Aug. '97, Jerusalem Steak House II couldn't have chosen a better location. Surprisingly, it is the first and only steak house on the block. Identical to the original eatery except this one takes credit cards.

Hours: **Sun-Thurs:** 11am-11pm   **Fri:** 11am-2:50pm
Sat: Opens 1 hr after Shabbos till 12:30am or 1am

Credit Cards Accepted: MC, Visa, AmEx, Discover

Restaurant Discount:

Borough: Brooklyn
Section: Midwood

The Authoritative New York City Kosher Dining Guide

Restaurant: Garden of Eat-In

Phone Number: (718) 252-5289
Fax: (718) 252-1856

Address: 1416 Avenue J (bet. E. 14th St. - E. 15th St.)

Hechsher: Vaad Harabbanim of Flatbush, also Kehilah Kashrus (Cholov Yisroel)

Proprietor/Manager:

Type(s) of Food: Dairy, Vegetarian - American, Italian

Price Range:

	Lunch	Dinner	Take out
Entrées:	$13.95-$15.95	Same	Same - Free Local Delivery
Desserts:	$1.50-$5.50	**Sandwiches:** $3.50-$7.95	**Pastas:** $9.95-$13.95
Drinks:	$ .75-$2.25	$1.50-$2.95 (Malts/Ice Cream Sodas)	

Food Specialties: Sandwiches, Pasta, Salads, Pancakes, Omelets, Fish, Desserts

Description: The Baked Coho Salmon (stuffed with spinach, topped with mushrooms & tomatoes, served with baked potato & steamed vegetables) was somewhat dry. The Salmone Alla Griglia is better. Of the 3 soups we tried, the Pea Soup was the best. The extensive selection of desserts, ice cream, malteds and ice cream sodas gives this restaurant the feel of an old fashioned ice cream parlor. The malted is very thick (it passed the straw test) and was perfectly delicious. The cakes are very sweet.

Comments: As a family restaurant, Garden of Eat-In offers good value, fresh and often healthily prepared food in portions that are sure to be filling.

Ambiance (Decor): Café/diner atmosphere with a display counter and a rotating glass dessert showcase near the entry. Main area has both booths and tables with chairs. Mirrors alternate with panels of colored and stained glass floral patterns in a mauve, pink and white color scheme. The addition of a 2nd quieter, more subdued room has doubled seating capacity to 150 (75 seats/room).

Service: Diner service: informal, accommodating, but can be understaffed

General Comments: It caters to and meets the needs of its loyal customers well. Avoid mealtimes as they can be extremely noisy and service can suffer.

Hours: Sun-Thurs: 7am-10pm **Friday Closed**
Sat: (**Oct.-May**) 1½ hrs after Shabbos till 1am

Credit Cards Accepted: MC, Visa

Restaurant Discount:

48

Borough: Brooklyn
Section: Midwood

The Authoritative New York City Kosher Dining Guide

Restaurant: Sub-Sational

Phone Number: (718) 677-6987
Fax: None

Address: 992 E. 15th Street (bet. Ave. J - Ave. I)

Hechsher: Kehilah (Glatt Kosher)

Proprietor/Manager: Gary

Type(s) of Food: Meat – Submarine Sandwiches, Deli, Mexican

Price Range:

	Lunch	Dinner	Take Out
Entrées:	$3.99-$5.99	Same	Same – Free Local Delivery
Desserts:	None	**Burgers:** $3.99-$5.99	(Min. $15)
Drinks:	$1.00	**Subs:** $3.99-$4.99	

Food Specialties: Subs, Chicken Nuggets, Burgers, Steaks, Tortillas, Tacos, Burritos

> **Description:** The submarine reigns in this fast food eatery. Where else can one find a kosher Italian Meatball Sub (sans cheese), or how about Italian Veal Sausage? Philly Steak (also sans cheese), BBQ Sliced Steak and Super Sensational Mad Rib-Eye Steak share the bill with Crazy Chicken and Mexican favorites such as Burritos and Tacos (no cheese here either). Add some Chicken Nuggets, Cajun and French Fries, and you have an idea how the menu develops. Soup of the Day and homemade bread make you wonder how they manage in the tiny kitchen.

> **Comments:** Surprisingly, good food for a fast food type establishment. Mexican food (quite good) and subs are good choices.

Ambiance (Decor): Compact and unpretentious, straddling the line between a take out and a sit down eatery. 4 tables (10 seats) and a couple additional tables outside in warm weather. A small glass display counter divides the kitchen from the eating area. Restaurant is a step above street level. Bathroom is very narrow.

Service: Self-serve

General Comments: Good value and good quality: a nice combo. Long lead-time on orders. Not good for fast meals, but food is worth the wait, >10 min when busy.

Hours: **Sun-Thurs:** 11am-12pm   **Fri:** 11am-2 hrs. before Shabbos
Sat: 9:30pm-1am

Credit Cards *Not Accepted*: CASH ONLY

Restaurant Discount: 10% Off

☒ ☒ ☒ ☒ ☒ ☒ **$$**

The Authoritative New York City Kosher Dining Guide

Restaurant: Weiss' *Phone Number:* (718) 421-0184
Fax: None

Address: 1146 Coney Island Avenue (bet. Ave. H - Foster Ave.)

Hechsher: Vaad Harabbanim of Flatbush (Cholov Yisroel)

Proprietor/Manager: Lenny Cohen (manager)

Type(s) of Food: Dairy, Vegetarian - American, Italian, Eclectic

Price Range: *Lunch* *Dinner* *Take out*
    Entrées: $10.00-$18.50 $16-$19 (Sp Th), $8.00-$14.00 Delivery Avail.
    Desserts: $4.00-$9.00 *Smorgasbord:* $13.99 (Mon: 6pm-10pm)
    Drinks: $ .65-$1.00, $2.75-$4.75/gl, $8-$22/btl (W), $4.50-$6.50 (Mx.Drnk)

Food Specialties: Tuna Teriyaki, Norwegian Salmon, Eggplant Rollentine Parmesana

> *Description:* The portions are respectable. Everything is à la carte, except for Monday when there is an all you can eat buffet.

> *Comments:* The preparation is uneven and often leaves much to be desired. The Smorgasbord spread is impressive, but although the dishes look appetizing and effort at their presentation is evident, they are tasteless. There is a decided scarcity of refinement in the cooking, particularly in the use of seasoning. Everything is either seasoned in a similar manner and thus tastes the same, or the seasonings used don't work well together. This lack of expertise culminates in boring, and sometimes nasty results. Two soups we recently sampled, the vegetable and the mushroom barley, both suffered from a sour aftertaste. The mushroom sauce that topped both my salmon and the vegetable liver blintz appetizer was thick, heavy with corn starch, and overpowered with salt.

Ambiance (Decor): Tastefully decorated in muted colors, this spacious eatery is now worn. A small water fountain is the visual focus in the room. Casual.

Service: If they're busy, be prepared to wait. Ranges from good to questionable.

General Comments: This restaurant has its devotees, but I fail to see why. I was prepared to write a wonderful review and am disappointed that I cannot. There is no reason why Weiss' cannot be first rate. I'm sorry to say it isn't as of yet.

Hours: (Winter) **Sun-Thurs:** 12-9:30pm **Friday Closed** Sat: 1½ hrs after Shabbos
(Summer) **Sun-Thurs:** 12pm-10pm **Friday Closed** **Saturday Closed**

Credit Cards Accepted: MC, Visa

Restaurant Discount:

Borough: Brooklyn
Section: Midwood

The Authoritative New York City Kosher Dining Guide

Restaurant: Famous Pita　　　　　　**Phone Number:** None
　　　　　　　　　　　　　　　　　　Fax: None
Address: 935 Coney Island Avenue (bet. 18th Ave. - Webster Ave.)

Hechsher: Kosher "K" Mehadrin Supervision

Proprietor/Manager:

Type(s) of Food: Meat - Middle Eastern

Price Range:　　**Lunch**　　　**Dinner**　　　**Take out**
　　Entrées:　$3.50 Falafel　$6.15 Schwarma　$4.65 Burger
　　Desserts:　None
　　Drinks:　$1.46 Mitzli　$1.62 בירה שחורה

Food Specialties: Falafel Bar, Shawarma Bar

　　Description: Do it yourself pita sandwiches: you get a pita with falafel or
　　　　shawarma and then you proceed to fill it up with your choice of the
　　　　perfunctory fixings.

　　Comments: Fast food: fresh salad at the falafel/salad bar.

Ambiance (Decor): Brightly lit with fluorescent lights. Small, crowded, warm.
　　Informal, cafeteria style eatery.

Service: Self-serve

General Comments: Open late, and after 11pm, may be your only option in the area.
　　Salad bar was okay. No frills eating. Oily, fried foods.

Hours: **Sun-Thurs:** 11am-3am　**Fri:** 11am-2hrs before Shabbos
　　Sat: Opens 1 hr after Shabbos till 3am

Credit Cards Not Accepted: CASH ONLY!

Restaurant Discount:

51

The Authoritative New York City Kosher Dining Guide

Pizzerias:

Kosher Pizza - Pasta
1220 Avenue M
Association for Reliable Kashruth

Tel: (718) 336-4024
(800)-870-2173

Jerusalem II Pizza
1424 Avenue M
Rabbi Yisroel P. Gornish

Tel: (718) 645-4753

Chadash Pizza
1919 Avenue M
Vaad Harabbanim of Flatbush
also Kehilah Kashrut

Tel: (718) 253-4793

Knish King (Pizza & Falafel)
2916 Avenue M
Vaad Harabbanim of Flatbush

Tel: (718) 377-6218

Pizza Island
568 Coney Island Avenue
Vaad Harabbanim of Flatbush

Tel: (718) 253-1400

Kosher Pizza World
3005 Avenue K
Vaad Harabbanim of Flatbush

Tel: (718) 692-2800

Tel Aviv Pizza
1387 Coney Island Avenue
Vaad Harabbanim of Flatbush

Tel: (718) 377-7720

Kosher Pizza Plus
1427 Coney Island Avenue
Vaad Harabbanim of Flatbush

Tel: (718) 258-0392

Jerusalem II Pizza
1312 Avenue J
Vaad Harabbanim of Flatbush

Tel: (718) 338-8156

The Authoritative New York City Kosher Dining Guide

Pizza Time   *Tel:* (718) 252-8801
1324 E. 14th Street (cor. Avenue J)
Rabbi Samuel David Beck
(Cholov Yisroel)

Natanya Fast Food & Pizza   *Tel:* (718) 258-5160
1506 Avenue J
Vaad Harabbanim of Flatbush

Student's Choice   *Tel:* (718) 859-1151
Campus Road & Hillel Place
(Brooklyn College--Boylin Hall)
Vaad Harabbanim of Flatbush

Donut Shops:

Dunkin' Donuts   *Tel:* (718) 336-2641
1611 Avenue M
ב-K

Dunkin' Donuts   *Tel:* (718) 692-1939
1410 Avenue J
ב-K

HOW DO YOU GET
PEOPLE TO CONTRIBUTE
TO YOUR CAUSE?

 **IT'S SIMPLE!**

OFFER THEM SOMETHING:

- THAT THEY ALREADY WANT
- THAT THEY CAN REALLY USE
- THAT WILL SAVE THEM MONEY
- THAT THEY CAN ENJOY ALL YEAR LONG
- THAT WILL SIMPLIFY THEIR LIVES
- THAT SUPPORTS THE COMMUNITY
- THAT IS CONVENIENT & EASY TO USE
- THAT IS VERSATILE & SERVES MANY NEEDS

THE AUTHORITATIVE
NEW YORK CITY
KOSHER DINING GUIDE
MAKES FUND-RAISING EASY!

Borough Park
Sunset Park
(Bush Terminal)

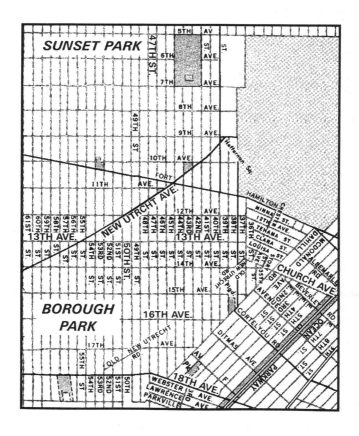

Borough: Brooklyn
Section: Borough Park

 **$$**

The Authoritative New York City Kosher Dining Guide

Restaurant: Uzbekistan   **Phone Number:** (718) 436-8400
                                                    Fax: None

Address: 4310 18ᵗʰ Avenue (bet. E. 2ⁿᵈ St. - McDonald Ave.)

Hechsher: Rabbi Jacob Nasirov (Glatt Kosher, Mashgiach Temidi)

Proprietor/Manager: Terry

Type(s) of Food: Meat – Russian, Asian

Price Range: **Lunch**   **Dinner**   **Take Out**
    Entrées: $4.99 (Special) $12.00-$15.00 $1.50-$4.99
    Desserts: $2.00-$3.00   Free Local Delivery ($15 Min.)
    Drinks: $2.00-$4.00, $4/gl (beer), $7/gl (Wine), $7/gl (Mixed Drinks)

Food Specialties: Caucasian Shish Kebobs, Soup, Chicken Tabaka, Lamb Balls

Description: A menu with a mix of Euro-Asian and Russian favorites. Some
fish entrées including Salmon Steak and Karp grilled in garlic sauce.
Kebob choices range from the familiar beef, chicken and lamb to
"Kaukasian Lamb" and "Kaukasian" Chicken. Beef Stroganoff is one of
11 Hot Entrées along with Steak New York and Basturma. Soups start
with Borsht and become increasingly more exotic as with the Mastava,
Lagman, Shurpa, Solyanka and finally the Ravioli in Broth. Appetizers
form the largest category on the menu & include separate lists of hot,.
cold, meat, and fish selections.

Comments: A menu that probably tastes more familiar than it sounds.

Ambiance (Decor): 400 seats, a spacious dining room, a wood dance floor that
dominates the center of the room, and a full bar standing to its right, invokes a
nightclub atmosphere. Evident is a partiality for colorful plastic flowers which
conflict with the nightclub setting. Table linens and candles lend a sense of
formality. For lunch, the tablecloths are removed uncovering sleek laminate
tables. Live music and dancing are featured on Saturday & Sunday nights.

Service: Standard

General Comments: Check closing times; they fluctuate depending on business.

Hours: **Sun-Thurs:** 10am-12pm   **Friday Closed**   **Sat:** 2 hrs after Shabbos till 1am

Credit Cards Accepted: MC, Visa, Discover

Restaurant Discount: 10% Off for Bills Over $25

Borough: Brooklyn
Section: Borough Park

The Authoritative New York City Kosher Dining Guide

Restaurant: Glatt Kosher Family   **Phone Number:** (718) 972-8061
                                                Fax: (718) 972-8086
Address: 4305 18th Avenue (bet. McDonald Ave. - E. 2nd St.)

Hechsher: Vaad Harabbanim of Flatbush (Glatt Kosher, Mashgiach Temidi)

Proprietor/Manager: Shing Sheung Chent

Type(s) of Food: Meat - Chinese

Price Range: **Lunch** (11am-3:30pm)   **Dinner**   **Take Out**
    Entrées: $5.50-6.95 (Special) $10-15.90   Same – Delivery Available
    Desserts: $ .50-$2.00   **Combo Platters:** $7.65-$8.95
    Drinks: $1.00-$1.20   **Special Diet Dishes:** $8.00-$11.00

Food Specialties: Sesame Chicken, 7 Stars Around the Moon, Da Chien Chicken

Description: Chicken and beef dishes dominate the menu, but veal and duck dishes have some presence. 5 choices of Chow Ho Fun (wide rice noodles) and Chow Mai Fun (thin rice noodles) dishes. 8 vegetable selections available for those watching their meat intake. The Lunch Specials and Combination Platters include fried rice and a choice between Wonton or Egg Drop Soup or an Egg Roll. Newly introduced fish specialties include General Tso's Fish, Sesame Fish, Salmon Steamed Steak w/ BBQ Sauce, Fish w/ Mixed Vegetables & Fish Soup.

Comments: The food may well be the best of the Chinese fast food/take out establishments, both in preparation and taste.

Ambiance (Decor): Newly opened, the restaurant sports a modern Chinese theme in a slick fast food setting. Bright fluorescent lighting, tables w/ red plastic tablecloths, large glitzy cityscapes framed in stainless, and Chinese fans (the only traditional references) decorate the walls. Seats 50. Neon window sign.

Service: Standard

General Comments: New Chinese eatery serving Hunan & Cantonese style cooking. Great take out that is better than a lot of Chinese restaurants. Good value!

Hours: **Sun-Thurs:** 11am-11pm   **Fri:** 11am-1hr before Shabbos
    Sat: 1 hr after Shabbos till 12pm

Credit Cards Accepted: MC, Visa, AmEx

Restaurant Discount: 10% Off On Orders of $15 or Over

Borough: Brooklyn
Section: Borough Park

The Authoritative New York City Kosher Dining Guide

Restaurant: Dalya & Zion Burger Restaurant   Phone Number: (718) 871-9467
                                              Fax: None
Address: 4102 18th Avenue (cor. E. 4th St.)

Hechsher: Vaad Harabbanim of Flatbush (Glatt Kosher, Kemach Yashan)

Proprietor/Manager: Dalya, Zion

Type(s) of Food: Meat - Middle Eastern

Price Range: Lunch   Dinner   Take out
    Entrées: $6.00-$15.00 $8.00-$18.00   Same – Delivery Available
    Desserts: $ .75-$2.50   Breakfast: $3.50-$4.50
    Drinks: $1.00-1.50   Sandwiches: $2.50-$7.00

Food Specialties: Grilled Meats, Kebobs, Schnitzel, Stuffed Grape Leaves, Falafel

Description: Chicken, beef and lamb kebobs, Rib Steak and Lamb Chops
    share the entrée list with cooked items such as Stuffed Peppers and
    Goulash. Entrées are served w/ pita, pickles, mini eggplant and Turkish
    salads and a choice of 2 side dishes. Appetizers offer Israeli favorites
    like Babaganoush, Moroccan Cigars, Kibbeh, Chummus and Techina.
    Some salads are Israeli, Turkish and Eggplant. Among the five soups are
    Calf Leg, Lamb, Meat, Bean, Chicken and Vegetable. Sandwiches come
    with homemade pita or on a bun with one side dish and salad. All food
    is made fresh daily from scratch.

Comments: "Heimishe, Chassidic, Israeli, yeshivaish" (owner's
    characterization) describes the home-style food as well as the clientele.

Ambiance (Decor): Renovated two years ago, but has already lost its new luster.
    Glass topped green & white checkered table-clothed tables accommodate 70.
    Brightly lit. Mirrors track across the walls to expand the space. Informal.

Service: Waitress

General Comments: An unpretentious and informal restaurant.

Hours: Sun-Thurs: 10am-1am   Fri: 10am till 2 hrs before Shabbos
    Sat: Opens 1½ hrs after Shabbos till 1am (Winter Only)

Credit Cards Accepted: MC, Visa, Discover ($20 Min.)

Restaurant Discount:

The Authoritative New York City Kosher Dining Guide

Restaurant: Edna's Restaurant & Deli   *Phone Number:* (718) 438-8207
                                          Fax: (718) 438-7306
Address: 125 Church Avenue (bet. McDonald Ave. - E. 2nd St.)

Hechsher: Vaad Harabbanim of Flatbush, also Rabbi Shmuel Krauz (Glatt Kosher)

Proprietor/Manager: Josh (Manager)

Type(s) of Food: Meat - Deli, Jewish-American

Price Range: *Lunch*   *Dinner*   *Take out*
Entrées: $12.25-$25.00   Same $12.45-$21.25 – Free Local Del. ($15 Min)
Desserts: $2.40-$3.00   *Sandwiches:* $5.45-$9.95, $12.75-$14.50 (Hot Open)
Drinks: $ .90-$1.25, $2.25-$3.00 (Beer)   *Dinner Specials:* $12.20-$22

Food Specialties: Potted Veal, Breast of Veal, Brisket, Steaks

Description: A full service deli menu featuring all the expected deli favorites.
Deli sandwiches, of course, and a fairly extensive array of cooked dishes
with poultry, beef, veal and fish. Broiler selections include London Broil
w/ Mushroom Sauce, Lamb Chops, and Rib Steak. Each entrée comes
with two vegetable side dishes. Dinner specials include cup of soup,
entrée, cole slaw, dessert, and tea or coffee. Old fashioned heimishe
cooking in which all the ingredients are fresh and all the food is
"homemade." Ample portions.

Comments: The corned beef and pastrami are lean and moist with good
traditional flavor, delicious. Texture not in the least bit stringy or chewy.

Ambiance (Decor): Besides the obligatory deli counter, there are tables (seating 70
people) with tablecloths, linen napkins and occasionally flowers making this
restaurant perfect for family outings. Informal, traditional deli setting. If you're
in the mood for a good old fashioned, heimishe deli experience, you'll find it
here. **HANDICAP NOTE:** No handicap stall in the bathroom.

Service: Standard

General Comments: With 40 years behind them, what could be bad?

Hours: **Sun-Thurs:** 9am-10pm   **Fri:** 9am-2 hrs before Shabbos
         Saturday Closed

Credit Cards Accepted: MC, Visa, AmEx

Restaurant Discount: 10% Off

Borough: Brooklyn
Section: Borough Park

The Authoritative New York City Kosher Dining Guide

Restaurant: The Bagel Spot   *Phone Number:* (718) 853-4450
                                                Fax: None
Address: 4305 14th Avenue (bet. 43rd St. - 44th St.)

Hechsher: Rabbi Chaim Yakarov (Chalov Yisroel Mehadrin, Pas Yisroel)

Proprietor/Manager:

Type(s) of Food: Dairy - American

Price Range: *Lunch*   *Dinner*   *Take out*
   Entrées: $4.00-$6.00   Same   Same
   Desserts: $1.00   *Lunch Special:* $4.00-$6.00
   Drinks: $ .25-$1.25

Food Specialties: Bagels Sandwiches, Cookies, Pastries & Cakes, Fresh Fish, Salad

   Description: All baking is done on the premises and consequently all the
      baked goods are very fresh. Many varieties of bagels are served with a
      choice of assorted fills, such as tuna, egg, cheese, white fish, etc. The
      Lunch Special consists of a fish entrée (flounder, salmon, white fish or
      gefilte) 2 sides, salad, a bagel and coffee.

   Comments: Not gourmet, but heimishe food served in satisfying portions.

Ambiance (Decor): Nothing fancy. A cross between a luncheonette and a bakery.
   The atmosphere is casual in the chassidic style, reflecting the restaurant's
   clientele. 35 seats.

Service: Self-service

General Comments: A fast food eatery convenient to 13th Avenue shopping. Also
   functions as a bakery and take out establishment.

Hours: **Sun-Thurs:** 6am-2am   **Fri:** 6am-3 hrs before Shabbos
      Sat: 1½ hrs. after Shabbos till 2am

Credit Cards Not Accepted: CASH ONLY!

Restaurant Discount:

60

Borough: Brooklyn
Section: Borough Park

The Authoritative New York City Kosher Dining Guide

Restaurant: Shem Tov Restaurant   **Phone Number:** (718) 438-9366
                                             Fax: None
Address: 5326 13th Avenue (bet. 53rd St. - 54th St.)

Hechsher: CRC

Proprietor/Manager: Yaakov Yisroel & Pincus Levy Steinmetz

Type(s) of Food: Dairy - Hungarian, Jewish

Price Range:	Lunch	Dinner	Take out
Entrées:	$7.95-$11.50	Same	Same
Desserts:	$1.00-$4.00	**Breakfast Special:** $3.00	
Drinks:	$ .60-$2.50	**Sandwiches:** $2.95-$4.50	

Food Specialties: Salmon Steak, Rainbow Trout, Tuna Cutlet, Soups, Salads

Description: Home style cooking. The Breakfast Special (7am-11am) includes 2 eggs, roll, home fries, salad, and coffee or orange juice. Entrées heavily favor fresh fish and include White Fish in Tomato Sauce, Baked Salmon, Tuna Cutlet, Rainbow Trout, Halibut Steak and Flounder, etc. Eggplant Parmegian, Stuffed Peppers and Lasagna are offered, as well. Soups, Salads, Omelets, and side dishes that include various blintzes round off the menu.

Comments: A chassidishe restaurant with its roots originating from Hungary. It is unpretentious, and offers generous portions of home-style food.

Ambiance (Decor): Heimishe, relaxed, but pleasantly decorated. This restaurant seats up to 30 people at laminate topped tables. Although attractively wallpapered, the atmosphere is mostly defined by the largely Chassidic clientele. The irregular shaped interior results from the odd shaped corner the restaurant occupies. The dining room is 2 steps above street level.

Service: Self-serve

General Comments: A pleasant eatery that offers good value for fish lovers.

Hours: Sun-Thurs: 6:30am-11pm   Fri: 6am-12pm   <u>**Saturday Closed**</u>

Credit Cards Not Accepted: CASH ONLY!

Restaurant Discount:

Borough: Brooklyn
Section: Borough Park

The Authoritative New York City Kosher Dining Guide

Restaurant: Deli 52 (formerly Guttman's)   *Phone Number:* (718) 871-9654
Fax: (718) 436-4830
Address: 5120 13th Avenue (bet. 51st St. - 52nd St.)

Hechsher: Rabbi Amrum Roth (Glatt Kosher)

Proprietor/Manager: Heshy & Lipa

Type(s) of Food: Meat - Deli

Price Range: *Lunch*   *Dinner*   *Take out*
     Entrées: $12.00-$18.00   Same   Same - Delivery ($30 Min.)
     Desserts: $2.00-$2.75 *Sandwiches:* $5.50-$8.95 *Ladies' Mon. Special*
     Drinks: $1.00-$1.50 *Tues-Wed Special:* Entrées include soup & dessert

Food Specialties: Tongue Polonaise, Goulash, Brisket, Fried Chicken, Chulent

> *Description:* This is a standard deli menu with traditional appetizers, soups,
> hot and cold sandwiches, salads and cooked entrées (beef, veal, chicken
> and turkey). Eggs and omelets made with assorted deli meat come with
> lettuce, tomato, and homemade curly fries. Hungarian Specialties.

> *Comments:* Good quality meats and traditional preparation. The corned beef is
> particularly good. The heimishe vegetable soup is based in split pea,
> potato, mushrooms, and celery. Portions are large.

Ambiance (Decor): A deli take out counter up front leads to a separate dining area in
the rear with seating for 60. Recently renovated and decorated with black and
white tiles on floor and walls, the interior is bright and fresh. Childproof
environment, perfect for family meals. Casual, with place mats on the tables.

Service: Friendly and attentive (Except Friday when there is no waiter service)

General Comments: A neighborhood fixture for 25 years now under new ownership.
An attractive contemporary take on the traditional deli. **Handicap Note:** Dining
Room is on street level, but the bathroom is in the basement.

Hours: **Sun-Thurs:** 12:30pm-10:30pm   **Fri:** 8am-2 hrs before Shabbos (Take Out
or Self-serve Only)   **Saturday Closed**

Credit Cards Accepted: MC, Visa, AmEx, Discover

Restaurant Discount: One Time Free à la carte Dinner

Borough: Brooklyn
Section: Borough Park

The Authoritative New York City Kosher Dining Guide

Restaurant: Matamim Dairy Restaurant

Phone Number: (718) 437-2772
Fax: None

Address: 5001 13th Avenue (cor. 50th St.)

Hechsher: CRC

Proprietor/Manager: Moshe Teitelbaum

Type(s) of Food: Dairy - Jewish American

Price Range:	*Lunch*	*Dinner*	*Take out*
Entrées:	$9.95-$11.95	Same	Same - Delivery Available
Desserts:	$ .85-$3.50		(3 block radius $15 Min., $25 Min.
Drinks:	$ .60-$3.00		

Food Specialties: Stuffed Trout, Broiled Salmon, Pastas, Soups, Salads,

> *Description:* Heimishe food with home cooked flavor. Fish entrées come with 2 side dishes. No frills, nothing exotic. In response to popular demand, plans for a complete menu overhaul are currently on hold. A heavy emphasis on fish entrées and home cooked dishes.

> *Comments:* Nothing fancy for now, just home cooking that comes in generous portions. The owner's ambition to inject some sophistication and variation into his menu have been dashed. Too bad! The introduction of unique international dishes would have distinguished this Borough Park dairy establishment. A place for heimishe, filling meals.

Ambiance (Decor): A typical luncheonette which features a take-out counter with stools, booths, and some tables in the back (total seating capacity 40). Plastic utensils and styrofoam plates.

Service: Self-serve

General Comments: Despite the owner's aspirations of offering his customers something a little different, it appears that the restaurant's customers prefer to keep things heimishe. Plans to introduce Mexican cuisine with a focus on health are on hold indefinitely.

Hours: **Sun-Thurs:** 7am-10pm **Fri:** 7am-1pm <u>**Saturday Closed**</u>

Credit Cards Not Accepted: CASH ONLY!

Restaurant Discount: 15% Off or Buy One Meal & Get The 2nd One Of Equal Or Lesser Value At Half Price.

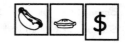

The Authoritative New York City Kosher Dining Guide

Restaurant: Crown Deli

Phone Number: (718) 853-9000
Fax: None

Address: 4909 13th Avenue (bet. 49th St. - 50th St.)

Hechsher: NO HECHSHER (Glatt Kosher)

Proprietor/Manager: Yachov Chavanow

Type(s) of Food: Meat - Deli, Jewish American

Price Range:

	Lunch	Dinner	Take out
Entrées:	$6.49-$14.49	Same	Same – No Delivery Available
Desserts:	$1.50	**Deli Sandwiches:**	$3-$6.99 (Reg.), $7-$8.49 (Hot Open)
Drinks:	$ .60-$1.95, $1.75 (Beer), $2.75 (Premium Beer)		

Food Specialties: Deli, Beef Stew, Steaks, Lamb Chops, Broiled Rib Steak, Roasts

Description: A standard traditional deli menu with the heimishe touch. A choice of deli platters and sandwiches, as well as a variety of home cooked dishes. Add $3.99 to the price of the entrée for the Special Deluxe Dinner consisting of appetizer, soup, entrée with 2 sides, dessert and tea. A choice of five soups $1.75-$2.49.

Comments: All the usual deli favorites are represented. Good value.

Ambiance (Decor): Usual deli layout with 65 seat capacity. Seating is concentrated in the back. Flannel backed, plastic tablecloths set the tone in this wood paneled eatery. Antiqued mirrors line the walls and tiffany styled pendants provide the somewhat subdued ambient lighting.

Service: Waiter service or self-serve

General Comments: A heimishe establishment which has become known as a place for good, hearty, home-style cooking with a chassidishe taam and reasonable prices.

Hours: Sun-Thurs: 10am-10pm **Fri:** 10am-3pm (depends on Shabbos)
Saturday Closed **Sun:** 11am-10pm

Credit Cards Accepted: MC, Visa

Restaurant Discount:

Borough: Brooklyn
Section: Borough Park

The Authoritative New York City Kosher Dining Guide

Restaurant: Chefah

Phone Number: (718) 972-0133
Fax: None

Address: 4810 13th Avenue (bet. 48th St. - 49th St.)

Hechsher: Rabbi Menachem Fischer, VIN (Glatt Kosher, Chasidishe Shechita)

Proprietor/Manager: Shlomy Steinberg (Manager)

Type(s) of Food: Meat – Deli, Jewish-American

Price Range: **Lunch** (11am-4pm)   **Dinner**   **Take Out**
    Entrées: $4-$8 (Specials) $6.99-$11.99   Same – Free Local Delivery
    Desserts: $1.5-$2.00 **Monday Night Smorgasbord:** $12.99 (6pm-10pm)
    Drinks: $ .90-$1.25   **Dinner Special:** $8   **Sandwiches:** $4.99-$7.99

Food Specialties: Deli Sandwiches, BBQ Wings, Goulash, Southern Fried Chicken

Description: Traditional Jewish fare dominates but menu also includes some
eclecticism with items like Stuffed Capon, Hawaiian Chicken, Chicken
Chow Mein, Pepper Steak and Swedish Meatballs. Good quality
heimishe food prepared fresh daily. Lunch Specials include soup, salad,
entrée and a beverage. The Monday Night All-You-Can-Eat
Smorgasbord menu changes weekly and features seasonal options. The
meat is smoked on premises. **Deli Sandwiches:** $6.99 **Deli Deluxe
Special:** $7.99 (includes pastrami or corned beef sandwich, French
fries and soda) applies to eat-in diners only.

Comments: Not only is providing fresh meat here not a problem, the quality
appears to be first rate. Impressive meats are on display in the front.

Ambiance (Decor): Spacious butcher shop/restaurant combo with a large display
case dominating the front area and the informal dining area is in the back.
Mirrored walls contribute to the roomy feel. Brightly lit and child friendly with
laminate top tables, tiled floors and wrought iron backed chairs. 40 seats.

Service: Self-serve

General Comments: A restaurant that makes eating out with the whole family easy.

Hours: **Sun-Thurs:** 9am-10pm   **Fri:** 8am-2 hrs before Shabbos   <u>**Saturday Closed**</u>

Credit Cards Accepted: MC, Visa, AmEx

Restaurant Discount: 10% Off on Thursdays Only On Eat In Dinners

Borough: Brooklyn
Section: Borough Park

The Authoritative New York City Kosher Dining Guide

Restaurant: Weiss Luncheonette

Phone Number: (718) 438-9721
Fax: None

Address: 1305 47th Street (bet. 13th Ave. - 14th Ave.)

Hechsher: NO HECHSHER (Cholov Yisroel, Pas Yisroel, Kemach Yoshon)

Proprietor/Manager: Mayer Weiss

Type(s) of Food: Dairy - American

Price Range:	Lunch	Dinner	Take Out
Entrées:	$3.65-$5.75	Closed	Same
Desserts:	$ .85-$2.00	Sandwiches: $1.00-$4.60	
Drinks:	$ .85-$1.25		

Food Specialties: Sandwiches, Platters, Omelets, Hungarian Rice, Eggplant, Soup

Description: A breakfast and lunch menu. Variety is not its strong point, but the selections should satisfy most. The single soup offered alternates between vegetable and potato every few months. Platters are either tuna, salmon (from a can or as a cutlet), or egg. The fresh vegetable salad is modified to taste. Cakes, ice cream, or seasonal fruit salad for dessert. Beverage choices include: malteds, juices, coffee, tea, sodas, and cream sodas.

Comments: A true but concise luncheonette menu.

Ambiance (Decor): A very small establishment with two tables and two eating counters that together seat 16. Its appearance is described as being like an old-fashioned candy store. Don't dress up!

Service: Owner cooks, serves, cleans and personally pampers customers.

General Comments: Operating for 17 years, Weiss Luncheonette harks back to the uncomplicated past, when mom & pop stores were not as rare as they are today.

Hours: Sun-Thurs: 7am-4:30pm   Fri: 7am-1pm   **Saturday Closed**

Credit Cards Not Accepted: CASH ONLY!

Restaurant Discount:

Borough: Brooklyn
Section: Borough Park

The Authoritative New York City Kosher Dining Guide

Restaurant: Avenue Plaza Hotel

Phone Number: (718)
Fax: (718)

Address: 13ᵗʰ Avenue (cor. 47ᵗʰ St.)

Hechsher: To Be Announced

Proprietor/Manager:

Type(s) of Food: Dairy

Price Range: *Lunch*   *Dinner*   *Take Out*
   Entrées: $
   Desserts: $
   Drinks: $

> The hotel is currently under construction and details about the 2 restaurants planned are still sketchy. Both restaurants will be dairy & open to the public. The hotel is scheduled to open about Pesach time.

Food Specialties:

Description:

Comments:

Ambiance (Decor): Two restaurants are planned in the hotel: one enclosed in glass on the roof which will hold up to 150 people and will also function as a party room. The second on the basement level will accommodate 75-80 people.

Service:

General Comments:

Hours: **Sun-Thurs:**   **Fri:**
      Sat:

Credit Cards Accepted:

Restaurant Discount:

Borough: Brooklyn
Section: Borough Park

The Authoritative New York City Kosher Dining Guide

Restaurant: China Glatt

Phone Number: (718) 438-2576
Fax: (718) 438-2436

Address: 4413 13th Avenue (bet. 44th St. - 45th St.)

Hechsher: Rabbi Fishel Senderowitz - Kahal Addas Vishnitz (Chassidishe Shechita)

Proprietor/Manager: Sholom Witriol

Type(s) of Food: Meat - Chinese, American

Price Range:

	Lunch	Dinner	Take out
Entrées:	$5.49-$8.95	$9.50-$19.95	**Lunch:** $5.49-$7.95
Desserts:	$1.95-$8.95/2	**Dinner Special:** $49.95/4	**Dinner:** $8.50-$17.00
Drinks:	$1.25/gl-$3.50/ btl.	$3-$4/gl, $8-$19/btl. (Wine)	

Food Specialties: Lin's Nest, Sesame Chicken, Goi Lan Steak, N.Y. Style Rib Steak

Description: Ample menu includes: beef, chicken, veal, duck, fish and vegetarian possibilities. Dietetic, American, Kid's, and Family Combo categories are offered, as well as numerous Chef Specialties. Every dish is freshly made to order and modified to suit your taste.

Comments: The beef, veal, and chicken are of excellent quality. All are tender, flavorful, and juicy. The carefully prepared and crispy vegetables lend a satisfying texture to the dishes. The sauces are seasoned with an experienced hand and are a delicious enhancement. If you are not sure, ask the waiters to recommend something, they're usually right!

Ambiance (Decor): Accommodates 85 people comfortably, in an attractive, not particularly Oriental dining room in peach, hunter green and beige. Colors are repeated in the tablecloths and cloth napkins . Currently undergoing renovations to spruce up the restaurant façade, entry, bathroom, main dining room and kitchen. Appropriate for family dining as well as social engagements. Upstairs party room. Semi-formal.

Service: Courteous and attentive, the Chassidic owner, usually in attendance, is a gracious and generous host who makes his guests feel cared for and welcome.

General Comments: The only regular Chinese restaurant in the area, it offers not only well prepared, good tasting food, but a pleasant setting to dine in. Conveniently located on 13th Ave., central to Borough Park shopping. Heimishe ownership and management. Dining room & restroom 1 step above street level.

Hours: Mon-Thurs: 11am-11pm **Friday Closed** **Saturday Closed**
Sun: 12:30pm-11pm (last order 10:30pm)

Credit Cards Accepted: MC, Visa, AmEx, Discover

Restaurant Discount: One Time 10% Off With Cash Only

Borough: Brooklyn
Section: Borough Park

The Authoritative New York City Kosher Dining Guide

Restaurant: Kosher Delight
Phone Number: (718) 435-8500
Fax: (718) 435-1669

Address: 4600 13th Avenue (cor. 46th St.)

Hechsher: Rabbi Pinchos D. Horowitz - Chuster Rav (Glatt Kosher)

Proprietor/Manager:

Type(s) of Food: Meat - Chinese, Deli

Price Range: *Lunch*   *Dinner*   *Take out*
  Entrées: $8.00-$16.50   Same   Same – Local Delivery Available
  Desserts: $1.50-$1.95   *Chinese Entrées:* $10.95-$15.95
  Drinks: $ .60-$1.30   *Sandwiches:* $5.50-$8.25   *Hero:* $20.95/ft.

Food Specialties: Burgers, Grill, Kebobs, Fried Chicken, Deli, Chinese Menu, Ribs

  Description: The fast food chain store menu of burgers and fries has been
      extended to include Chinese and deli. Chinese dishes are made fresh to
      order w/o MSG. Hero by the Foot has been added to the deli sandwich
      selections. Fried chicken is sold by the piece in various box sizes,
      buckets, etc. Soups and salads are also offered.

  Comments: The food tends to be greasy, but it has its devotees. Portions are
      scant and everything is à la carte.

Ambiance (Decor): Plastic everything, with trays to eat on. Tends to be hot, smoky,
      and crowded during meal hours. A favorite with families with small children
      and consequently noisy and chaotic. Expect long lines which wind through the
      store. Typical fast-food restaurant decor of the McDonalds genre.

Service: Self-serve, difficult to get service at counter plus a long wait in line,
      especially during typical meal times, otherwise, minimal wait.

General Comments: The mystique of fast food: the chicken lacks meat, the burgers
      are small and unspectacular, the food in general is prepared in a haphazard
      manner, and there is no health consciousness in sight, but people love it!

Hours: **Sun-Thurs:** 11am-11pm **Fri:** 11am-4pm
      Sat: Opens 1 hr after Shabbos till 1am (Winter Only) (Summer Closed)

Credit Cards Accepted: MC, Visa, AmEx, Discover

Restaurant Discount:

Borough: Brooklyn
Section: Borough Park

The Authoritative New York City Kosher Dining Guide

Restaurant: Mazal Restaurant   *Phone Number:* (718) 854-3753
                                        Fax: None

Address: 4807 New Utrecht Avenue (bet. 48th St. - 49th St.)

Hechsher: CRC (Bodek Vegetables, Pas Yisroel)

Proprietor/Manager: David

Type(s) of Food: Dairy, Vegetarian - American

Price Range: *Lunch*   *Dinner*   *Take out*
    Entrées: $6.00-9.00   Same   Same
    Desserts: $1.25-$2.50
    Drinks: $ .75-$2.25

Food Specialties: Stuffed Cabbage, Fresh Fish, Baked Ziti, Eggplant Parmesana

   Description: Everything is made fresh; nothing is frozen or pre-packaged, from Cheese cake to a large assortment of homemade knishes.

   Comments: A fast food establishment, which leans heavily towards its catering operation.

Ambiance (Decor): The establishment seems somewhat dingy, but appears to be a popular choice for simchas. It has a dual personality: by day it is a small, fast food restaurant seating only 70 and in the evening, the space is expanded to an adjacent area to bring seating capacity to 150 people.

Service: Self-serve, but waiter service for parties

General Comments: Plans for extending the restaurant have fallen by the wayside in favor of catering. Remains a small, fast food eatery.

Hours: **Sun-Thurs:** 9:30am-5pm (after 6pm reservations are needed!)
    Fri: 9:30am-3pm **Saturday Closed**

Credit Cards Not Accepted: CASH ONLY!

Restaurant Discount:

Borough: Brooklyn

Section: Sunset Park (Bush Terminal Area)

The Authoritative New York City Kosher Dining Guide

Restaurant: 3rd Avenue Kosher Dairy Restaurant   **Phone Number:** (718) 492-2000
                                                             Fax: None

Address: 274 47th Street (bet. 2nd Ave. - 3rd Ave.)

Hechsher: OK Labs, also Rabbi Shraga Fievish Hager (Vishnitz)

Proprietor/Manager: Mr. Leizer Neuhause

Type(s) of Food: Dairy, Vegetarian - American

Price Range:	Lunch	Dinner	Take out
Entrées:	$1.50-$4.25	None	Same
Desserts:	$1.00-$1.25	**Breakfast Special:** $2.75	
Drinks:	$ .50-$1.25	**Sandwiches:** $1.75-$4.00	

Food Specialties: Baked Salmon, Lox Salad, Tuna Salad, Grilled Cheese

> **Description:** Sandwiches, lasagna, stuffed peppers, and other unadorned fare, in a surprising breadth of variations. Breakfast and lunch specials change daily.

> **Comments:** Fast food: quite decent for what it is. Hearty, but not nothing to rave about. Heimishe food for the local work force.

Ambiance (Decor): This is a heimishe luncheonette/cafeteria type establishment, located in the Bush Terminal commercial, manufacturing center. A counter mounted display presents the day's offerings and substitutes for a printed menu. Wood chairs and plastic laminated tables can accommodate up to 40 diners. A non-descript restaurant that services local workers.

Service: Self-serve

General Comments: In their words, "its dead after 4:30pm." An oasis for kosher diners in an otherwise kosherless area. It serves it purpose. The food served is actually quite satiating, but lacks the accompaniments and polish of a more sophisticated restaurant (e.g. No tartar sauce for a fish sandwich).

Hours: **Mon-Thurs:** 7am-4:30pm   **Fri:** 7am-12pm   <u>**Saturday Closed**</u>
         <u>**Sunday Closed**</u>

Credit Cards Not Accepted: CASH ONLY!

Restaurant Discount:

The Authoritative New York City Kosher Dining Guide

Mazal Pizza Luncheonette
4807 New Utrecht Avenue
CRC
Tel: (718) 854-3753

Rishon Pizza
5114 13th Avenue
Star-K
Tel: (718) 438-9226

Garden 13 Restaurant
4905 13th Avenue
CRC
Tel: (718) 437-1962

Amnon Kosher Pizza Inc.
4814 13th Avenue
OU, KAJ, Rabbi Yechiel Kaufman
Tel: (718) 851-1759

Benny's Famous Pizza Plus
4514 13th Avenue
Star-K
Tel: (718) 438-2369

16th Avenue Bagel & Pizza
4303 13th Avenue
Star-K
Tel: (718) 853-5397

Pardes Kosher Pizza
4001 13th Avenue
Star-K
Tel: (718) 633-9138

Naim Kosher Pizza
3904 15th Avenue
Rabbi Yechiel Babad
Tel: (718) 438-3569

Dairy Delight
5320 16th Avenue
CRC
Tel: (718) 854-6650

Dagan Pizza
4820 16th Avenue
OK Labs
Tel: (718) 435-5711

Mendel's 18th Avenue Pizza
4923 18th Avenue
Rabbi Shmuel Dovid Krauz
Tel: (718) 438-8493

Mendelsons 18th Avenue Kosher Pizza
4418 18th Avenue
Rabbi Binyamin Gruber
Tel: (718) 854-0600

Are you aware that...

Authoritative Kosher Dining Guides make terrific party planners?

For family get-togethers, office parties, birthdays, anniversaries, retirement parties, graduation celebrations, sheva brachos, or for any occasion - know where to go and where to order from - all the facts before you call save the hassle & running around!

Crown Heights
Brooklyn Heights
Bklyn Navy Yard
Williamsburg

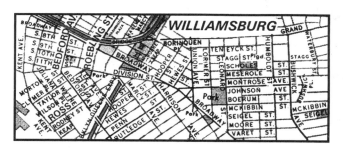

Borough: Brooklyn
Section: Crown Heights

The Authoritative New York City Kosher Dining Guide

Restaurant: Mermelstein Kosher Delicatessen   *Phone Number:* (718) 778-3100
                                                 Fax: None

Address: 351 Kingston Avenue

Hechsher: Bais Din of Crown Heights

Proprietor/Manager:

Type(s) of Food: Meat - Deli

Price Range:	*Lunch*	*Dinner*	*Take out*
Entrees:	$5.50-$8.50	Same	None
Desserts:	None		
Drinks:	$ .90-$1.25		

Food Specialties: Deli Sandwiches, Stuffed Cabbage, Salads, Burgers, Soup

> *Description:* Standard deli fare with a chassidishe taam. No surprises here just home cooked food.

> *Comments:* Heimishe, good quality, homemade food.

Ambiance (Decor): This small (16 seats) and unpretentious restaurant is an old timer that is undistinguished in its decor. A heimishe deli that caters to a Chassidishe clientele. Paper plates and plastic utensils set the tone.

Service: Self-serve

General Comments: Struggling to keep up with the more modern and child friendly Kosher Delight, this neighborhood institution keeps chugging along.

Hours: **Sun-Thurs:** 9am-9pm   **Fri:** 9am-1 hr before Shabbos
Saturday Closed

*Credit Cards **Not** Accepted:* CASH ONLY!

Restaurant Discount:

Borough: Brooklyn
Section: Crown Heights

The Authoritative New York City Kosher Dining Guide

Restaurant: Crown Bagel

Phone Number: (718) 493-4270
Fax: None

Address: 333A Kingston Avenue

Hechsher: Bais Din of Crown Heights

Proprietor/Manager:

Type(s) of Food: Dairy - Jewish American

Price Range:	*Lunch*	*Dinner*	*Take out*
Entrées:	$3.00-$5.50	Same	No Delivery Available
Desserts:	$2.00	*Breakfast Special:* $3.00	
Drinks:	$1.00-$1.50		

Food Specialties: Sandwiches, Fresh Fish, Lasagna, Blintzes, Salads, Desserts

Description: This no-frills, heimishe eatery offers light dairy meals. The Breakfast Special includes a bagel, scrambled egg, home fries, salad, and coffee. A variety of salads, spaghetti, lasagna, blintzes, pancakes, and sandwiches are sold. Fish platters featuring white fish, salmon, or flounder with two side dishes cost $5.50 and come with a bagel. Cheesecake, homemade apple pie, and pudding are some desserts. Various juices, tea and coffee make up the beverage selection.

Comments: The menu is not printed lending a sense of informality. No pretensions here, just simple home cooking. I'm told the portions are generous.

Ambiance (Decor): A luncheonette set up with seating for 19. No decor to speak of. Laminate tables, display counter, etc. Dining on paper plates with plastic utensils.

Service: Self-serve

General Comments: An inexpensive, no frills, fast food eatery.

Hours: **Sun-Thurs:** 7am-10pm **Fri:** 7am-2½ hrs before Shabbos
Sat: 1 hr after Shabbos till 11pm

Credit Cards Not Accepted: CASH ONLY!

Restaurant Discount:

Borough: Brooklyn
Section: Crown Heights

The Authoritative New York City Kosher Dining Guide

Restaurant: Esther Grill & Deli

Phone Number: (718) 735-4343
Fax: (718) 953-7219

Address: 463 Albany Avenue (bet. Montgomery St. - Empire Blvd.)

Hechsher: Bais Din of Crown Heights

Proprietor/Manager: David Dery

Type(s) of Food: Meat - American, Deli, Chinese, Middle Eastern

Price Range:	Lunch	Dinner	Take out
Entrées:	$6.95-$15.95	Same	Same - Delivery Available
Desserts:	$3.50		(Immediate area free, others $15 Min)
Drinks:	$1.00-1.75	Motzei Shabbos Shawarma Special:	$5.95

Food Specialties: BBQ Ribs Southern Style, Deli, Grill, Chinese, Shawarma

> *Description:* Fairly large portions, standard deli selections, 15 Chinese selections. They maintain that everything is prepared fresh daily.

> *Comments:* "Best food in the neighborhood" and "excellent food" are the descriptions used by the staff. We'll let you know.

Ambiance (Decor): A fairly new restaurant (a little over a year old) with a standard deli layout, starting with the deli service/display counter by the entrance. Laminate tables and wood chairs that seat 45 people follow. Casual and family oriented.

Service: Standard

General Comments: A fast food type restaurant that offers a surprisingly varied menu. The owner also operates the Deli Kasbah restaurants in Manhattan. So if experience counts, I would expect the food to be decent.

Hours: **Sun-Thurs:** 12pm-12am **Friday Closed**
Sat: Opens 1 hr after Shabbos till 12am

Credit Cards Not Accepted: MC, Visa, Discover

Restaurant Discount:

Borough: Brooklyn
Section: Brooklyn Heights

The Authoritative New York City Kosher Dining Guide

Restaurant: Pastrami Box

Phone Number: (718) 246-7089
Fax: (718) 246-7092

Address: 82 Livingston Street (bet. Court St. - Boerum Pl.)

Hechsher: Rabbi Israel Steinberg

Proprietor/Manager: Boris

Type(s) of Food: Meat - Deli

Price Range:

	Lunch	*Dinner*	*Take out*
Entrées:	$6.95-$9.95	Same	Same - Free Local Delivery
Desserts:	$1.50-$1.90	*Sandwiches:* $4.50-$9.55	*Breakfast:* $1.50-$4.75
Drinks:	$ .75-$1.25	*Hot & Cold Cut Platters:* $7.55-$8.95	

Food Specialties: Jumbo Hamburgers, Eggs & Omelets, Split Knish, Sandwiches

Description: Deli menu replete with sandwiches: Overstuffed, Triple Deckers, Combos, Deli & Egg, Open Faced, and Jumbo Deli Hamburgers. Most come with cole slaw, fries or other sides. Salad platters and Chef Salads. Cold or hot platters come with sides, as do entrées. Split Knishes consist of corned beef or pastrami on an open knish ($7.10). From The Sea selections offer lox, white fish or gefilte fish platters. Deli favorites are spiced up with the addition of newcomers like the Jumbo Deli Hamburgers (Mushroom & California varieties) and the split knish.

Comments: The corned beef and pastrami sandwiches are quite good.

Ambiance (Decor): This 2 year old restaurant integrates an old fashioned deli atmosphere with a modern gray, burgundy, and black décor. Deli meats hang from the ceiling over the large glass display counter. Quirky decorative touches include caricature drawings, an employee uniform, and an "Eat Well, Live Well" motto. A flower box is a nice addition. Capacity is 50 seats.

Service: Standard

General Comments: Finally, a kosher meat restaurant in this part of town! Located in the hub of Brooklyn's court district, and the Brooklyn Heights historic district.

Hours: **Mon-Thurs:** 6:30am-8pm **Fri:** 6:30am-1hr before Shabbos
Saturday Closed   Sunday Closed

Credit Cards Accepted: MC, Visa, AmEx

Restaurant Discount:

79

Borough: Brooklyn
Section: Brooklyn Heights

The Authoritative New York City Kosher Dining Guide

Restaurant: The Green's Vegetarian Restaurant   *Phone Number:* (718) 246-1288
Fax: (718) 935-9304
Address: 128 Montague Street 1ˢᵗ Floor (cor. Henry St.)

Hechsher: Rabbi Aron L. Raskin

Proprietor/Manager: Mr. Pan (Manager)

Type(s) of Food: Vegetarian - Chinese

Price Range: *Lunch*   *Dinner*   *Take out*
    Entrées: $7.50-$10.45   Same   Same - Free Local Delivery
    Desserts: None   *Lunch Special:* $5.25 (Mon-Fri: 11am-3:30pm)
    Drinks: $1.00-$2.75

Food Specialties: Buddha's Delight, Yin-Yang, Sunrise On The Pagoda

> *Description:* Contemporary Vegetarian Chinese cuisine with a health
> conscious attitude: low in fat, salt, and cholesterol, while high in fiber,
> protein, and vitamins. Clever manipulation of soy bean gluten and soy
> protein as meat and poultry substitutes.

> *Comments:* Particularly intriguing is the variety of dishes derived from all
> vegetable ingredients. Quality, presentation and taste of the food is first
> rate. A refreshing change of pace!

Ambiance (Decor): The first floor corner location of Green's affords a good view of
Montague and Henry streets below. Designed in green with pink accents, the
modern dining room is furnished with stained oak tables and 55 wood chairs
arranged along the large windows. High ceilings give the room a spacious feel,
while three large landscape paintings dominate the walls and enhance the mood.
Lighting is soft and spotlights the individual tables. Casual, café style.

Service: Chinese waitresses with limited facility in English

General Comments: A burgundy canopy marks the entry of this fairly new
restaurant. An opportunity to dine at this charming eatery deserves serious
consideration. First floor location requires walking up a flight of stairs.

Hours: **Mon-Thurs:** 11am-10:30pm   **Fri:** 11am-2 hr before Shabbos
    Sat: 1½ hr after Shabbos till ? (Call)   **Sun:** 1pm-10:30pm

Credit Cards Accepted: MC, Visa

Restaurant Discount: 10% Off

Borough: Brooklyn
Section: Brooklyn Navy Yard

The Authoritative New York City Kosher Dining Guide

Restaurant: Hall Street Kosher Café

Address: 7 Hall Street (cor. Flushing St.)

Phone Number: (718) 802-9638
Fax: (718) 802 9645

Hechsher: CRC

Proprietor/Manager: Shloma Friedman

Type(s) of Food: Dairy, Vegetarian - American

Price Range:
	Lunch	*Dinner*	*Take out*
Entrées:	$1.00-$8.00	Same	Same
Desserts:	$1.00-$3.00		Delivery Available
Drinks:	$ .75-$1.50		

Food Specialties: Sandwiches, Salads, Omelets, etc.

Description: Standard diner fare made fresh to order.

Comments: Simple, but good hearty food for the neighborhood workforce or any hungry passerby. An acquaintance and a frequent customer here tells me, often and emphatically, that the food is really terrific. The restaurant will also accommodate diners by preparing custom dishes by request.

Ambiance (Decor): Although a diner in a trailer is a common feature in the American landscape, it is a rarity in kosher circles. In fact, this is possibly, the one and only kosher restaurant with that description. Seats 25.

Service: Self-serve

General Comments: Located in an industrial, commercial area, serving mostly truckers and local workers. If you find yourself in this neighborhood, its nice to know there's a kosher diner near-by.......only in New York City!

Hours: **Mon-Thurs:** 7:30am-7pm **Fri:** 7:30am-4pm (Summer) or 2pm (Winter)
Saturday Closed **Sun:** 9am-4pm

Credit Cards Not Accepted: CASH ONLY!

Restaurant Discount:

Borough: Brooklyn
Section: Williamsburg

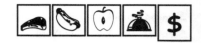

The Authoritative New York City Kosher Dining Guide

Restaurant: Landau's Glatt Kosher Deli   *Phone Number:* (718) 782-3700
                                              Fax: Same

Address: 65 Lee Avenue (Ross & Rodney St.)

Hechsher: NO HECHSHER (Glatt Kosher, Chassidishe Shechita)

Proprietor/Manager: Sam Landau

Type(s) of Food: Meat – Traditional Jewish

Price Range: *Lunch*   *Dinner*   *Take Out*
   Entrées: $7.00-$12.00   Same   Same – Delivery for Large Orders
   Desserts: $2.00
   Drinks: $1.00-$1.25

Food Specialties: Deli, Sauteed Liver, Cholent, Stuffed Cabbage, Knishes, Kugel

   Description: All the traditional cooked favorites that were born of Europe and
      have become Jewish American standards, from soup to dessert.
      Vineland Chicken is used exclusively. Homemade food, freshly made
      daily.

   Comments: Right out of grandma's kitchen. Yiddishe taam in a heimishe
      atmosphere.

Ambiance (Decor): Small, just 16 seats, with laminate tables. Casual and
   unpretentious, décor takes second stage here. Nondescript.

Service: Self-serve

General Comments: Hearty and economical meals are the focus here.

Hours: **Sun-Thurs:** 12:30pm-12 or 1 am **Fri:** 11:30am-1 hr before Shabbos
   Saturday Closed

Credit Cards Accepted: MC, Visa

Restaurant Discount:

Borough: Brooklyn
Section: Williamsburg

The Authoritative New York City Kosher Dining Guide

Restaurant: Golden King Restaurant   *Phone Number:* (718) 384-6577
                                              Fax: None

Address: 595 Bedford Avenue (cor. Keap St.)
          (near the Brooklyn.-Queens Expressway Kent Avenue Exit)
Hechsher: CRC

Proprietor/Manager: Barry Klein (Manager)

Type(s) of Food: Dairy - American, Middle Eastern

Price Range:	Lunch	Dinner	Take out
Entrees:	$4.25-$6.25	Same	Same
Desserts:	$ .75-$1.10	*Sandwiches:* $2.25-$2.75	
Drinks:	$ .85-$1.25	*Breakfast Special:* $3.00	

Food Specialties: Sandwiches, Falafel, Cheese Blintzes, Fried Flounder, Gefilte Fish

>   *Description:* Fast food with a familiar taam. The only real entrée served is the
>   fried flounder which comes with mashed potatoes. The most important
>   mealtime is breakfast. The $3.00 special gives the diner a complete meal
>   that includes eggs, bread, vegetables and coffee. The rest of the menu is
>   a potpourri of vegetable dishes (eggplant, spinach, etc.), latkes, kugels,
>   knishes and sandwiches. The sandwiches are limited to tuna fish and egg
>   salads. Falafel and fries are the big winners with the regulars. Vegetable
>   soup is a standard menu item.

>   *Comments:* The menu is quite limited, but for quick meal, it suffices.

Ambiance (Decor): Located in the center of a small triangular "park," right off the
          L.I.E. this luncheonette type establishment can accommodate between 24-26
          seated diners. A total renovation is planned this year, sometime before Pesach.

Service: Self serve

General Comments: Light eating, convenient for breakfasts or lunches on the go.

Hours: **Sun-Thurs:** 6am-8pm **Fri:** 6am-2pm **<u>Saturday Closed</u>**

Credit Cards Not Accepted: CASH ONLY!

Restaurant Discount:

Borough: Brooklyn
Section: Williamsburg

The Authoritative New York City Kosher Dining Guide

Restaurant: Gottleib Zoltan

Phone Number: (718) 384-6612
Fax: None

Address: 352 Roebling Street (off Bedford Ave.)

Hechsher: CRC (Glatt Kosher)

Proprietor/Manager:

Type(s) of Food: Meat - Deli, Hungarian

Price Range:	Lunch	Dinner	Take out
Entrées:	$8.50-$15.00	Same	Same
Desserts:	$1.50		
Drinks:	$ .75-$1.00		

Food Specialties: Stuffed Cabbage, Lamb Stew, Rib Steak, Grilled Chicken

> **Description:** You'll find ample portions here with a heimishe taam. Home cooked meals like Bubbe used to make, (if she happened to be Hungarian, spoke only Yiddish and came from Europe) but not limited to just goulash or veal cutlets. They have a deli menu as well.

> **Comments:** Heimishe cooking for a heimishe crowd.

Ambiance (Decor): Seating 50 people, this small restaurant is an old-time, somewhat worn deli with plastic laminate tables, no tablecloths, and no frills; and they apparently like it that way.

Service: Standard

General Comment: Now celebrating their 36th year: A neighborhood old timer whose staying power attests to the loyalty of its Chassidic customers and the restaurant's ability to serve their needs.

Hours: **Sun-Thurs:** 11am-9pm **Fri:** 11am-3pm **Saturday Closed**

Credit Cards Not Accepted: CASH ONLY!

Borough: Brooklyn
Section: Williamsburg

The Authoritative New York City Kosher Dining Guide

Restaurant: Williamsburg Pizza & Restaurant   *Phone Number:* (718) 384-2540
                                                Fax: None

Address: 214 Ross Street (bet. Lee Ave. – Marcey Ave.)

Hechsher: CRC

Proprietor/Manager:

Type(s) of Food: Dairy - Hungarian American, Italian

Price Range:	Lunch	Dinner	Take out
Entrées:	$5.50-$7.95	Same	Same
Desserts:	$1.25-$1.75		
Drinks:	$ .60-$1.25		

Food Specialties: Fish Cutlets, Blintzes, Pizza, Salads, Kugels

> *Description:* A heimishe restaurant which has a fairly extensive menu 16 different salads, 3 soups, a variety of blintzes, a choice among 5-6 different fresh fish dishes, different kugels, and various cooked dishes made fresh daily. And of course, there's pizza.

> *Comments:* Home cooking away from home. No frills, just nice hearty meals.

Ambiance (Decor): This mid-sized restaurant with between 60-70 seats, is best described as a luncheonette. Casual in the Williamsburg (not VA) style.

Service: Self-serve

General Comments: In the heart of Jewish Williamsburg, a restaurant we are not yet familiar with.

Hours: **Sun-Thurs:** 7am-7pm   **Fri:** 7am-2pm
         Sat: Opens ½ hr after Shabbos till 11:30pm

Credit Cards Not Accepted: CASH ONLY!

The Authoritative New York City Kosher Dining Guide

The perfect
guide for all
your kosher guests.

Whether on
business
or pleasure,
The Guide
is indispenable.

Remember to
take the Kosher
Privilege Card
wherever you go.

It's the gift
your friends
will thank you
for all year long.

JFK Int Airport
Kew Gardens
Forest Hills
Rego Park

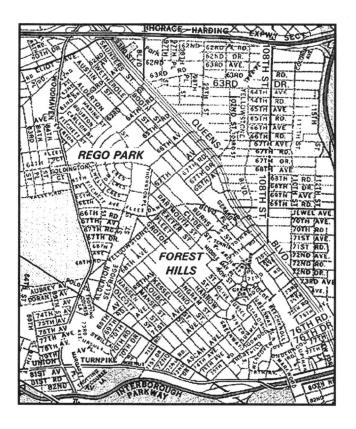

Borough: Queens
Section: J.F.K. International Airport

The Authoritative New York City Kosher Dining Guide

Restaurant: Kosher International Restaurant   *Phone Number:* (718) 656-1757
                                                  Fax: (718) 253-7163

Address: J.F.K. Airport, West Wing - 2nd Floor
   International Arrivals Building - Across El-Al Terminal (bet. Gates 32 - 33)

Hechsher: Rabbi Yechiel Babad - Tartevkov Rav - (Glatt Kosher, Bodek Vegetables)

Proprietor/Manager: Shaul, Shlomo

Type(s) of Food: Meat - Deli

Price Range: *Lunch*   *Dinner*   *Take out*
   Entrées: $5.95-$7.95   Same   Same
   Desserts: $1.75-$1.95
   Drinks: $1.07-$1.75   *Deli Sandwiches:* $3.50 (Jr.), $5.50-$7.45 (Combo)

Food Specialties: Deli Sandwiches, Salads, Tuna Platter, Falafel, Shawarma

   Description: Decent sized portions, fast food with a heimishe flavor. The meat
      comes from Meal Mart and the baked and cooked foods come from the
      kitchen of the Goldberg Supermarket in Borough Park. All sandwiches
      are served with pickle, lettuce, tomato & cole slaw.

   Comments: The limited menu has an assortment of foods that are familiar but
      not related in any discernible way. Thus, you can order an egg roll, but
      that is the only Chinese item offered. You can also choose between a
      Schnitzel Sandwich, Falafel in a Pita, and a Corned Beef or Pastrami
      Sandwich.

Ambiance (Decor): Large cafeteria style restaurant seating up to 200 people. Airport
   dining facility with laminate tables and cafeteria chairs. Disposable utensils and
   plates.

Service: Self-serve

General Comments: A convenient airport eatery and the only kosher facility.

Hours: **Sun-Thurs:** 1pm-10pm   **Friday Closed**
      Sat: (November-March) Opens 2 hrs after Shabbos till 10pm

Credit Cards Accepted: MC, Visa, Amex, Discover, Diners Club

Restaurant Discount: 10% Off Excluding Specials

Borough: Queens
Section: Kew Gardens

The Authoritative New York City Kosher Dining Guide

Restaurant: Ruchel's Kosher Kettle   **Phone Number:** (718) 441-5886
                                                    Fax: None
Address: 123-04 Metropolitan Avenue (bet. 123rd St. - 124th St.)

Hechsher: Vaad Harabonim of Queens (Glatt Kosher)

Proprietor/Manager: Habib

Type(s) of Food: Meat – Traditional Jewish

Price Range:	Lunch	Dinner	Take out
Entrées:	$7.00-$14.00	Same	$7.00-$9.00 - Delivery ($30 Min.)
Desserts:	$1.50-$2.00	Deli Sandwiches: $3.50-$8.00	
Drinks:	$1.00-$1.50		

Food Specialties: BBQ Chicken, Deli, Leek Pie, Stuffed Cabbage, Rib Steak

> **Description:** Although its parameters are set, specific contents of the menu
> remain fluid. With definite origins in European cuisine, the eclectic
> nature of this traditional Jewish menu includes items such as Stuffed
> Cabbage, Kasha Varnishkes, Matzah Ball Soup, Soufflés, Shlishkes,
> homemade Knishes, etc. form its basis and items like BBQ Chicken and
> deli sandwiches have been adopted and are now identified as integral to
> that cuisine. Some Armenian dishes of rice and stews can be found, as
> well. All pastries, rugalech and other baked goods are homemade too.
> Everything is made fresh w/ Ruchel's loving care. Beer license pending.

> **Comments:** New to us, but comes with a history as the former, and popular,
> Kosher Kettle (previously at a different location.)

Ambiance (Decor): A grocery/eatery combo: 20 seats divided among 2 booths and
several small tables. Bright and cheerful in wood tones and mirrors. Casual.

Service: Self-serve or owner will accommodate

General Comments: Have breakfast or lunch while you shop, or stay for dinner. Real,
homemade food without having to bother. Family owned and operated.

Hours: **Sun-Thurs:** 9am-9pm **Fri:** 9am-2 hrs before Shabbos
Sat: 2hr after Shabbos till 10pm (Winter Months Only)

Credit Cards _Not_ Accepted: CASH ONLY! (Charge Cards Planned In Future)

Restaurant Discount: 10% Off Only With A $20 Minimun Order.

Borough: Queens
Section: Forest Hills

The Authoritative New York City Kosher Dining Guide

Restaurant: Club Rafael Restaurant   *Phone Number:* (718) 268-3308
                                          Fax: (718) 268-3264
Address: 116-33 Queens Boulevard (off Union Tpk.)

Hechsher: Rabbi Avraham Aicenman (Glatt Kosher, Mashgiach Temidi)

Proprietor/Manager: David (owner)

Type(s) of Food: Meat - Russian, Euro-Asian, American Middle Eastern

Price Range: *Lunch*   *Dinner*   *Take out*
     Entrées: $7.50-$12.50   ┌─────────────────────────────────────┐
     Desserts: $1.50-$3.00   │ PRICES ARE DUE TO CHANGE IN JANUARY. │
     Drinks: $1.00-$1.50   └─────────────────────────────────────┘
                           $5/gl. (Mixed Drinks), $3.50/gl., $10/botl. (Wine)

Food Specialties: Baked Salmon, Lamb Chops, Steak New York, Kebobs

> *Description:* The menu represents a "melting pot" with items like rice pilafs
> from Asia, lamb kebobs from the Middle East,and steaks from the USA.
> Dishes are authentically prepared and generously apportioned.

> *Comments:* The menu has a mix of Russian, Middle Eastern, and American
> influences, which reflect both the restaurant's ownership and its patrons.

Ambiance (Decor): Used primarily as a catering hall in 1998, this establishment will
focus more on the restaurant aspect of the business after Dec. 26. With a total
capacity of 550 people between 2 rooms (350 and 200), the facility was totally
renovated about 2 years ago and transformed into a modern, sumptuous
environment with the liberal use of marble and red wall covering. Live music
(beginning about 7pm-8pm) is planned for the weekends. An inviting dance
floor adds to the nightclub atmosphere. Semi-formal or formal.

Service: Standard

General Comments: This restaurant embodies the Russian zest for getting out and
socializing, as well as the love of the modern style. Speaking Russian is a plus.

Hours: **Mon-Thurs:** 12pm-12am **Friday Closed**
         Sat: Opens 1 hr after Shabbos till 1am   **Sun:** 11am-12am

Credit Cards Accepted: CASH ONLY!

Restaurant Discount:

Borough: Queens
Section: Forest Hills

The Authoritative New York City Kosher Dining Guide

Restaurant: Madras Hut   *Phone Number:* (718) 263-4733
                             Fax: (718) 263-2065

Address: 113-25 Queens Boulevard (bet. 76th Rd. - 76th Ave.)

Hechsher: Rabbi Israel Mayer Steinberg - RESTAURANT IS OPEN 7 DAYS
                                                            A WEEK

Proprietor/Manager: Rashid (Manager)

Type(s) of Food: Vegetarian, Dairy, Parve - Indian

Price Range:	*Lunch*	*Dinner*	*Take out*
Entrées:	$6.95-$12.95	Same	Same - Free Local Delivery
Desserts:	$2.50-$2.95	*Business Lunch Buffet:* $4.95 (Mon-Fri)	
Drinks:	$1.95-$2.95	$3.00 (Beer)	

Food Specialties: Dosai (Crepes), Uttapam (Pancakes), Thalis (Rice Dishes)

Description: Authentic Indian cuisine. Dairy and non-dairy menu items are specified. Most of the dishes are vegetarian. Nice selection of Indian specialties. No eggs or fish served. Bread is "Hamotzi."

Comments: Price ranges for "entrées" are difficult to assess since cost varies depending on which items are chosen by the diner. Familiar vegetables with exotic spices, characteristically Indian.

Ambiance (Decor): The restaurant's attractive interior (54 seats) is decorated in warm tones and it's Eastern theme is enhanced by the use of oriental archways, mirrors, and Indian styled paintings. Exotic smells and flavors which are richly evocative of India, further the exotic mood in the dimly lit room. Casual / semi-formal for social or family dining.

Service: Standard

General Comments: Authentic Indian cuisine served in an attractive setting. The owner is not Jewish, therefore, hashgacha permits Shabbos opening.

Hours: **Mon-Fri:** 12pm-10pm   **Sat:** 12pm-10:30pm
         Sun: 12pm-10:00pm - RESTAURANT IS OPEN 7 DAYS A WEEK

Credit Cards Accepted: MC, Visa, AmEx, Diners Club

Restaurant Discount:

Borough: Queens
Section: Rego Park

The Authoritative New York City Kosher Dining Guide

Restaurant: The Wok *Phone Number:* (718) 896-0310
  Fax: (718) 997-1007

Address: 100-21 Queens Boulevard (bet. 67th Rd. - 67th Ave.)

Hechsher: Vaad Harabonim of Queens (Glatt Kosher)

Proprietor/Manager: Nissan Douek

Type(s) of Food: Meat - Chinese

Price Range: **Lunch** **Dinner** **Take out**
  Entrées: $9.50-$14.95 Same Local Delivery Free
  Desserts: None $4.95-$5.75 (Sm. Portions) *Combo Platters:* $6-$7
  Drinks: $1.00 *Lunch Special:* $5.25 (11:30am-3:30pm)

Food Specialties: General Tso's Chicken, Fong Wong Gai, Tea-Smoked Duck

  Description: The menu is comprised of all the standard Chinese favorites
    featuring beef, veal, chicken, duck and vegetables. The selections in
    each category are numerous (e.g. 8 soup selections). Except for the
    specials, dishes come in both regular size and small portions, as well.
    There is also a dietetic menu which offers steamed selections. The
    restaurant will also package orders for travel. Dishes come with white
    rice. Fried rice is $ .50 extra.

  Comments: Custom sized portions (a thoughtful option) mean that you order
    and pay for only what you want to consume. This also offers children a
    greater selection beyond the ordinary Children's Menu choices.

Ambiance (Decor): A fast food Chinese restaurant and take-out. It offers a very
  small seating area (16 seats). Brightly lit and child proof.

Service: Self-serve

General Comments: This is a no-nonsense, no-frills Chinese fast-food establishment.
  Short on atmosphere, but family friendly.

Hours: **Sun-Thurs:** 11:30am-10pm **Fri:** 11:30am-Please Call
  Sat: (Winter) 1 hr after Shabbos till 11pm (Summer Closed)

Credit Cards Accepted: MC, Visa, Discover

Restaurant Discount: 10% Off On Dishes Except Combo Platters or Lunch Specials

Borough: Queens
Section: Rego Park

The Authoritative New York City Kosher Dining Guide

Restaurant: Empire Kosher Roasters #1   *Phone Number:* (718) 997-7315
                                             Fax: (718) 997-1007
Address: 100-19 Queens Boulevard (bet. 67th Ave. - 67th Rd.)

Hechsher: Vaad Harabonim of Queens

Proprietor/Manager: Malka Perlmutter

Type(s) of Food: Meat - American

Price Range:	*Lunch*	*Dinner*	*Take out*
Entrées:	$5.69-$13.99	Same	Free Local Delivery ($10 Min.)
Desserts:	$1.15-$2.45	*Sandwiches:* $2.99-$5.95, $4.99-$7.95 (Platter)	
Drinks:	$ .60-$1.25	*Children's Menu:* $2.99-$3.49	

Food Specialties: BBQ Chicken, Chicken Kebob, Rotisserie, Broiled Fish, Deli

> *Description:* Poultry served every which way (no surprise here), but fish and
> deli meat as well. The kid's menu includes French fries & soda.
> Sandwich platters come with two side dishes and a roll or muffin.

> *Comments:* Fast food with the emphasis on poultry and fish, instead of beef
> Lots of side dishes.

Ambiance (Decor): This Family friendly, cafeteria style, fast food restaurant is
similar to the Kenny Rogers/Boston Market restaurant chains. Colorful,
modern, well lit, child oriented eatery. Eat on regular dishes. Seats 50 people.

Service: Self-serve

General Comments: The first of three, this restaurant is a good answer to the
question of where to take young children for a meal where they will be
welcomed in a relatively tension free environment. The friendly proprietor is
usually on hand. Good value and quality makes it a popular lunch destination
for the working set.

Hours: **Sun-Thurs:** 11am-9:30pm
Fri: 9:30am-2:30pm (Winter) or 4pm (Summer)   **Saturday Closed**

Credit Cards Accepted: MC, Visa, Discover

Restaurant Discount: 10% Off Platters Only Excluding Lunch Specials & Buffets

Borough: Queens
Section: Rego Park

The Authoritative New York City Kosher Dining Guide

Restaurant: Pita House (Habayit) *Phone Number:* (718) 897-4829
Fax: None
Address: 98-102 Queens Boulevard (bet. 66th Ave. - 67th Ave.)

Hechsher: Rabbi Dovid Katz (Glatt Kosher, Chassidishe Shechita)

Proprietor/Manager: Tsvi

Type(s) of Food: Meat- Middle Eastern (Yeminite)

Price Range: *Lunch* *Dinner* *Take out*
  Entrées: $9.95-$13.95 Same Same - Local Free Delivery
  Desserts: $2.50 (Min $15)
  Drinks: $1.00-$1.50 *Pita Sandwiches:* $3.00- $4.95

Food Specialties: Kebobs, Steaks, Shawarma, Jachnoon, Cous-Cous, Melawach

Description: Homemade Yeminite cuisine. Grilled and cooked dishes, such as
  Baked Chicken Leg, Stuffed Pepper, Goulash, and Hamin (Chulent).
  Entries come with two vegetable side orders from a choice including:
  salad, rice, magadra, beans, and fries. The menu offers an array of soups
  (7, e.g. Yeminite Calf Leg Soup & Pea and Lentil), hot (7) and cold
  (10) appetizers, and pita sandwiches (15). Grills include beef, turkey,
  lamb, chicken and kufta (ground beef and lamb). Everything is prepared
  and spiced to taste. Nice portions.

Comments: An Israeli style steak house in the Yeminite tradition. Food is
  prepared in a homestyle, non-rigid fashion.

Ambiance (Decor): This small restaurant, seating 50 people, draws an Israeli crowd
  (the owner refers to it as a "small Israel"). Informal, relaxed atmosphere where
  tables are covered with tablecloths and topped with glass. Non-descript interior.

Service: Standard

General Comments: Cheaper than a plane ticket, catch up on the latest from Israel
  here. Formerly Habayit, the aim is still to make you feel at home.

Hours: **Sun-Thurs:** 10am-12pm **Fri:** 10am-1 hr before Shabbos
  Sat: Opens 1 hr after Shabbos till 1am

Credit Cards Accepted: MC, Visa, AmEx, Discover

Restaurant Discount: 10% Off

Borough: Queens
Section: Rego Park

The Authoritative New York City Kosher Dining Guide

Restaurant: Ben's Best Kosher Deli

Phone Number: (718) 897-1700
Fax: (718) 997-6503

Address: 96-40 Queens Boulevard

Hechsher: Vaad Harabonim Lemeshmeret Hakashrut Orthodox Rabbis –
Rabbi Israel Steinberg - RESTAURANT IS OPEN 7 DAYS A WEEK

Proprietor/Manager: Jay

Type(s) of Food: Meat – Deli

Price Range:

	Lunch	*Dinner*	*Take out*
Entrées:	$10.95-$17.75	Same	Same – Local Free Delivery ($15 Min.)
Desserts:	$1.50-$2.95 *Kid's Menu:*	$4.95	Charge For Greater Distance
Drinks:	$ .65-$2.25,	$2-$2.50 (Beer)	*Sandwiches:* $5.40-$10.95

Food Specialties: Daily Specials, Deli, 3 Egg Omelets, Fresh Fish, Salads

Description: An extensive menu that covers all the bases. 2 specials are
offered daily, dishes like Chicken Marsala, Pepper Steak and Stuffed
Peppers. Traditional favorites share the stage with some of a more
American nature, e.g. Stuffed Breast of Capon, Roast Maryland Turkey,
and Broiled fish (Flounder, Halibut & Salmon). Salad Platters and
Dieters Delights offer low fat options. Sandwich selections are listed as
"Overstuffed," "Hot," and "Celebrity." The "Celebrities" named,
however, are companies (NBO Special, Sears, Circuit City, Sterling
Optical Special, etc.) rather than personalities. The Dr. Ruth Westheimer
and the Congressman Gary Ackerman Special, are the only exceptions.

Comments: Enticing menu, tempting food and now under supervision!

Ambiance (Decor): Typical old fashioned deli setup, in a room seating 65 people.
Informal and family friendly. Scheduled for a facelift during Passover '99.

Service: Standard

General Comments: In business for 52 years, this restaurant must be doing
something right. Not to be confused with the Ben's chain of delis.

Hours: **Sun-Sat:** 9am-9:45pm - RESTAURANT IS OPEN 7 DAYS A WEEK

Credit Cards Accepted: MC, Visa, AmEx, Diners Club, Discover

Restaurant Discount:

Borough: Queens
Section: Rego Park

The Authoritative New York City Kosher Dining Guide

Restaurant: Chosen Garden   *Phone Number:* (718) 275-1300
                                                               Fax: (718) 275-1309
Address: 64-43 108th Street (bet. 64th Rd. - 65th Ave.)

Hechsher: Vaad Harabonim of Queens

Proprietor/Manager: Michael Mo/Neil Wallin

Type(s) of Food: Meat - Chinese

Price Range: **Lunch** (Special)   **Dinner**   **Take out**
   Entrées: $10.50-$10.95 $13.50-$19.95   20% off Dinner Menu
   Desserts: $2.95 $45.00/2 (Peking Duck)
   Drinks: $1.50, $3.50-$3.95 (Beer), $4.00-$4.95 (Mixed Drinks)
              $3.50/glass (House Wine), $12.00-$17.00/bottle (Wine)

Food Specialties: Szechuan, Hunan, Mandarin, Sushi

   Description: The news for 1999 is the introduction of a complete sushi menu.
      The regular menu boasts the usual chicken, beef and veal selections. A
      number of duck and fish selections expand the options further. The
      portions are nicely sized and attractively presented.

   Comments: The quality is good and there are many selections to choose from.

Ambiance (Decor): Although the restaurant seats 120, it is sectioned off into two
      rooms and thus doesn't appear large. In fact it could be regarded as somewhat
      intimate. The second room is closed off for private parties when needed. The
      decor is modern with some Chinese references. The atmosphere is relaxed.
      Dress can be casual or semi-formal.

Service: Accommodating, helpful

General Comments: The restaurant is located in a small shopping strip. This 7 year
      old restaurant is staffed by many from the defunct, but well remembered,
      "Moshe Peking." Its worth a try if you're in the neighborhood.

Hours: **Sun-Thurs:** 11am-10pm   **Friday Closed**
      Sat: Opens 1 hr after Shabbos till 12:30am

Credit Cards Accepted: MC, Visa, AmEx

Restaurant Discount:

Borough: Queens
Section: Flushing

The Authoritative New York City Kosher Dining Guide

Restaurant: Salut Kosher Restaurant

Phone Number: (718) 275-6860
Fax: None

Address: 63-42 108th Street (bet. 63rd Rd. - 63rd Dr.)

Hechsher: Rabbi Pesach Ackerman

Proprietor/Manager: Baruch Siyanov

Type(s) of Food: Meat - Middle Eastern, Russian

Price Range:

	Lunch	Dinner	Take out
Entrées:	$5.95 (Special)	$5.50-$10.50	Same – Delivery Available
Desserts:	$1.00-$2.50		
Drinks:	$1.00		

Food Specialties: Kholodets, Lula-Kebob, Khorovak, Uzbek Mantu, Chalokhoch

Description: That's Jellied Meat, Koufta Kebob, Veal, Meat Pie and Grilled Lamb Steak for the uninitiated. Just a sampling of the intriguing menu items that will transport you into the helpless realm of the foreigner, right in your own backyard! Hasib (chopped veal baked as a sausage) and Cheburekes (chopped meat baked with onion in pastry dough) are some other exotic sounding dishes. For the less adventurous, there are familiar dishes, as well, like Rib Steak, Grilled Salmon, Grilled Chicken Lamb Ribs. Not an extensive menu, but still, getting through it is arduous enough. Soups include Lagman (noodle soup), Pelmeni (with meat stuffed dumplings) and Shurpa (broth with lamb & beef).

Comments: A menu with Middle Eastern origins and Russian influences.

Ambiance (Decor): An unassuming interior with seating for 40 diners. Tables are covered with tablecloths, but the general mood is casual.

Service: Standard

General Comments: Home cooked ethnic meals that add up to an adventure in eating.

Hours: Sun-Thurs: 11am-12am **Fri:** 11am-½ hr before Shabbos
Sat: ½ hr after Shabbos till 1am

Credit Cards _Not_ Accepted: CASH ONLY!

Restaurant Discount: 15% Off

Borough: Queens
Section: Rego Park

The Authoritative New York City Kosher Dining Guide

Restaurant: Café Baba Restaurant

Phone Number: (718) 275-2660
Fax: None

Address: 91-33 63rd Drive (Off Austin St.)

Hechsher: Rabbi Charles Schulson (Glatt Kosher)

Proprietor/Manager: Alex Acksakalov

Type(s) of Food: Meat - International (Russian, Israeli, American)

Price Range:

	Lunch	*Dinner*
Entrées:	$10.00-$15.00	$23.00-$37.00/Prix Fix/p.p.
Desserts:	Included	
Drinks:	$4.00-$5.00 (Mixed Drinks)	

Food Specialties: Steaks, Kebobs, Fish, Goulash

   Description: Family style eating: serving platters are placed in center of the table and you help yourself.

   Comments: The food has a Russian influence and the Mashgiach tells me that it is very delicious.

Ambiance (Decor): A year ago, under new Russian ownership, this nightclub and restaurant combo went through extensive renovations. What emerged was a modern club that features entertainment, an expanded dance floor, and good food. The new, augmented space accommodates approx. 200 people. Singers, band, and belly dancers perform at 11pm.

Service: Standard

General Comments: One of the very few kosher nightclubs in the city. Call ahead to check if the restaurant is closed for private parties.

Hours: **Sun-Thurs:** 12pm-12am   **Fri:** 12pm-2 hrs before Shabbos
      Sat: Opens 1 hr after Shabbos till 1am

Credit Cards Accepted: MC, Visa

Restaurant Discount:

Borough: Queens
Section: Rego Park

 $$

The Authoritative New York City Kosher Dining Guide

Restaurant: Da Mikelle Glatt Kosher Ristorante   *Phone Number:* (718) 275-0988
                                                      Fax: Same
Address: 97-26 63ʳᵈ Road (bet. 97ᵗʰ St. - 98ᵗʰ St.)

Hechsher: American Association of Kosher Butchers - Rabbi Pesach Ackerman

Proprietor/Manager: Michael

Type(s) of Food: Meat – Italian, Eclectic

Price Range: *Lunch*   *Dinner*   *Take out*
     Entrées: $9.95-$17.95   Same   Same – Delivery Available
     Desserts: $3.95-$5.95   *Lunch Special:* $6.95   *Dinner Special:* $10.95
     Drinks: $1.25-$3.00, $2.50/gl (Wine), $3-$4.50/gl (Mixed Drinks)

Food Specialties: Grills, Kebobs, Carpaccio di Salmone, Vitello alla Marsala

   Description: A fairly extensive offering of classic Italian dishes. Entrées
        encompass chicken, veal, beef, and fish recipes. Nice selection of salads
        and pasta as well. The Lunch Special (Noon-4pm) and the Dinner
        special (5pm-8pm) both offer complete dinners from select menus.
        There is an accommodation for children @ $4.95-$5.95.

   Comments: The menu is well developed and impressive in scope. It indicates a
        familiarity with Italian cuisine that is both sophisticated and schooled.

Ambiance (Decor): As described, the setting is romantic, with dim lights, fresh
        flowers, and candles on tables, covered with green linen tablecloths, white top
        cloths and linen napkins. Italian paintings adorn the walls. The dining room
        offers banquette seating along with tables and chairs (80 total). There is live
        music on the Saturday and Sunday nights (8pm-closing). A second room on the
        basement level (capacity for approx. 50 people) is used for parties. Full bar.

Service: Standard

General Comments: A promising dining prospect for the coming year.

Hours: **Sun-Thurs:** 11am-11pm   **Fri:** 11am-1 hr before Shabbos
        Sat: 1 hr after Shabbos till 12am

Credit Cards Accepted: MC, Visa, AmEx

Restaurant Discount:

99

The Authoritative New York City Kosher Dining Guide

Sam Kosher Pizza　　　　　　　　　　*Tel:* (718) 459-6183
63-46 108th Street
Vaad Harabonim of Queens

Dan Carmel Ice Cream & Pizza　　　　*Tel:* (718) 544-8530
98-98 Queens Boulevard
Vaad Harabonim of Queens

Panorama Pizza　　　　　　　　　　　*Tel:* (718) 275-3992
102-11 Queens Boulevard
Vaad Harabonim of Queens

Kew Gardens Hills
Flushing
Fresh Meadows

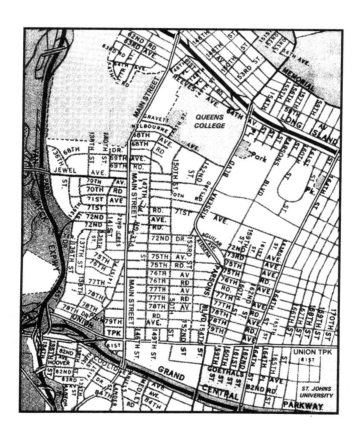

Borough: Queens
Section: Kew Gardens Hills

The Authoritative New York City Kosher Dining Guide

Restaurant: Hapisgah

Phone Number: (718) 380-4449
Fax: (718) 591-8991

Address: 147-25 Union Turnpike (bet. 147th St. - 148th St.)

Hechsher: Vaad Harabonim of Queens (Glatt Kosher)

Proprietor/Manager: David Brachiyahu

Type(s) of Food: Meat - Middle Eastern

Price Range:

	Lunch (12pm-6pm)	*Dinner*	*Take out*
Entrées:	$2.75-$7.95 (SP)	$10.95-$23.95	Same- No Delivery
Desserts:	$2.25-$3.25		
Drinks:	$1.75-$2.50	$4.00/gl. (Wine),	$3.00-$3.50 (Beer)

Food Specialties: Steaks, Kebobs, Grilled/Fried Fish, Shawarma, Sweet Breads

> *Description:* Not merely a steak house, this restaurant offers: an extensive menu of House Specials such as Cous-Cous, Goulash w/ Potatoes, Chulent and Baked Chicken. Cold and hot appetizers feature various salads and Middle Eastern specialties. 7 different soups (from Vegetable to Calf Leg Soup), and 22 different entrées. An aside from the expected Steaks, Grills, and Kebobs, are the Sweet Breads, Schnitzel, and Shawarma. There is also a large sandwich & dessert selection. A kid's menu provides for the little ones.

> *Comments:* The food is of high quality and well prepared. The lentil soup is full bodied and flavorful, as is the vegetable. The portions are filling, but make sure you leave room for the delicious desserts.

Ambiance (Decor): What was already a large (150 seats), light, airy, & attractive place has been expanded for the 2nd time in 7 years, adding another room. The main dining room remains the same smoke free oasis. The grills are visible in the back, but are far enough away to allow for smoke free dining. Take-out traffic is sectioned off from the seating area, so dining here is relaxed and pleasurable. The new room seats 40 with a full bar, dimmed lighting, & jazz piped in for easy listening. Smoking is permitted by the bar. Free valet parking.

Service: Friendly and responsive

General Comments: You won't leave hungry from this very popular restaurant. Sat. night RSVP a must. Long lines are not uncommon. Dining room no smoking rules are strictly enforced (Imagine a room full of young Israelis & no smoke!).

Hours: **Sun-Thurs:** 12pm-12am   **Closed Friday**
Sat: Opens 1 hr after Shabbos till 12am (Summers till 1am)

Credit Cards Accepted: MC, Visa

Restaurant Discount:

The Authoritative New York City Kosher Dining Guide

Restaurant: Tashkent Glatt Kosher Restaurant   *Phone Number:* (718) 969-9810
                                                    Fax: None

Address: 149-15 Union Turnpike (bet. 149th St. - 150th St.)

Hechsher: Vaad Harabonim of Queens

Proprietor/Manager: Joseph

Type(s) of Food: Meat - Middle Eastern, Eastern European

Price Range:	*Lunch*	*Dinner*	*Take out*
Entrées:	$5.00-$7.00	$9.00-$15.00	10%-20% less (off Lunch)
Desserts:	$2.50-$9.95	Same	Free local Delivery Available
Drinks:	$1.20-$3.00	*Lunch Special:* $5.95	*Dinner Special:* $9.95

Food Specialties: Beef Stroganoff, Russian Cuisine, Kiev Chicken, Steaks, Kebobs

> *Description:* The menu is replete with dishes that ferry you across several
> continents. Beef Stroganoff, Goulash stews, Borsht, ravioli and other
> European favorites are served alongside kebobs, steaks, and an array of
> salads. Persian dishes are well represented with items like Mastava soup,
> Dolma, Babaganush, and many kebobs [beef, lamb, Lula (ground beef),
> chicken, turkey, Horovak (sweet bread), and vegetable]. You can order
> Rassolnik Soup (barley and meat) or Ukranian Borscht, Chicken Tabaka
> (grilled chicken Caucas style) or Zharkoe (fried meat with vegetables).
> Seafood entrées consist of either trout or salmon baked or fried.

> *Comments:* This is not just another Israeli Steakiya with a Russian or a
> European accent. The menu offers a truly interesting mix of ethnic
> delicacies. The brick oven bread that we left with was delicious.

Ambiance (Decor): The street level main dining area accommodates 65 people. The
basement level room holds 40 people and is used primarily for private parties.
A casual, somewhat tacky restaurant bathed in turquoise and hot pink. Plastic
flowers. Live entertainment on Saturday and Sunday, beginning at 6pm-closing.

Service: Standard

General Comments: One of the few kosher Russian restaurants in operation. Under
new ownership. Go for the good, freshly made ethnic food.

Hours: **Sun-Thurs:** 11am-11pm   **Friday Closed**   **Sat:** 1 hr after Shabbos till 2am

Credit Cards Accepted: MC, Visa, AmEx

Restaurant Discount: 10% Off

Borough: Queens
Section: Kew Gardens Hills

$$$

The Authoritative New York City Kosher Dining Guide

Restaurant: Stargate   **Phone Number:** (718) 793-1199
                                                   Fax: (718) 793-0293

Address: 73-27 Main Street (cor. 75th Ave.)

Hechsher: Vaad Harabonim of Queens (Mashgiach Temidi, Glatt Kosher)

Proprietor/Manager: Samson Abitbol

Type(s) of Food: Meat – Italian, Chinese, French, Mexican, Middle Eastern

Price Range: **Lunch**   **Dinner**   **Take out**
  Entrees: $11.95-$26.95   Same   **Child Menu:** $6-$8 (Del. Avail.)
  Desserts: $2.95-$4.50 **Dinner Specials:** $12-$21   **Late Menu:** $8-$12
  Drinks: $1.25-$4.00, $2.50-$5/gl $10-$30/btl(Wine), $4/gl (Mix Drk)

Food Specialties: Cordon Bleu, Cajun Rib Eye, Rosemary Veal Roast Medallions

> **Description:** Totally revamped, the menu has been expanded not only in
> length, but in breadth. Salads, deli sandwiches, burgers, shish kebobs,
> pastas and vegetarian pizza make up the varied and well balanced
> selection. Start off with the Pea Soup. The Steak Au Poivre is a
> delicious entrée choice, but you can't go wrong with the Entrecote a La
> Bearnaise Sauce, Grilled Baby Lamb Chops A La Merlot, Chicken
> Picata, Scalloppine A La Marsala, Grilled Halibut, etc. Or try the
> Fajitas, Kabobs or Salmon of the Great Wall for a change of pace.

> **Comments:** An enticing and sophisticated menu, carefully prepared cuisine.

Ambiance (Decor): Newly renovated, the space accommodates 180 diners, but can
  be sectioned off for parties. Crème walls with mahogany trim present a neutral
  background for future embellishments. Recessed ceiling domes, dotted with
  stars and giving off blue light, punctuate the ceiling. These are the sole
  references to the restaurant's name. Burgundy linen. Full bar. Informal.

Service: Standard

General Comments: Here's one good reason to visit Queens!

Hours: Sun-Tues: 12pm-9:30pm **Wed-Thurs:** 12pm-10pm **Friday Closed**
  Sat: 1 hr after Shabbos till 12am (Oct.-May) (Summers Closed)

Credit Cards Accepted: MC, Visa, AmEx, Diners Club

Restaurant Discount: **Mon-Thurs:** 15% Off (Max. 6 People), **Sat-Sun:** Free glass
  Of Wine (Up To Four People); also, 1x Special: Buy One Entrée Get The 2nd
  Lower Priced Entrée For Free. Not To Be Combined With Any Other Offer.

Borough: Queens
Section: Kew Gardens Hills

The Authoritative New York City Kosher Dining Guide

Restaurant: Kosher Corner

Phone Number: (718) 263-1177
Fax: (718) 263-8974

Address: 73-01 Main Street (cor. 73rd Ave.)

Hechsher: Vaad Harabonim of Queens (Cholov Yisroel)

Proprietor/Manager: Samson Abitbol

Type(s) of Food: Dairy - Italian, American

Price Range:	*Lunch*	*Dinner*	*Take out*
Entrées:	$7.95-$15.95	Same	10% off dinner prices
Desserts:	$2.75-$3.00		Delivery - 15 Block Radius $15 Min.
Drinks:	$ .70-$4.00	*Breakfast Special:* $1.50-$4.00	

Food Specialties: Fish, Pasta, Pan Pizza, Blintzes, Chinese, Stuffed Baked Potato

Description: The extensive menu is predominately Italian and (Jewish) American, but some Middle Eastern dishes can be found. Dairy and vegetarian entrées, fresh fish, pasta, gourmet salads, omelets and pan pizza, Lo-Cal and Lafah Melt are options. Breakfast specials can be a simple bagel w/cream cheese and coffee or can be expanded with eggs and juice. Stuffed potatoes, homemade blintzes, Tortellini Alfredo, Red Snapper Filet (of 8 fish choices), Salad Nicoise and Sauteed Vegetables with Halibut chubs (salmon, halibut or tuna chubs), are possibilities.

Comments: There is so much to choose from! Everything sounds delicious.

Ambiance (Decor): A café-like ambiance pervades this mid-size restaurant which accommodates 50-55 people. Tables are covered with tablecloths and topped with glass in the rather ordinary dining room. The atmosphere is casual and relaxed: nothing fancy. Suitable for informal entertaining and family dining.

Service: Standard

General Comments: Owned by the same restaurateur who brings us the Stargate a few doors down the street, and run with the same concern for detail.

Hours: **Sun-Thurs:** 9:30am-10pm   **Fri:** 8am-2:30pm (May be closed in Winter)
Sat: Opens 1 hr after Shabbos till 1:30am

Credit Cards Accepted: MC, Visa, AmEx, Diners Club ($20 min.)

Restaurant Discount: **Mon-Thurs:** 15% Off (Up To 6 People Max.) Does Not Include House Specials & Not To Be Combined With Any Other Offers.

Borough: Queens
Section: Kew Gardens Hills

The Authoritative New York City Kosher Dining Guide

Restaurant: Annie's Kitchen

Phone Number: (718) 268-0960
Fax: None

Address: 72-24 Main Street (cor. 72nd Rd.)

Hechsher: Vaad Harabonim of Queens

Proprietor/Manager: Pei Man Chan

Type(s) of Food: Meat - Chinese

Price Range: **Lunch** (11am-3pm) *Dinner* *Take out*
   Entrées: $8.95-$15.50   Same   Same - (Free Local Delivery
   Desserts: None   *Lunch Special:* $4.60-$6.50   bet. 5pm-9pm)
   Drinks: $1.00-$1.25   *Special Combination Dinner:* $6.95-$11.95

Food Specialties: Fong Wan Gai, Orange Beef, Sesame & General Tso's Chicken

   Description: A fairly large selection for a fast food/take-out restaurant. Small
      and large portions are offered to accommodate diners with different
      capacities to devour food. The Special Lunch Combination includes
      soup and fried rice. The Special Combination Dinner, however, is
      served with fried rice and an egg roll (no soup). Food can be spiced to
      taste.

   Comments: We have yet to try the food, but we're working on it.

Ambiance (Decor): There are tables and chairs to seat 38 people, in this casual,
   Chinese restaurant. In the back, an order food counter separates the dining area
   from the kitchen. Noisy during dinnertime, amplified by sounds bouncing off
   the hard surfaces. Family oriented and child friendly.

Service: Self-serve during the day, however, at night table service is available

General Comments: The bulk of this establishment's business is take-out. Standard
   Chinese for when you're really informal or on the go. Frozen dinners available.

Hours: **Sun-Thurs:** 11am-10pm **Fri:** 10am-1 hr before Shabbos
   Sat: 1 hr after Shabbos till 12am (Winter Only)

Credit Cards Accepted: MC, Visa

Restaurant Discount:

Borough: Queens
Section: Kew Gardens Hills

The Authoritative New York City Kosher Dining Guide

Restaurant: Jerusalem Cafe   *Phone Number:* (718) 520-8940
                                 Fax: None
Address: 72-02 Main Street (cor. 72nd Ave.)

Hechsher: Vaad Harabonim of Queens (Cholov Yisroel, Pas Yisroel)

Proprietor/Manager: Eli Gluska

Type(s) of Food: Dairy - Appetizing, Bakery

Price Range: *Lunch*   *Dinner*   *Take out*
    Entrées: No Cooked Entrées   None   Same
    Desserts: $1.00-$2.00   *Salads:* $2.00-$4.00   *Pastas:* $3.50-$4.00
    Drinks: $ .65-$2.00   *Sandwiches:* $ .80-$4.00

Food Specialties: Salads, Pastas, Soups, Borekas, Bagels

> *Description:* The duel nature of this establishment is characterized as both a
> bakery and dining area. The dining menu is made up of light fare for
> quick meals or a dessert stop over. There are no entrées. Offered are
> selections of borekas, pastas, soups, and salads complemented by
> sandwiches on either bagels or rolls.

> *Comments:* Light eating for quick, casual, no-frills meals.

Ambiance (Decor): In a nutshell, Jerusalem Café is a bakery with an area set off for
café style eating. There are approximately 12 tables and seating for 48.

Service: Self-serve

General Comments: Light dining while you eye all the possible desserts!

Hours: **Sun-Thurs:** 7am-6:30pm   **Fri:** 7am-1 hr before Shabbos
        Saturday Closed

Credit Cards Not Accepted: CASH ONLY!

Restaurant Discount:

Borough: Queens
Section: Kew Gardens Hills

The Authoritative New York City Kosher Dining Guide

Restaurant: Hapina

Phone Number: (718) 544-6262
Fax: None

Address: 69-54 Main Street (cor. Jewel Ave.)

Hechsher: Vaad Harabonim of Queens (Glatt Kosher)

Proprietor/Manager:

Type(s) of Food: Meat - Middle Eastern

Price Range:	*Lunch*	*Dinner*	*Take out*
Entrées:	$8.95-$12.95	Same	Same
Desserts:	$2.00	*Grilled Sandwiches:* $3.70-$5.00	
Drinks:	$ .75-$1.50	*Free Salad Bar*	

Food Specialties: Cornish Hen & Turkey Shawarma, Salad Bar, Falafel

> *Description:* Entrées come with French fries or rice and salad. The salad bar, featuring (14) different salads, is included free with entrée orders and sandwiches. Vegetarian sandwiches include salad in a pita only. These contain falafel, chummus, babaganoush and vegetable latkes. The (4) soups are homemade and are served with pita bread. Add $1.50 for laffah-esh tanoor with grilled sandwiches.

> *Comments:* What they don't give you in atmosphere they give you in value.

Ambiance (Decor): Located on the corner of Main Street and Jewel Avenue (hence the name), this mid-size (60 seats), no-frills restaurant, is not meant to impress with its decor. It is a brightly lit, bustling, upbeat environment for casual eating. The laminate tables and tiled floors are family friendly. A relaxed atmosphere pervades and takes its cue from the mostly Israeli clientele

Service: Standard

General Comments: An inexpensive restaurant where the focus is on eating, not decor. A good choice for families with children. Note the late closing times. Also one of the few places that offers the aish tanoor. The food is a bit oily, but quite good. Salad bar is ok. Fast turnover insures freshness.

Hours: **Mon-Thurs:** 11am-1am **Fri:** 11am-2 hrs before Shabbos
Sat: 1 hr after Shabbos till 2am **Sun:** 11am-2am

Credit Cards Not Accepted: CASH ONLY!

Restaurant Discount:

108

Borough: Queens
Section: Kew Gardens Hills

The Authoritative New York City Kosher Dining Guide

Restaurant: Burger Nosh

Phone Number: (718) 520-1933
Fax: None

Address: 69-48 Main Street (cor. Jewel Ave.)

Hechsher: Vaad Harabonim of Queens (Glatt Kosher)

Proprietor/Manager: Mark Bauer (Manager)

Type(s) of Food: Meat - American

Price Range:

	Lunch	Dinner	Take out
Entrées:	$7.50-$9.95	Same	Same
Desserts:	None	**Sandwiches:** $1.50-$6.95	
Drinks:	$ .89-$1.35		

Food Specialties: Burgers, Steaks, Chicken Nuggets, Deli, Fried Chicken, Grills

Description: Fast Food on a bun, kaiser roll, or platter. The menu holds no surprises. Chicken is skewered, marinated, grilled, in a salad, or in a pot pie. The beef comes in the form of Sino Steak (sandwich or platter), roast beef (sandwich), or in assorted burgers. Turkey breast can be ordered in a salad or as a sandwich. Tuna and tossed salad are also available. The side orders include: egg roll, knishes, chili, soup, etc. The Lite-Line, presumably offering low fat selections, is grilled chicken served three different ways. The fried chicken can be ordered in various box sizes, buckets, and barrels.

Comments: A small menu that doesn't mince meat and gets right to business. It has all the elements for a successful dinnertime with the kids.

Ambiance (Decor): Set in the "Burger King" mold, Burger Nosh is a modern, brightly colored, well lit, and a child friendly environment that seats up to 50 diners in molded plastic seats. Dining is à la trays and with disposable plates & utensils. Don't dress up!

Service: Self-serve

General Comments: Burger Nosh is an option for when you go to eat out with the children. However, children are not a prerequisite.

Hours: **Sun-Thurs:** 11:30am-10pm   **Friday Closed**   **Saturday Closed**

Credit Cards Not Accepted: CASH ONLY!

Restaurant Discount: 10% Discount Not To Be Combined With Any Other Offer

Borough: Queens

Section: Kew Gardens Hills (Queens College)

The Authoritative New York City Kosher Dining Guide

Restaurant: Kosher Heaven

Phone Number: (718) 261-0149
Fax: None

Address: 65-30 Kissena Boulevard

Hechsher: Vaad Harabonim of Queens

Proprietor/Manager: Moshe Harary

Type(s) of Food: Meat - Deli

Price Range: *Lunch*   *Dinner*   *Take out*
Entrées: There is no printed menu. Rating above is based on
Desserts: the fact that it is located in Queens College and caters mostly to
Drinks: students, is self-serve and is short on amenities.

Food Specialties:. Deli Sandwiches, Salads

Description: A limited menu of deli sandwiches designed to feed the student population of Queens College.

Comments: College eatery we haven't tried.

Ambiance (Decor): Large seating capacity in a cafeteria style dining room. Located in Queens College, this is a fast food college dining facility with no frills. Disposable plates and cutlery.

Service: Self-serve

General Comments:

Hours: **Mon-Thurs:** 8:30am-7pm   **Fri:** 8:30am-1:30pm
Saturday Closed   Sunday Closed

Credit Cards Not Accepted: CASH or CHECK ONLY!

Borough: Queens
Section: Fresh Meadows

The Authoritative New York City Kosher Dining Guide

Restaurant: Pninat Hamizrach   *Phone Number:* (718) 591-3367
                                        Fax: None
Address: 178-07 Union Turnpike (bet. 178th St. - Surrey Pl.)

Hechsher: Vaad Harabonim of Queens (Glatt Kosher)

Proprietor/Manager: Neil, Shalom, & Yehuda (Owners)

Type(s) of Food: Meat - Middle Eastern, American

Price Range: *Lunch*   *Dinner*   *Take out*
  Entrées: $ $9.00-$14.95   Same
  Desserts: $ 2.50-3.00 *Lunch Special:* $6-$7 *Kid's Menu:* $4.95
  Drinks: $1-$1.50, $3.50-$4.50 (Beer), $4-$5/gl, $15-$27/btl (Wine)

Food Specialties: Shawarma, Kebobs, Grills, Fresh Fish, Salads, Chummus Combos

  Description: The menu features grills, which aside from Rib Steaks and
  burgers, offers a wide array of kebob possibilities including: beef,
  turkey, chicken, veal, and lamb. "In a Pita" selections, Shish Kabob,
  Cutlets, Steak, etc. stuffed in a pita, are quite reasonably priced ($4.75-
  $5.75). The lunch specials include a soup and entrée. All entrées include
  2 side dishes. Portions are generous. Free salad bar has been introduced.

  Comments: The fairly extensive menu offers a nice variety of meats and
  dishes whose origins span the Middle East. Also, has a children's menu.

Ambiance (Decor): Israeli landscapes, in relief form, hang on the walls and provide
  the backdrop to the dining experience. Seating 75-80 people at marble topped
  tables, this informal restaurant is the scene for family meals and "lots of
  sheduchim." Known for its "cheerful and friendly" atmosphere.

Service: Cheerful and friendly

General Comments: With the new management, this restaurant will no doubt retain
  its reputation for hospitality. The introduction of live music is a nice touch.

Hours: **Sun-Thurs:** 11:30am-11pm   **Friday Closed**
        Sat: 1 hr after Shabbos till 12am

Credit Cards Accepted: MC, Visa, AmEx, Carte Blanche, Diners Club

Restaurant Discount: 10% Off

Borough: Queens
Section: Fresh Meadows

The Authoritative New York City Kosher Dining Guide

Restaurant: Surrey Kosher Restaurant & Deli   *Phone Number:* (718) 658-9243
                                                  Fax: None
Address: 179-08 Union Turnpike (bet. 179th St. - 180th St.)

Hechsher: NO RABBINIC HECHSHER - RESTAURANT IS OPEN 7 DAYS
                                                           A WEEK
Proprietor/Manager:

Type(s) of Food: Meat - Deli

Price Range: *Lunch*   *Dinner*   *Take out*
    Entrées: $6.75-$8.95 (Sand.) $8.95-$17.95
    Desserts: $1.75-$2.95   *Early Bird Dinner Special:*$7.95-$9.95
    Drinks: $1.00-$1.35 $2.75-$2.95 (Beer)   *Sandwiches:* $6.75-$8.95

Food Specialties: Pastrami & Corn Beef Sandwiches, 5¢ Hot Dogs*

> *Description:* Fresh, delicious, generous portions of food if the owner is
> accurate. They serve only Hebrew National meats. The Early Bird
> Dinner Special (available only 4:00pm-6:00pm) includes a full meal
> consisting of soup, appetizer, main course with vegetable and potato and
> dessert, but no drink. The Hot Dog Special: *Buy 1, the 2nd costs $.05

> *Comments:* Typical deli menu.

Ambiance (Decor): 48 seats in this standard deli set up. Laminate tables.

Service: Standard

General Comments: The owner's son is carrying on in the family's thirty year
tradition by having recently taken over the restaurant. They appear to be very
busy and that speaks for itself. However, after an extended conversation, it was
my impression that the current management has limited knowledge of or
background in Kashrus concerns.

Hours: **Sun-Sat:** 9am-8:30pm - RESTAURANT IS OPEN 7 DAYS A WEEK

Credit Cards Accepted: MC, Visa, AmEx

Restaurant Discount:

Borough: Queens
Section: Fresh Meadows

The Authoritative New York City Kosher Dining Guide

Restaurant: Empire Kosher Roasters #2   *Phone Number:* (718) 591-4220
                                              Fax: (718) 997-1007
Address: 180-30 Union Turnpike (bet. 180ᵗʰ St. - 181ˢᵗ St.)

Hechsher: Vaad Harabonim of Queens (Pas Yisroel)

Proprietor/Manager: Ezra Douek

Type(s) of Food: Meat - American

Price Range: *Lunch*   *Dinner*   *Take out*
  Entrées: $5.69-$13.99   Same   Free Local Delivery ($10 Min.)
  Desserts: $1.15-$2.45   *Sandwiches:* $2.99-$5.95, $4.99-$7.95 (Platter)
  Drinks: $ .60-$1.25   *Children's Menu:* $2.99-$3.49
  Sunday-Tuesday Buffet: (4:30pm-9pm) $6.99/pp, $3.99/child under 9

Food Specialties: BBQ Chicken, Chicken Kebob, Broiled Fish, Deli Sandwiches

  Description: Poultry served every which way with fish and deli, as well. The
    fish choices include tuna, whitefish, salmon, and herring salads; broiled
    salmon and broiled flounder. The children's menu selections include
    French fries & soda. Deli favorites come in both adult and children sized
    portions. Sandwich platters come with two side dishes and a roll or
    muffin. The buffet features chicken, fried or BBQ, and rice, pasta,
    potato, salads, vegetable, dessert, muffins, coffee or tea or soda.

  Comments: Fast food with an emphasis on poultry and fish, instead of beef. A
    welcome change of pace.

Ambiance (Decor): An attractive setting for family dining. Cafeteria style, fast food
    restaurant in the "Kenny Rogers" mold. It is well lit, colorful and child friendly.
    Regular dishes and cutlery are used. Seats 44 people.

Service: Self-serve

General Comments: Originally in Manhattan, but relocated to Queens. Good solution
    for families looking for a place to eat with small children or for anyone wanting
    a good meal without the fuss. Good value in an attractive setting.

Hours: **Sun-Thurs:** 11am-9:30pm
         Fri: 9:30am-2:30pm (winter) or 4:30pm (summer)   **Saturday Closed**

Credit Cards Accepted: MC, Visa

Restaurant Discount: 10% Off On All Platters Except Lunch Specials & Buffets

113

Borough: Queens
Section: Fresh Meadows

 $$

The Authoritative New York City Kosher Dining Guide

Restaurant: Glatt Wok Palace

Phone Number: (718) 740-1362
Fax: (718) 740-4570

Address: 190-13 Union Turnpike (bet. 190th St. - 192nd St.)

Hechsher: Vaad Harabonim of Queens (Glatt Kosher, Chassidishe Shechita)

Proprietor/Manager: Yossi

Type(s) of Food: Meat - Chinese, American

Price Range: *Lunch* (11:30am-4pm) *Dinner* *Take out*
  Entrées: $5.50 (Special) $9.95-$15.95 Same – Del. Avail.($20 Min.)
  Desserts: $3.00-$3.50 *Monday Buffet:* (6:30pm-9:30pm) $13.95/pp
  Drinks: $1.25 *Children's Special:* $3.25-$5.50 *Combo Platters:* $7

Food Specialties: Spare Ribs, General Tso's Chicken, Mandarin Steak, Hunan Duck

> *Description:* A traditional Chinese menu replete with just about anything you
> would fancy. Chow Fun, beef, chicken, duck, veal, and vegetable
> selections. The luncheon special is only available weekdays and not on
> holidays. It includes soup, entrée and fried rice. (19) specialties offer
> beef, chicken, and duck selections. All dishes can be prepared to taste.

> *Comments:* Mark this restaurant for future reviews.

Ambiance (Decor): This fairly large-sized restaurant seats 120 people in an informal
but purportedly elegant dining room. Manhattan sophistication is coupled with a
casual atmosphere that is suitable for both family and social occasions.

Service: Standard

General Comments: A moderately priced and pleasant family restaurant. The new all
you can eat buffet on Monday evenings makes it even more attractive. They
have a separate take out business next door.

Hours: **Sun-Thurs:** 11:30am-10:30pm
  Fri: (Winter Closed!), 11:30am-3pm (Summer)
  Sat: 1 hr after Shabbos till 1am (Nov-March) (Summer Closed!)

Credit Cards Accepted: MC, Visa, AmEx

Restaurant Discount:

Borough: Queens
Section: Fresh Meadows

The Authoritative New York City Kosher Dining Guide

Restaurant: Deli Master   *Phone Number:* (718) 353-3030
                                   Fax: (718) 353-8256
Address: 184-02 Horace Harding Expressway (bet. 184ᵗʰ St. - 185ᵗʰ St.)

Hechsher: NO HECHSHER - RESTAURANT IS OPEN 7 DAYS A WEEK

Proprietor/Manager: Jonathan

Type(s) of Food: Meat - Deli, Middle Eastern, American

Price Range: *Lunch*   *Dinner*   *Take out*
  Entrées: $10.95-$16.95   *Dinner Special* Same - Delivery Available
  Desserts: $2.00-$2.95   *Sandwiches:* $5.95-$9.95, *Combos:* $7.50-$13.50
  Drinks: $ .95-$1.60   *Hot Open:* $10.95-$11.95   *Kid's Corner:* $6.95

Food Specialties: Tongue Polonaise, Chicken Paprika, Chicken In A Pot, BBQ Ribs

  Description: The menu is extensive. Aside from the many deli sandwiches
      you would expect (regular, triple deckers, combo & hot open) you'll
      find traditional specialties, vegetarian selections, Israeli Specialties (e.g.
      Chummus, Techina, Babaganoush, Israeli Combo Platter & Falafel,
      etc.), Grills, Three Egg Omelets, À la carte Entrées (BBQ Ribs, 16 0z.
      Prime Rib Steaks, Roast Turkey, etc.), and a kid's menu. Dinner
      Special: for an additional $3 entrées become full dinners consisting of
      soup, entrée, dessert, and coffee or tea.

  Comments: Maintain they are strictly kosher by New York State Standards,
      but does not have a rabbinic hechsher. Hebrew National meats and
      Empire poultry served exclusively.

Ambiance (Decor): This informal deli seats 90 at both separate tables and booths. No
    tablecloths, but chandeliers and piped in music to eat by.

Service: Standard

General Comments: The variety offered in the menu makes this restaurant worthy of
    a try if the absence of a mashgiach is not an issue for you. This is an old
    fashioned "traditional" Jewish deli with a Middle Eastern connection.

Hours: **Sun-Sat:** 10am-9pm - RESTAURANT IS OPEN 7 DAYS A WEEK

Credit Cards Accepted: MC, Visa, AmEx, Discover, Diners Club, Carte Blanche

Restaurant Discount: 10% Off Eat-in Only w/ Regular Menu (Not to be Combined)

115

The Authoritative New York City Kosher Dining Guide

Flushing:

Benjy's Pizza
72-73 Main Street
Vaad Harabonim of Queens

Tel: (718) 268-0791

Guy's Pies
75-43 Main Street
Vaad Harabonim of Queens

Tel: (718) 793-0710

Naomi's Kosher Pizza
68-28 Main Street
Vaad Harabonim of Queens

Tel: (718) 520-8754

Shimon's Pizza & Falafel
71-24 Main Street
Vaad Harabonim of Queens

Tel: (718) 793-1491

Manna Kosher Pizza
68-28 Main Street
Vaad Harabonim of Queens

Tel: (718) 520-8754

Moshe's Kosher Pizza
181-30 Union Turnpike
Vaad Harabonim of Queens

Tel: (718) 969-1928

Bellerose:

Spencer's Pizza
248-06 Union Turnpike
Vaad Harabonim of Queens

Tel: (718) 347-5862

Whitestone
Bayside
Little Neck

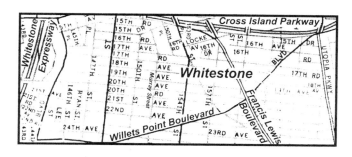

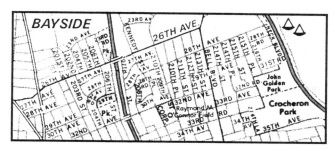

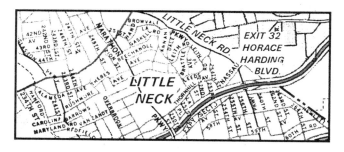

Borough: Queens
Section: Whitestone

The Authoritative New York City Kosher Dining Guide

Restaurant: Celebrity Kosher Gourmet   *Phone Number:* (718) 746-9222
                                                Fax: None
Address: 2014 Francis Lewis Boulevard (bet. Willets Point Blvd. - 20th Rd.)

Hechsher: NO HECHSHER – RESTAURANT IS OPEN 7 DAYS A WEEK

Proprietor/Manager:

Type(s) of Food: Meat - Deli

Price Range:	Lunch	Dinner	Take out
Entrées:	$11.95-$15.95	Same	Same – Delivery Available
Desserts:	$1.75-$2.75	Lunch & Dinner Specials Available	
Drinks:	$ .95-$2.50	Deli Sandwiches: $6.25-$9.95	

Food Specialties: Boiled Beef Flanken, Stuffed Cabbage, Potato Pancakes, Burgers

> *Description:* Strictly a deli menu except for the falafel. Entrée selection is limited, offering several choices of beef and poultry and a few additional cooked items like: Stuffed Cabbage, Chicken or Boiled Beef Flanken in a Pot, etc. Omelets, Soups, Platters, and sandwiches, sandwiches, sandwiches. Adding $3 to the price of an entrée entitles the diner to a full course dinner consisting of choice of appetizer or soup, entrée, dessert and tea or coffee. The Lunch Special (Mon-Fri, 11am-3pm) offers a free cup of soup du jour with every deli sandwich and beverage.

> *Comments:* Not one of the most extensive menus, but it manages to cover enough of the bases.

Ambiance (Decor): 65 seats. A typical and traditional deli.

Service: Standard

General Comments: It's a deli!

Hours: **Sun-Sat:** 10am-8pm - RESTAURANT IS OPEN 7 DAYS A WEEK

Credit Cards Accepted: AmEx

Restaurant Discount:

Borough: Queens
Section: Bayside

The Authoritative New York City Kosher Dining Guide

Restaurant: Ben's Bayside Kosher Deli   *Phone Number:* (718) 229-2367
                                            Fax: (718) 229-3066
Address: 211-37 26th Avenue (bet. 211th St. - 212th St. in Bay Terrace Shppg Ctr.)

Hechsher: Rabbi Israel Steinberg - RESTAURANT IS OPEN 7 DAYS A WEEK

Proprietor/Manager: Ronnie Dragoon / Scott Dragoon (Manager)

Type(s) of Food: Meat - Deli

Price Range: *Lunch*   *Dinner*   *Take out*
  Entrées: $10.95-$19.95   Same   Delivery via Delivery Service only
  Desserts: $2- $3.25 *Sandwiches:* $5.95-$11.95   *Kid's Menu:* $5.25
  Drinks: $1.25-$1.55, $3.25-$3.95 (Beer), $4-$5/gl $10-$20/btl (Wine)

Food Specialties: Sandwiches, Burgers, Homemade Soup, Stuffed Cabbage, Salads

  Description: An extensive deli menu with all the favorites and then some.
    Tongue & corned beef are cured on premises. Nice selection of freshly
    made salads and cold platters. 3 egg omelets are served with choice of
    potato pancake and apple sauce or fries. Poultry, beef, veal, and fresh
    salmon entrées come with 2 vegetables. Traditional specialties e.g.
    Hungarian Goulash, Chicken Fricassee, Boiled Beef In The Pot
    (flanken) are offered, alongside pasta dishes e.g. Primavera or
    Marinara. 3 homemade soups, including mushroom barley, chicken, and
    soup of the day. Large selection of side dishes and appetizers.

  Comments: Empire and Hebrew National meats are featured. The menu has
    just about everything to satisfy anyone's deli cravings. The restaurant is
    one of 7 in Ben's deli chain. If their professionalism is extended to the
    quality & preparation of their food, you won't be disappointed.

Ambiance (Decor): A capacity of 150 seats, in a modern, attractive setting. I'm told
    that each of the restaurants in this chain has its own individual character,
    reflecting its location and clientele, and that none could be described as typical.

Service: Standard

General Comments: A slick organization with all aspects of marketing down pat.

Hours: **Sun-Sat:** 9am-9:30pm - RESTAURANT IS OPEN 7 DAYS A WEEK

Credit Cards Accepted: MC, Visa, AmEx, Discover, Diners Club

Restaurant Discount:

The Authoritative New York City Kosher Dining Guide

Restaurant: Masur's   *Phone Number:* (718) 428-5000
                               Fax: (718) 631-2952
Address: 254-51 Horace Harding Boulevard (cor. Little Neck Pwy.)
                               (L.I.E. Exit 32)
Hechsher: Vaad Harabonim of Long Island (Glatt Kosher, Mashgiach Temidi)

Proprietor/Manager:

Type(s) of Food: Meat - American, Deli

Price Range:	*Lunch*	*Dinner*	*Take out*
Entrées:	$7.95-$15.95	Same	Only Sandwiches: $4.50-$5.95
Desserts:	$1.50-$2.50	*Specials: Lunch:* $12-$15, *Dinner:* $6-$7	
Drinks:	$ .85-$1.25	*Sandwiches:* $4.95-$10.45 (Hot)	
	$3.00/gl. (Wine), $2.00-$2.50 (Beer)		

Food Specialties: Deli, Steaks, Burgers

> *Description:* Typical deli menu with all the popular dishes served in standard portions. The daily changing Lunch Specials include an entrée and soup. The Dinner Specials offer soup or salad with an entrée and dessert.

> *Comments:* The meat, poultry and produce are understandably very fresh, coming from the family owned supermarket next door. You probably never have to hear, "Sorry, we're out of it" from this establishment.

Ambiance (Decor): The restaurant shares its name with its other half, the supermarket next door. Having a separate entrance though, the restaurant space is entirely unencumbered. Newly renovated in modern style, this mid-size restaurant seats 90. Informal, with tablecloths covering the tables.

Service: Standard

General Comments: After operating the market for 31 years, the Masurs opened the restaurant 11 years ago. On the border between Queens and Nassau, it is the only glatt kosher eatery in the area. Handicapped accessible.

Hours: **Sun-Thurs:** 11am-8:30pm **Fri:** 11am-2:30pm **Saturday Closed**

Credit Cards Accepted: MC, Visa, AmEx, Diners Club, Discover

Restaurant Discount:

Westerleigh
Willowbrook
Staten Island Mall

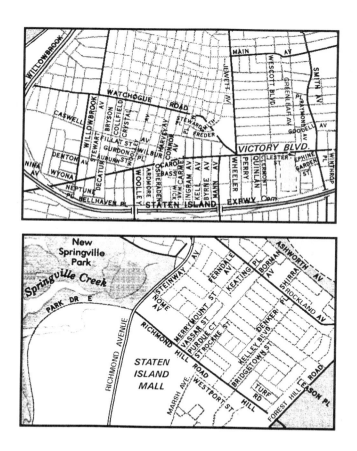

Borough: Staten Island

Section: Westerleigh (near Willowbrook)

The Authoritative New York City Kosher Dining Guide

Restaurant: Jerusalem Kebob House Restaurant   *Phone Number:* (718) 447-1400
Fax: (718) 982-6337

Address: 1980 Victory Boulevard

Hechsher: Vaad Harabonim of Staten Island (Glatt Kosher, Mashgiach Temidi)

Proprietor/Manager: Abraham Magoli

Type(s) of Food: Meat - Middle Eastern

Price Range:	Lunch	Dinner	Take out
Entrées:	$8.50-$13.50	Same	Same - Free Local Delivery ($10 Min)
Desserts:	$1.50-$2.00	*Thursday Schwarma Special:* $4.00	
Drinks:	$1.00-$1.50	*Kid`s Menu:* $4.00	*Salad Bar*

Food Specialties: Shawarma, Shish Kebob, Falafel, Chicken Nuggets, Rib Steak

> *Description:* The scaled back menu (the Chinese dishes have been dropped) features Middle Eastern kebobs, shawarma and grills, the mainstays of the restaurant. Nice size portions. The Kid's Special comes with fries. The Israeli salads and a choice of three soups are made fresh daily. Most selections are offered either served in a pita or on a plate.

> *Comments:* This Israeli steakia, the only glatt kosher restaurant in Staten Island, now has a new chef to tantalize locals. The pita sandwiches make for nutritious, and relatively low fat, fast food alternatives.

Ambiance (Decor): An unpretentious restaurant with large mirrored pictures depicting Israeli sites and landscapes decorating the walls. The 42 seats have been modernized and a salad bar has been added. A take-out display counter dominates the front. Lends itself to informal lunches and family dinners.

Service: Standard

General Comments: The only glatt kosher restaurant in Staten Island. A possible alternative to pizza for informal or children's parties.

Hours: **Sun-Thurs:** 11:30am-9:30pm **Friday Closed** **Saturday Closed**

Credit Cards Not Accepted: CASH ONLY!

Restaurant Discount: 10% Off

Borough: Staten Island
Section: Westerleigh (near Willowbrook)

The Authoritative New York City Kosher Dining Guide

Restaurant: Good Appetite Café

Address: 1980 Victory Boulevard

Phone Number: (718) 981-5458
Fax: None

Hechsher: Vaad of Staten Island

Proprietor/Manager: Mickey Simantov

Type(s) of Food: Dairy, Health Food - American

Price Range:
	Lunch	*Dinner*	*Take out*
Entrées:	$6.49.50-$13.99	Same	Same - Delivery Available ($30 Min)
Desserts:	$2.50-$ 2.75	*Breakfast Specials:* $1.20-$1.95	
Drinks:	$1.25-$ 3.25	*Sandwiches:* $ 2.95-$6.49	*Daily Specialties*

Food Specialties: Fresh Fish, Omelets, Sandwiches, Pancakes, Waffles, Bourekas

Description: They feature low cholesterol, low calorie, low sugar foods. The menu includes fresh salads, sandwiches, fish platters, various omelets, homemade crepes, pancakes, waffles, homemade desserts, and a gourmet coffee selection. Portions are fairly large. Gourmet coffee can be bought by the pitcher (1¾ cups). Although the menu is mostly American, a few ethnic foods are offered e.g. Borekas and Melawach.

Comments: Don't miss the homemade waffles! They're very delicious, as is the super light cheesecake. The parve matzah ball chicken soup is very convincing and quite good. Choose the fresh fish for a satisfying entrée.

Ambiance (Decor): This small restaurant has a bright color scheme of pink and turquoise, and a feel reminiscent of ice cream parlors or coffee shops of small town America straight out of the '50's. The pace is easy going and friendly. Laminate tables and chairs seat 35 or eat on a stool by the counter.

Service: Owner doubles as a server

General Comments: Lunchtime is the busiest for this comfortable eatery. With its focus on healthy eating, it's a find in the desolate world of kosher SI eateries.

Hours: **Sun-Thurs:** 7am-9pm   **Fri:** 7am-3pm
Sat: Open 1 hr after Shabbos till 1am

Credit Cards Not Accepted: CASH ONLY!

Restaurant Discount: 10% Off

Borough: Staten Island
Section: Willowbrook

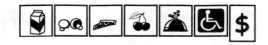

The Authoritative New York City Kosher Dining Guide

Restaurant: Dairy Palace

Phone Number: (718) 761-5200
Fax: None

Address: 2210 Victory Boulevard

Hechsher: Vaad Hakashrus of Staten Island (Rabbi Yaachov Marcus)

Proprietor/Manager: Weiss Family

Type(s) of Food: Dairy, Vegetarian - Eclectic

Price Range:

	Lunch	Dinner	Take out
Entrées:	$5.00-$12.99	Same	Same – Free Local Delivery ($15 Min.)
Desserts:	$1.50		
Drinks:	$ .90-$2.00		

Food Specialties: Pizza, Vegetarian Chinese, Mexican, Italian, Middle Eastern

Description: The extensive menu has just about everything. It starts with a large selection of pizzas, falafel, salads, sandwiches on bread or bagels; a varied fish selection (Salmon, Flounder Red Snapper, Brook Trout, Halibut, Maui Maui & Sole), a respectable pasta list, 9 different stuffed potatoes, beverages, knishes, & desserts! A potpourri of hot dishes from assorted ethnicities: a Chinese menu where the "meats" are all vegetarian in dishes like Pepper Steak, Sesame Chicken, & Beef with Broccoli. The "Hot Steaming Foods" include Stuffed Burritos, Mexican Chili, Eggplant Parmigiana, and Stuffed Cabbage. There are diet selections, 7 soups, even Cholent. Middle Eastern items: Shawarma, Babaganoush, Malawach & Moroccan Cigars.

Comments: Established in 1986, this restaurant tries single-handedly to satisfy all the kosher culinary needs of Staten Island in a heimishe way.

Ambiance (Decor): A hybrid of a pizzeria and a fast food restaurant. Children don't pose a problem here with the laminate tables, washable chairs (55) & tiled floor.

Service: Self-serve or restaurant will accommodate

General Comments: A family pizzeria with an ambitious menu.

Hours: **Sun-Thurs:** 11am-8:30pm **Fri:** 11am-3pm
Sat: ½ hr after Shabbos till 12:30am

Credit Cards _Not_ Accepted: CASH ONLY!

Restaurant Discount:

Borough: Staten Island

Section: Staten Island Mall (near New Springville)

The Authoritative New York City Kosher Dining Guide

Restaurant: Golden's Kosher Deli & Restaurant   **Phone Number:** (718) 494-6000

Fax: None

Address: 2845 Richmond Avenue

Hechsher: NO HECHSHER - RESTAURANT IS OPEN 7 DAYS A WEEK

Proprietor/Manager:

Type(s) of Food: Meat - Deli, American

Price Range:

	Lunch	Dinner	Take out
Entrées:	$9.75 - $16.95	Same	Same - Delivery Available
Desserts:	$1.35 - $ 2.50	**Sandwiches:** $5.75 - $7.10	
Drinks:	$ .85 - $ 2.25	$2.50 - $2.95 (Wine/Beer)	

Food Specialties: Deli sandwiches, BBQ or Buffalo Wings, Prime Rib Steak

Description: Sandwiches, platters, and hot entrées such as Breaded Veal Chops, Romanian Steak, and Hungarian Goulash. Hebrew National meats served. Omelets and egg sandwiches are a breakfast possibility. Burger selection: turkey (99% fat free, served with lettuce, tomato, and French fries) as well as beef (served the same way). Kid's menu (under 12) available: $6.75 for a choice of entrée, fries, soda, cookie, or jello.

Comments: Nice selection. A revised menu is planned in the coming months.

Ambiance (Decor): This large dining room accommodates an old 1930's subway car in the middle of the restaurant in which you can sit and eat. Relaxed and casual this is a very nice space with a clean appearance. A separate smoking room is in the back of the restaurant. Bustling during the weekend and at meal times.

Service: Standard, also take-out counter

General Comments: This is an old fashioned deli with all the deli favorites in a novel and attractive setting in the Staten Island Mall complex. Owner maintains he strictly abides by NY State kosher guidelines. Despite size, diners may still encounter lines waiting to be seated during busy periods.

Hours: Sun-Thurs: 9am-10pm   **Fri-Sat:** 9am-11pm
- RESTAURANT IS OPEN 7 DAYS A WEEK

Credit Cards Accepted: MC, Visa, AmEx, Diner's Club, Discover

Restaurant Discount:

The Authoritative New York City Kosher Dining Guide

Dairy Palace   *Tel:* (212) 761-5200
2210 Victory Boulevard
Vaad of Staten Island

Financial District
Tribeca
Lower East Side

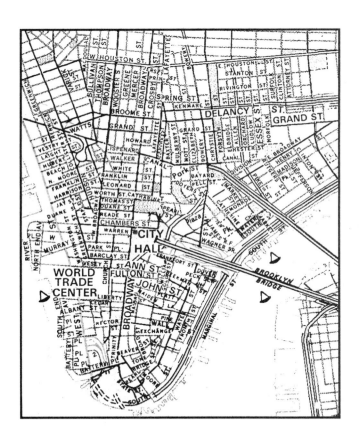

Borough: Manhattan
Section: Financial District

The Authoritative New York City Kosher Dining Guide

Restaurant: American Café & Health Bar   *Phone Number:* (212) 732-1426
                                              Fax: (212) 732-1728
Address: 160 Broadway (Basement) (bet. Liberty St. - Maiden Ln.)

Hechsher: ⊃ - K (Cholov Yisroel, Mashgiach Temidi)

Proprietor/Manager: Dan

Type(s) of Food: Dairy - International

Price Range: *Lunch*   *Dinner*   *Take out*
   Entrées: $5.95-$6.25   Same   Same - Free Local Delivery ($5 Min.)
   Desserts: $1.50-$2.95   *Sandwiches:* $4.95-$6.95
   Drinks: $ .65-$3.00   *Breakfast:* $2.50-$3.75

Food Specialties: Fish Of The Day, Deep Pan Pizza, Health Salads & Drinks, Soups

Description: The menu claims "We start fresh everyday with love and other
   natural ingredients." The focus is on health, with fresh, low calorie, high
   quality food as the stated aim. You'll find a fairly extensive salad
   selection (at least eight choices), and a wide variety of vegetable and
   fruit juices and shakes. Entrées include Eggplant Scaloppini, Fetuccini
   Casserole, Curried Vegetables, and Quiche of the Day. The Deep Dish
   Pizzas come with Tossed Salad, and the sandwiches are served with
   House Salad & French fries.

Comments: It has been a while since we ate here, but I do remember that the
   portions are quite large and filling. There are many viable choices.

Ambiance (Decor): The basement location of this restaurant requires descending a
   flight of stairs. There is a large display for take-out. A counter ($3.00 min), and
   tables ($4.00 min) in the main dining area comprise your seating options.
   Catering to office workers in the area, the decor takes second place to the food.

Service: Standard

General Comments: The largest kosher eatery in the area. Not handicapped friendly.

Hours: **Mon-Thurs:** 7am-8pm   **Fri:** 7am-2 hrs before Shabbos
         Saturday Closed   Sunday Closed

Credit Cards Accepted: MC, Visa, AmEx

Restaurant Discount: 10% Off After 3pm.

Borough: Manhattan
Section: Financial District

The Authoritative New York City Kosher Dining Guide

Restaurant: Deli Glatt Kosher Sandwich Shop   *Phone Number:* (212) 349-3622
                                                  Fax: (212) 374-9130
Address: 150 Fulton Street

Hechsher: Vaad Harabbanim of Flatbush

Proprietor/Manager: Melvin Sternfield

Type(s) of Food: Meat – Deli, Middle Eastern

Price Range:	*Lunch*	*Dinner*	*Take out*
Entrées:	$5.59-$6.49	Same	Same – Free Local Delivery
Desserts:	$1.29-$2.29	*Deli Sandwiches:* $3.99-$7.29	
Drinks:	$ .69-$1.50	*Breakfast Special:* $1.19-$1.69	

Food Specialties: Deli & Parve Sandwiches, Salads, Hot & Cold Platters, Falafel

Description: Succinct menu for a fast lunch or a supper on the go. Deli, Burgers and parve sandwiches are the mainstays. A short "From The Grill" selection offers BBQ Chicken, Pepper Steak w/ rice and Chicken Cutlet. Hot and cold platters include beef stew w/ rice, meatballs w/ spaghetti, Broiled Salmon, tuna, chicken, turkey, falafel and something called a sub platter. Soup of the Day. Side dishes include a variety of salads and knishes, along with the usual fries. The "Breakfast Special" offers various combinations of bagels with tea or coffee, and in some cases, eggs or lettuce & tomato. Side dish selection is expanding.

Comments: Catering to the luncheon needs of the local working hordes.

Ambiance (Decor): Very small, unadorned: seating for 4 at a counter. Don't look for ambiance, there is none. Largely take-out business. Hard to spot from the outside, it is the door just west of the building's large entry.

Service: Self-serve

General Comments: This is one of those establishments that stretches to the limit the definition of a restaurant. But you can eat here, and in a pinch it can be helpful to know it exists. Not far from Battery Park, making for possible outdoor eating.

Hours: **Mon-Thurs:** 7:30am-6pm   **Fri:** 7:30am-2 hrs before Shabbos
Saturday Closed   **Sunday Closed**

Credit Cards Not Accepted: CASH OR CHECK ONLY!

Restaurant Discount:

The Authoritative New York City Kosher Dining Guide

Restaurant: Pita Express

Phone Number: (212) 571-2999
Fax: Same

Address: 15 Ann Street (bet. Broadway - Nassau St.)

Hechsher: Rabbi Avraham Shlomo Fishelis

Proprietor/Manager: Yossi

Type(s) of Food: Meat - Middle Eastern

Price Range:	Lunch	Dinner	Take out
Entrées:	$8.00-$15.95	Same	Same
Desserts:	$2.50		Free Local Delivery
Drinks:	$1.00-$1.50	Sandwiches: $3.00-$6.00	

Food Specialties: Cous-cous, Shish Kebob, Rib Steak, Moroccan Fish, Shawarma

Description: The menu consists of Middle Eastern favorites. Eleven salads are offered by the pound. Seven soups include: Vegetable, Split Pea, Lentil, Bean, Chicken Noodle, Yemenite style meat soup, and a soup of the day. House Specials feature: Baked Chicken, Fish and Chips, Moroccan Cigars, and Kibbeh, among others. Entrées feature: Baby Lamb Chops, Chicken, Beef, and/or Koufta Kebob; Falafel Plate, and Burgers, which can be bought as sandwiches in pita as well.

Comments: A small, but adequate menu that has something for most everyone.

Ambiance (Decor): This newest of the chain of three restaurants accommodates 50 people. A modern, fast food restaurant with a café casualness. A hunter green color scheme sets the background for the laminate tables, wood backed café chairs, and neon light accents. A modern, recently renovated option downtown.

Service: Self-serve

General Comments: Steps from the World Trade Center, Wall Street, and Battery Park City, it is the third fast food, kosher meat restaurant to open in the area. Near the Jewish Heritage Museum.

Hours: **Mon-Thurs:** 9am-8pm **Fri:** 9am-2 hrs before Shabbos
Saturday Closed   Sunday Closed

Credit Cards Accepted: MC, Visa, AmEx

Restaurant Discount: 10% Off For Orders Over $10

Borough: Manhattan
Section: Financial District

The Authoritative New York City Kosher Dining Guide

Restaurant: Garden American Health Bar   **Phone Number:** (212) 587-8485
     Deli & Shawarma   **Fax:** (212) 587-8101
Address: 49 Ann Street (bet. William St. - Nassau St.)

Hechsher: OK Labs (Cholov Yisroel, Glatt Kosher, Pas Yisroel, Masgiach Temidi)

Proprietor/Manager: Meir Sarfehzadh (Owner), Sam (Manager)

Type(s) of Food: Dairy, Meat- Italian, Middle Eastern, Deli, Chinese American

Price Range: *Lunch*   *Dinner*   *Take out*
   Entrées: $4.95-$7.25 (Dairy), $5.95-$8.25 (Meat) Same- Free Local Delivery
   Desserts: $ .90-$2.95   **Breakfast:** $2.75-$4.75/platter, $.65-$3.99/sandwich
   Drinks: $ .60-$2.99 **Pizza:** $1.50-$2.50/sl, **Sandwiches:** $4.25-$6.95

Food Specialties: Pastas, Salads, Pizza, Fish, Shish Kebob, Shawarma, Deli

   Description: Two separate kitchens, and two distinct menus. The dairy
     stresses homemade food: Hot Plate Platters (w/ 2 veg) include Baked
     Spinach Quiche, Eggplant Parmigiana (w/pasta), & Salmon Cutlet.
     Fresh fish are baked, broiled, or fried. Hot or cold pastas, pizzas, salads,
     soups and sandwiches are offered. There are juices & shakes. Desserts
     include Blintzes, Frozen Yogurt, etc. In the adjacent room, deli and
     parve sandwiches, grilled fish platters, pasta, various kebobs, BBQ
     chicken, and hot or cold platters are offered. Knishes, soups and Middle
     Eastern specialties, such as Chicken Baglipolo and Koresh Bedenjun are
     offered along with falafel, chummus and babaganoush. Grilled /baked
     snapper or salmon are served w/ 2 veg.

   Comments: A fast food establishment with a surprisingly extensive and varied
     menu, now expanded even further and with a full meat selection.

Ambiance (Decor): Cleaved into two distinct eateries. Dairy seats 70, and meat 45.
   No air conditioning, when needed a large fan blows air through the restaurant.

Service: Self-serve

General Comments: Located mid-block, on an old, narrow, hard to find street.

Hours: **Mon-Thurs:** 6am-7pm   **Fri:** 6am-2 hrs before Shabbos
     <u>**Saturday Closed**</u>   **Sun:** 10am-5pm

Credit Cards Accepted: MC, Visa, AmEx, Discover, Carte Blanche, Diners Club

Restaurant Discount: 10% Off

Borough: Manhattan

Section: Tribecca (City Hall Area)

The Authoritative New York City Kosher Dining Guide

Restaurant: Yummi

Phone Number: (212) 228-2429

Fax: None

Address: 63 Reade Street (bet. Broadway - Church St.)

Hechsher: Rabbi Shmuel Fishelis (Glatt Kosher)

Proprietor/Manager:

Type(s) of Food: Meat - Middle Eastern, American

Price Range:

	Lunch	*Dinner*	*Take out*
Entrées:	$4.95-$12.95	Same	Same- Local Free Delivery Avail.

Desserts: $1.25-$1.50 *Sandwiches:* $1.50-$8.95 *Daily Specials:* $5-$6

Drinks: $ .50-$1.25 *Student Special:* 10% Discount

Food Specialties: Shish Kebob, Shawarma, Lamb Chops, Grills, BBQ Chicken

> *Description:* Middle Eastern specialties, and American staples (beef burgers, fried & BBQ chicken, frankfurters). Many kebobs including: beef, chicken, turkey, and lamb. Ten salads are served in either a pita ($3) or a platter ($3.50). A Combo Salad ($6), four different salads, includes three falafel balls. A Soup of the Day is one of five soups ($2.50). Monday's Special: Jerusalem Mix in a pita with fries and drink ($5.99). Friday's Special: Shawarma in a pita with fries and drink ($4.99).

> *Comments:* To date, we've only tried falafel in a pita here. The salad was fresh and the falafel crisp on the outside and soft on the inside as it should be. Unlimited condiments such as olives, sour pickles and sauerkraut are self-served.

Ambiance (Decor): Though only a year old, this small and very narrow eatery is worn and unattractive. The take-out counter / showcase dominates the front area. Seating, for about 24 patrons, is located in the back. Not a place to linger.

Service: Self-serve

General Comments: Located near City Hall, this restaurant focuses on their take-out business and seems disinterested in attracting in-restaurant diners.

Hours: **Mon-Thurs:** 8:30am-8pm **Fri:** 8:30am-2 hrs before Shabbos
Closed Saturday **Sun:** 10am-5pm

Credit Cards Not Accepted: CASH ONLY!

Restaurant Discount:

The Authoritative New York City Kosher Dining Guide

Restaurant: The Grand Deli (aka. Tricom)   *Phone Number:* (212) 477-5200
                                                Fax: (212) 477-3515
Address: 399-401 Grand Street (bet. Clinton St. - Suffolk St.)

Hechsher: OU (Glatt Kosher, Chassidishe Shechita, Masgiach Temidi)

Proprietor/Manager: Chaim

Type(s) of Food: Meat - Deli, Chinese, American

Price Range: *Lunch* (11am-4pm) *Dinner*   *Take out*
Entrees: $9.00 special $12.00-$28.00   Same
Desserts: $3.00-$3.75   Delivery Available
Drinks: $1.00-$1.50   *Early Dinner Menu:* $10.95 (4pm-6pm)

Food Specialties: Sino-Steak, Ribs, Pastrami, General Tso, BBQ Breast of Veal

Description: Extensive deli, and a complete Chinese menu. Also, Shish
Kabob, a Dieters Delights list, and grilled items. The Chinese menu
includes chicken, beef, veal, & duck favorites. Portions-small side.

Comments: The quality of the meat is uneven: the texture has often been
chewy and always fatty, however, it appears that their customers like it
for just those reasons. The application of salt tends to be heavy-handed.
With the Chinese menu, however, you can specify low sodium, no
MSG, spice to taste, & low fat preparations. Everything is à la carte, but
Midweek Luncheon & Early Dinner Menus are available.

Ambiance (Decor): Bright dining room, well air conditioned. Seats 60 in a relaxed
setting. The neon ceiling lights give a nice soft white glow, in contrast to the
bright wall sconces. The reflective surfaces, in the long, narrow room tend to
amplify the noise level, so it gets loud regardless of the number of people.

Service: Old time Jewish waiters: can be unresponsive and sometimes hard to find.

General Comments: Management assures me that any prior problems are diligently
being attended to. They are up for a new review in next year's edition.

Hours: **Sun-Thurs:** 11am-10:00pm   **Fri:** 8am-2 ½ hrs before Shabbos (Winter)
        Saturday Closed   8am-3:30pm (Summer)

Credit Cards Accepted: MC, Visa, AmEx, Discover, Diners Club, Carte Blanche

Restaurant Discount:

Borough: Manhattan
Section: Lower East Side

The Authoritative New York City Kosher Dining Guide

Restaurant: Gertel's Bakery & Sandwich Shop   *Phone Number:* (212) 982-3250
                                                  Fax: (212) 677-2870

Address: 53 Hester Street (bet. Essex St. - Ludlow St.)

Hechsher: CRC

Proprietor/Manager:

Type(s) of Food: Dairy - American

Price Range: *Lunch*   *Dinner*   *Take out*
   Entrées: $1.50 (for a schmear)- $4.75 (Sandwiches)
   Desserts: $ .80-$6.00/lb.   Delivery Available
   Drinks: $ .65-$1.25

Food Specialties: Sandwiches, Salads, Hot Soups, Omelets, Baked Goods

   Description: The menu features various sandwiches, tuna, egg salad, cheese,
   lox & cream cheese, etc. 2-3 different salads made fresh daily, as well as
   the Soup of the Day (served with bread). For breakfast, your choice of
   eggs prepared as you like. And then there is all that the bakery makes
   for dessert.

   Comments: A good quick stop for a light bite and unlimited dessert choices.

Ambiance (Decor): A bakery with 5 tables.

Service: Self-serve or they will bring the food to the table for you after you order

General Comments: Friday afternoon the food selection runs low.

Hours: **Sun-Thurs:** 6:30am-5:30pm **Fri:** 6:30am-3pm <u>**Saturday Closed**</u>

Credit Cards Accepted: MC, Visa

Restaurant Discount:

134

Borough: Manhattan
Section: Lower East Side

The Authoritative New York City Kosher Dining Guide

Restaurant: Ratner's   **Phone Number:** (212) 677-5588
                                                Fax: (212) 473-4860

Address: 138 Delancy Street (bet. Suffolk St. - Norfolk St.)

Hechsher: Ɔ-K

Proprietor/Manager: Robert or Fred Harmatz

Type(s) of Food: Dairy, Vegetarian - Jewish American

Price Range:	Lunch	Dinner	Take out
Entrées:	$9.95 - $18.95	Same	Delivery Available
Desserts:	$2.75 - $4.50	**Daily Specials:**	$9.25-$14.95
Drinks:	$1.25-$3.75	$4.00/glass average	(Alcoholic Beverages)

Food Specialties: Soups, Blintzes, Fish, Vegetarian Dishes, Salads, Bakery

Description: Traditional Jewish-American fare: standard vegetarian (Protose steak, kasha varnishkes, etc.), Fish (grilled or fried) served with two vegetables and even some Italian specialties are offered. Baked goods are fresh and very good. Satisfying Daily Soup Specials.

Comments: Reminiscent of eating in an old Catskills hotel dining room. The soups are particularly good. Portions aren't as filling as they once were.

Ambiance (Decor): The large dining room has a cafeteria feel. There is a take out counter up front as well as a 2nd counter for bakery sales. There is no attempt to create atmosphere. You go there to eat, it's as simple as that.

Service: Jewish style. Can range from "what's the matter, you're not hungry?" (if you haven't finished everything on your plate), to impatience (if the waiter has had a hard day). Some waiters are helpful and hover over you, "Eat it, it's good." Once you've ordered, service is fast. The waiter may return to verify that his suggestions have met your expectations or to make sure you've eaten.

General Comments: A Jewish New York eating experience, a relic of another time when life was simpler in many ways and there were only three or four kosher restaurants in all of Manhattan. Stop in if only to catch a glimpse of the past.

Hours: **Sun-Thurs:** 6am-11pm **Fri:** 6am-3pm
        Sat: Opens 1 hr after Shabbos till 2am (Winter Only)

Credit Cards Accepted: MC, Visa, AmEx, Discover

Restaurant Discount: 10% off, dine in only, max. 4 people

Borough: Manhattan
Section: Lower East Side

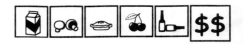

The Authoritative New York City Kosher Dining Guide

Restaurant: Lansky Lounge

Phone Number: (212) 677-9489
Fax: (212) 473-4860

Address: 104 Norfolk Street (bet. Delancy St. - Rivington St.)

Hechsher: Ɔ-K

Proprietor/Manager: Ted

Type(s) of Food: Dairy, Vegetarian - Jewish American, Eclectic

Price Range:	Lunch	Dinner	Take out
Entrées:	Closed	$5.00-$15.00	None
Desserts:		$6.00	
Drinks:	$2.00-$3.00	$6-$7/glass	$30-$40/bottle (Wine)	$4-$7 (Beer)
	$5-$12/glass (Single Malts)		$5-$12/glass (Mixed Drinks)

Food Specialties: Fresh Fish, Perogies, Salads, Pasta, Wild Mushroom Halibut

Description: An extremely limited menu, with a total of 12 selections ranging from something to nosh on like Mushroom and Nut Pate with Toast Points or Wild Mushroom Kugel, to true entrées like Mango Dijon Glazed Sole with Caviar Potato Salad and Green Beans, or Macadamia Crusted Halibut with Pilaf and Glazed Carrot. Dessert is a choice between White Chocolate Mousse and Grand Marnier Truffles. Full bar.

Comments: The chef, Michael Young, apprenticed at Patria, a non-kosher restaurant in New York City. An appeal to sophisticated taste, though not what you'd expect in this part of town.

Ambiance (Decor): Lounge setting carved from the back of Ratner's, reflecting the bygone era of the twenties. Reminiscent of a speakeasy from prohibition days, with red mahogany coupled with cold rolled steel. A formal and plush decor.

Service: Formal

General Comments: A unique backdrop for dining and drinking. Getting inside is not very convenient. There is only an unmarked entrance to an alley on the street. After walking down this rather unattractive alley you go up a flight of stairs.

Hours: Sun-Thurs: 7pm-4am   **Friday Closed**   Sat: Opens 1 hr aft Shabbos till 4am

Credit Cards Accepted: MC, Visa, AmEx, Discover

Restaurant Discount:

136

Borough: Manhattan
Section: Lower East Side

The Authoritative New York City Kosher Dining Guide

Restaurant: Le Petit Cafe   *Phone Number:* (212) 473-5488
                                 Fax: None
Address: 96 Orchard Street (bet. Broome St. - Delancey St.)

Hechsher: Rabbi Fishelis

Proprietor/Manager: Erez

Type(s) of Food: Dairy - American

Price Range:	*Lunch*	*Dinner*	*Take out*
Entrees:	$3.00-$8.00	Same	Same – Free Local Delivery
Desserts:	$.20-$1.50	*Sandwiches:* $3-$4.50	*Lunch Special:* $4-$5
Drinks:	$1.50-$3.50	*Breakfast Special:* $1-$1.50	*Mon-Thur Special*

Food Specialties: Fresh Fish, Pasta, Salads, Quiche, Soups, Potatoes

> *Description:* A small, select menu where the only thing French is the fries, despite the name. It is designed to meet the needs of this unique neighborhood. Soup of the Day changes each day, as does the fish. The fish, salmon for example, comes with 2 side dishes for a price of $5.00. The Lunch Special is your basic sandwich and soda. The Breakfast Special is even more basic: coffee with a bagel and spread. A Monday and Thursday Special offers free cappuccino or latte to diners spending $7 or more.

> *Comments:* Having just opened within the past year, the restaurant continues to fine-tune its menu.

Ambiance (Decor): With a total seating of 15, divided up between counter seats and several tables, space is at a premium. What space there is, is distinguished more by what is hanging on the walls: unique silver on wood photos, which have the appearance of being antique are framed in metal and are for sale. Themes are Jewish in black and white. Café is about 6 steps above street level.

Service: Self-serve or owner will serve

General Comments: For locals and shoppers to enjoy as a mid day respite.

Hours: **Sun-Thurs:** 8am-6pm   **Fri:** 8am-2 hours before Shabbos
        Saturday Closed

Credit Cards Not Accepted: CASH ONLY!

Restaurant Discount: Free Dessert To 2 Or More Diners

137

The Authoritative New York City Kosher Dining Guide

Financial District:

American Café and Health Bar *Tel:* (212) 732-1426
160 Broadway
כ-K

Garden American Health Bar *Tel:* (212) 587-8101
49 Ann Street
OK Labs

Tribecca (City Hall Area):

Mizrachi Kosher Pizza & Falafel *Tel:* (212) 964-2280
105 Chambers Street
Certified Kosher Underwriters

The Lower East Side:

Essex Kosher Pizza *Tel:* (212) 358-9218
21 Essex Street
Rabbi Shmuel Fishelis

Shalom Chai Pizza *Tel:* (212) 598-4178
359 Grand Street
Rabbi Pinchos Horowitz

East Village
Union Square
Stuyvesant Town
Chelsea

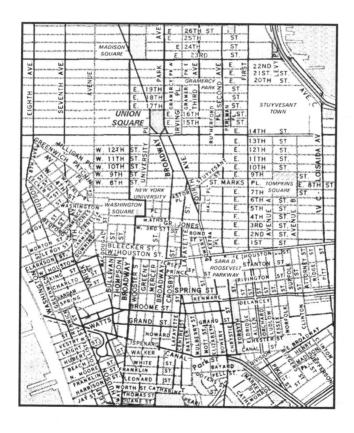

Borough: Manhattan
Section: East Village

The Authoritative New York City Kosher Dining Guide

Restaurant: Caravan of Dreams   *Phone Number:* (212) 254-1613
    Fax: Same
Address: 405 East 6th Street (bet. 1st Ave. - Ave. A)

Hechsher: Rabbi Harry Cohen – RESTAURANT IS OPEN 7 DAYS A WEEK

Proprietor/Manager: Angel

Type(s) of Food: Vegetarian, Parve – Eclectic

Price Range:	Lunch	Dinner	Take out
Entrées:	$8.25-$12.95	Same	Same – Delivery Available
Desserts:	$4-$6	*Sandwiches:* $8.95-$9.50	
Drinks:	$1.50-$4.95	Wine & Beer Served	

Food Specialties: Caravan Burrito, Ginger Curry Stir Fry, Black Bean Chili

   Description: Entrées draw from different parts of the world, such as Angel's
      Caravan Pig-Out (polenta with sweet potato sautéed veggie burger with
      tahini, vegetables and mixed salad) or the Ginger-Curry Stir-fry (organic
      pasta, vegetables, fresh ginger, cumin and herbs). Organic, macrobiotic
      salads; breads, assorted appetizers, soup du jour, and rice & beans of the
      day augment original recipes that work wonders with bean sprouts,
      chummus, seaweed, tofu chunks, etc. All eggs are free range. Only
      "exceptionally purified water" served. Other potables range from fresh
      organic juices, health shakes, assorted coffees, teas, to wines and beers.

   Comments: A menu committed to health in a restaurant imbued with soul.

Ambiance (Decor): An artsy milieu which hosts local exhibits of photography and
      contemporary artwork as well as live music, ranging from classical to jazz
      (nightly after 8pm, no charge). Exposed brick walls, subdued lighting, wooden
      floor, and plants provide backdrop. Some tables feature original art under their
      glass tabletop integrating art into the process of eating. The aroma of fresh
      herbs fills the air. 45 seats.

Service: Standard

General Comments: A bit of the laid back West Coast transplanted to NYC!

Hours: **Sun, Tues-Thurs:** 11am-11pm **Mon:** 5pm-11pm **Fri-Sat:** 11am-12pm
      - RESTAURANT IS OPEN 7 DAYS A WEEK (Non-Jewish Ownership)

Credit Cards Accepted: MC, Visa, AmEx, Discover, Diners Club

Restaurant Discount: 10% Off

Borough: Manhattan
Section: East Village

The Authoritative New York City Kosher Dining Guide

Restaurant: 2nd Avenue Deli

Phone Number: (212) 677-0606
Fax: (212) 477-5327

Address: 156 Second Avenue (cor. E. 10th St.)

Hechsher: Rabbi Leonard Bronstein - RESTAURANT IS OPEN 7 DAYS A WEEK

Proprietor/Manager: Steve (Manager)

Type(s) of Food: Meat - Deli

Price Range:

	Lunch	Dinner	Take out
Entrées:	$10.95-$20.95	Same	Same - Delivery Available
Desserts:	$2.25-$3.50	**Sandwiches:** $6.25-$8.50 (Reg.), $10.95-$12.95 (Hot)	
Drinks:	$1.00-$3.50	**Healthy Alternative Menu:** $11.95-$14.50	

Food Specialties: Deli Sandwiches, Whole Filet of Smoked Trout, Roast Chicken

Description: The menu is traditional New York Deli, except for a selection of fresh fish dishes (e.g. Broiled Filet of Sole, Broiled or Baked Carp, Broiled Salmon). The Healthy Alternative menu features mainly broiled fish or poultry (e.g. Turkey Kebob, Grilled Chicken Breast or Broiled Chicken). Expanding upon the 5 regular soups, are the daily specials. Complete dinners (by adding $8.00 to the à la carte entrées) include appetizer and soup, entrée, dessert and coffee or tea.

Comments: Old fashioned Jewish cooking and long standing deli favorites are what you can expect to find here: nothing gourmet, nothing fancy.

Ambiance (Decor): Standard deli ambiance pretty much describes this large restaurant (seats 125). Old fashioned, informal and somewhat worn.

Service: Standard

General Comments: A New York institution, this deli is a holdover from the days when 2nd Avenue was the center of Jewish cultural life in the city. Steps from the sites of the now mostly extinct Jewish theaters, it has managed to remain an enduring and popular fixture in the East Village, and for Jews around the world.

Hours: **Sun-Thurs:** 7am-12am   **Fri-Sat:** 7am-2am
- RESTAURANT IS OPEN 7 DAYS A WEEK

Credit Cards Accepted: MC, Visa, AmEx, Diners Club

Restaurant Discount: 10% Off

Borough: Manhattan
Section: East Village

The Authoritative New York City Kosher Dining Guide

Restaurant: Rectangles

Phone Number: (212) 677-8410
Fax: None

Address: 159 Second Avenue (cor. E. 10th St.)

Hechsher: Rabbi Leonard Bronstein - RESTAURANT IS OPEN 7 DAYS A WEEK

Proprietor/Manager: Gilli or Daniel

Type(s) of Food: Yemenite & Israeli Cuisine

Price Range:	*Lunch*	*Dinner*	*Take out*
Entrées:	$5.50-$17.50	$ 8.95 - $18.50	Local Free Delivery-$10.00 Min.
Desserts:	$3.00-$3.50	*Lunch Special:* $7.95 (M-F: 11:30am-3:30pm)	
Drinks:	$1.50-$3.00	$4-$4.75/gl, $16-$18/btl (Wine) $4-$5/gl (Mx Drinks)	

Food Specialties: Kebobs, Shawarma, Cous-cous, Grilled Fish, Soups

> *Description:* Homemade soups include Yemenite soup and calf leg soup along
> with the more common vegetable, white bean, and lentil soups.
> Appetizers such as Malawach (Yemenite pancake), Kibbeh (fried
> ground beef covered with crushed wheat and spices) and Tabouli are
> among the other exotic dishes. The entrées feature beef, chicken, and
> lamb kebobed, grilled, baked, roasted or sautéed, as well as fish.
> Jachnoon and Hamin (Chulent) are offered on Sat. & Sun. only.

> *Comments:* Authentically prepared Middle Eastern food featuring original
> Yemenite spices define this restaurant's cuisine.

Ambiance (Decor): East Village and therefore relaxed, and informal. Middle Eastern
flavor, wooden tables and chairs, and a bar lines the far wall. Outdoor sidewalk
eating area open when appropriate.

Service: Standard

General Comments: If you're from the Middle East and are homesick, or if you like
the East Village and Middle Eastern seasonings, this is the place for you. The
prices are reasonable (most entrées around $11-$12) and the atmosphere in
this part of town is unique.

Hours: **Sun-Thurs:** 11:30am-12am   **Fri-Sat:** 11:30am-1am
    - RESTAURANT IS OPEN 7 DAYS A WEEK

Credit Cards Accepted: MC, Visa, AmEx, Diners Club, Discover

Restaurant Discount:

Borough: Manhattan
Section: East Village

$$$

The Authoritative New York City Kosher Dining Guide

Restaurant: The Kosher Tea Room

Phone Number: (212) 677-2947
Fax: (212) 677-1211

Address: 193 Second Avenue (cor. E. 12ᵗʰ St.)

Hechsher: OK Labs, also Bais Din of Crown Heights (Glatt Kosher)

Proprietor/Manager: Reuben

Type(s) of Food: Meat - Italian, International

Price Range:

	Lunch	Dinner	Take out
Entrées:	$11.95-$15.95	$13.95-$25.95	
Desserts:	$4.00-$6.00		
Drinks:	$2.00-$4.00	Wine list available	

Food Specialties: Grill Prime Rib Eye Steak, Chicken Kiev, Seared Red Snapper

> *Description:* A few select entrées: one each of chicken, Cornish hen, lamb, veal, and steak, and a few fish and pasta choices. All are accompanied with vegetables. Predominately Italian, but the cuisine extends to other nationalities. One of two soups is Borscht a la Vielle Russe, an entrée is Grilled Cornish Hen Tabaka, and a Lylie Kebob is an appetizers.

> *Comments:* The scantly sized portions, are more than made up for by the careful, artistic, and elegant presentation. The meals are pleasing to the palate. The portions leave you wanting more, yet satisfied that you've had an exceptional culinary experience.

Ambiance (Decor): The room is elegant and upscale, in marble, granite, gold leaf and brass. Formal table settings, garnished with flowers and candlelight, establish the mood. The atmosphere is further enhanced by the live violin and/ or piano music (Classical or by request) which accompanies your meal. The music on our visit was spirited, well played, and enjoyable. European ambiance.

Service: French service - gracious

General Comments: Not the most elegant address but well worth the trip.

Hours: **Mon-Thurs: Lunch:** 12pm-3pm **Dinner:** 5pm-10:30pm
Friday Closed **Sat:** Opens 1 hr after Shabbos-12:30am
Sun: Lunch: 12pm-3pm **Dinner:** 4pm-10:30pm

Credit Cards Accepted: MC, Visa, AmEx, Discover, Diners Club

Restaurant Discount: 10% Off On Mondays, Tuesdays and Wednesdays Only

Borough: Manhattan
Section: East Village

▢ ⊘ 🍾 🛎 **$$**

The Authoritative New York City Kosher Dining Guide

Restaurant: Village Crown
Phone Number: (212) 777-8816
Fax: (212) 388-9639
Address: 94 Third Avenue (bet. E. 12th St. - E. 13th St.)

Hechsher: ⊃ - K (Cholov Yisrol, Pas Yisroel, Mashgiach Temidi)

Proprietor/Manager: Eli (Owner)

Type(s) of Food: Dairy - Italian

Price Range: **Lunch**   **Dinner**   **Take out**
Entrées: $6.95-$17.95   Same $9.95-$16.95
Desserts: $4.50-$5.50   Free Local Delivery, ($40 Min. on Distance)
Drinks: $1.50-$3.50 $3/btl. (Israeli Black Beer), $5/gl (Mixed Drinks)

Food Specialties: Pizza Bar, Pasta, Fish

Description: The Poached Salmon Pavarotti (salmon fillet poached in white wine, served in a light cream sauce, with smoked salmon and dried tomatoes) is a new addition. So is the Sauté Fillet of Sole "Zangara" (sole topped with marsala wine, mushrooms, tomatoes, olives, and capers). The Pasta Specialita, retains the Fettuccine Alfredo with Smoked Salmon (light cream butter, smoked salmon, scallions & fresh parmesan), but adds Baked Penne Tomato Cream (mushrooms, red pepper, zucchini, garlic, tomato, cream topped with mozzarella). The menu rounds off with a nice selection of Antipasti, Insalatas and Dolci.

Comments: A nice variety to choose from.

Ambiance (Decor): A relaxed, informal atmosphere permeates this small restaurant (12 tables). A shared, enclosed outdoor dining area (seats 100) is a nice option. Tablecloths, candles, and flowers on the tables.

Service: Standard

General Comments: The dairy counterpart to the meat restaurant, of the same owner, just next door. Food's okay. Reservations Recommended for Sunday.

Hours: Sun-Thurs: 11am-11pm   **Fri:** 11am-2 hrs before Shabbos
Sat: Opens 1 hr after Shabbos till 1am

Credit Cards Accepted: MC, Visa, AmEx, Discover

Restaurant Discount: 10% Off

144

Borough: Manhattan
Section: East Village

The Authoritative New York City Kosher Dining Guide

Restaurant: Village Crown Restaurant
& Garden Café
Address: 96 Third Avenue (bet. E. 12ᵗʰ St. - E. 13ᵗʰ St.)

Phone Number: (212) 674-2061
Fax: None

Hechsher: ב-K (Glatt Kosher, Chassidishe Shechita)

Proprietor/Manager: Eli (Owner)

Type(s) of Food: Meat, Vegetarian - Moroccan, Middle Eastern, American

Price Range:

	Lunch	*Dinner*	*Take out*	
Entrées:	$8.95-$15.95	$9.95-$17.95	$8.95-$14.95	Free Delivery
Desserts:	$4.50-$5.50	***Lunch Special:*** $5.95-$7.95		($25 Min Local)
Drinks:	$1.00-$1.50	$3/btl. (Israeli Black Beer),	$5/gl. (Mixed Drinks)	

Food Specialties: Kebobs, Steak, Cous-cous, Moroccan Chicken, Grilled Chicken

Description: The King's Special: rib steak, marinated chicken cutlets, beef, chicken, and Romanian kebobs for 2 to 3 people, is "the grill of your dreams." All entrées are served with two side orders. The appetizer Combination Platters can make a vegetarian meal. A variety of Pasta dishes and Salads are available. The entrées also come in smaller "Pita" sizes. Lunch Specials run from 11:30am-3pm and includes a cup of soup and soda. An American Hickory Grill section has been recently added.

Comments: Middle Eastern food with a Moroccan influence. Nice sized portions. The chef tends to favor salt and spices that make you thirsty.

Ambiance (Decor): "Clouds," hung from the ceiling with wires, are a fanciful but unsophisticated attempt to suggest an outdoor setting. The dining room can accommodate 100 people. A heated and covered outdoor space, shared with the dairy restaurant, can seat another 100. Tablecloths and candles give this casual and somewhat off-beat East Village restaurant a semi-formal touch.

Service: Exceptional in its responsiveness and desire to please

General Comments: Situated in the trendy and colorful East Village area, this restaurant offers a relaxed setting for an informal meal.

Hours: **Sun-Thurs:** 11am-11pm   **Fri:** 11:30am-2 hrs before Shabbos
Sat: Opens 1 hr after Shabbos till 1am

Credit Cards Accepted: MC, Visa, AmEx, Discover, Diners Club

Restaurant Discount: 10% Off

Borough: Manhattan
Section: Union Square

The Authoritative New York City Kosher Dining Guide

Restaurant: Tashi Awen   *Phone Number:* (212) 633-8823
    Fax: (212) 633-6271

Address: 210 West 14th Street (bet. 7th Ave. - 8th Ave.)

Hechsher: United Kosher Supervision

Proprietor/Manager: Emily (Manager)

Type(s) of Food: Vegetarian - Primarily Chinese

Price Range: *Lunch*   *Dinner*   *Take out*
    Entrées: $6.50-$13.50   Same   Same - Free local delivery
    Desserts: $1.50-$3.50   *Combination Platters:* $6.50
    Drinks: $1.50-$3.50   Juice Bar ($3.50/gl)

Food Specialties: Bird's Nest, Vegi-Oyster, Vegetable Bundle, Kung Po Vegi-Squid

> *Description:* A vegan oasis, meaning no dairy, animal by-products, fish or
> eggs. No MSG and restraint in fried selections reflects the menu's health
> consciousness. Faux meat and fish are convincing. Variety in texture
> and appearance makes for a palatable dining adventure. Juices are fresh.

> *Comments:* Beautifully prepared dishes are a visual treat. Seasoning is
> restrained so the sauces are mild. The masterfully presented vegetables
> retain their color and crisp texture. Soups lack kick but can be modified
> to taste. An evolving menu.

Ambiance (Decor): Dimly lit and subdued in its minimalist decor, it offers a
    soothing, unencumbered dining environment. Sparsely hung Chinese prints
    adorn the beige walls. Carpeting minimizes the noise level and aids in creating a
    relaxed milieu enhanced by piped in music. 100 seat capacity on the main floor
    (handicap ramp & bathroom facilities available). Additional 80 seats one flight
    up in a second dining/party room. Table linens add an elegant touch.

Service: Courteous

General Comments: Open just one year: this is a promising new place. The food is
    quite good and filling. Unique Oriental food items that are not available through
    general kosher distribution are made from scratch in house. $5/pp Dinner Min.

Hours: **Sun-Thurs:** 12pm-10:30pm   **Fri:** 12pm-Shabbos
    Sat: after Shabbos till 12am

Credit Cards Accepted: MC, Visa, AmEx

Restaurant Discount:

146

Borough: Manhattan
Section: Union Square

The Authoritative New York City Kosher Dining Guide

Restaurant: Penguin Restaurant *Phone Number:* (212) 255-3601
Fax: None

Address: 258 West 15th Street (bet. 7th Ave. - 8th Ave.)

Hechsher: Torah-K (Glatt Kosher)

Proprietor/Manager: Riki

Type(s) of Food: Meat - Middle Eastern

Price Range: *Lunch*   *Dinner*   *Take out*
    Entrées: $9.95-$13.99   Same   Same – Free Local Delivery
    Desserts: $1.00-$1.50
    Drinks: $1.00-$1.50

Food Specialties: Shawarma, Shish Kebob, Steaks, Soup

> *Description:* Still in the process of defining itself. Beef, Lamb, Chicken, and Turkey dishes dominate. 3 different soups are made fresh daily.

> *Comments:* Very new, more to come in our next edition.

Ambiance (Decor): 24 seats with laminate tables, modern and informal. An orange and brown color scheme with mirrors added to expand the space.

Service: Self-service or will accommodate

General Comments: Open just two months, this latest addition to the Middle Eastern restaurants in NYC is the only glatt kosher restaurant in the area. The owner is anxious to please and is concerned about the dining experience of her customers.

Hours: **Mon-Thurs:** 10am-10pm **Fri:** 10am-1½ hrs before Shabbos
    Saturday Closed **Sun:** 10am-8pm

Credit Cards Not Accepted: CASH ONLY!

Restaurant Discount: 10% Off

Borough: Manhattan
Section: Stuyvesant Town

The Authoritative New York City Kosher Dining Guide

Restaurant: Pita Express

Phone Number: (212) 533-1956
Fax: None

Address: 261 First Avenue (bet. E. 15th St. - E. 16th St.)

Hechsher: Rabbi Avraham Shlomo Fishelis (Glatt Kosher)

Proprietor/Manager: Yossi

Type(s) of Food: Meat - Middle Eastern

Price Range:

	Lunch	Dinner	Take out
Entrées:	$8.00-$15.95	Same	Same
Desserts:	$2.50		Free Local Delivery
Drinks:	$1.00-$1.50	Sandwiches: $3.00-$6.00	

Food Specialties: Cous-cous, Shish Kebob, Rib Steak, Moroccan Fish, Shawarma

Description: The menu consists of Middle Eastern favorites. Eleven salads are offered by the pound. Seven soups include: Vegetable, Split Pea, Lentil, Bean, Chicken Noodle, Yemenite style meat soup, as well as a soup of the day. House Specials feature Baked Chicken, Fish and Chips, Moroccan Cigars, Kibbeh, among others. Entrées feature Baby Lamb Chops, Chicken, Beef and/or Koufta Kebob, Falafel Plate, and Burgers, which can be bought as sandwiches in a pita as well.

Comments: The selections offer a nice variety of different foods, to please most palates.

Ambiance (Decor): A modern fast food restaurant, with no distinguishing traits, that can accommodate 40 people. Casual.

Service: Standard

General Comments: Part of a chain of three restaurants. This one is convenient to Beth Israel Hospital.

Hours: Sun-Thurs: 10am-10pm   Fri: 10am-1 hr before Shabbos
Saturday Closed

Credit Cards Not Accepted: CASH ONLY!

Restaurant Discount: 10% Off For Orders Over $10

Borough: Manhattan
Section: Stuyvesant Town

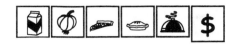

The Authoritative New York City Kosher Dining Guide

Restaurant: La Bagel

Phone Number: (212) 338-9292
Fax: (212) 260-5511

Address: 263 First Avenue (bet. E. 15th St. - E. 16th St.)

Hechsher: Rabbi Shmuel Fishelis (Midtown Board of Kashrus)

Proprietor/Manager: Nisson

Type(s) of Food: Dairy - American, Italian

Price Range:

	Lunch	Dinner	Take out
Entrées:	$4.95-$7.50	Same	Same
Desserts:	$1.25-$2.25		Delivery Available
Drinks:	$ .75-$2.25	**Daily Specials:** $2.95-$3.95	

Food Specialties: Pizza, Pasta, Baked Salmon, Salads, Knishes, Sandwiches

Description: They bake their own breads, cakes, cookies, and of course the bagels. In fact, I'm told their challah has become famous. Homemade soups are featured and are made fresh daily. Examples of the Daily Specials are Stuffed Peppers ($3.50), Tuna on a Bagel ($3.95), or a free cup of soda with an order of pizza.

Comments: A nice selection for light meals.

Ambiance (Decor): A mid-sized restaurant with a seating capacity of approximately 80. A café style establishment with a casual atmosphere.

Service: Self-serve

General Comments: Located by Beth Israel Hospital. The owner prides himself in the cleanliness of his restaurant.

Hours: Mon-Thurs: 6am-10pm **Fri:** 6am-3pm
Saturday Closed **Sun:** 6am-8pm

Credit Cards Not Accepted: CASH ONLY!

Restaurant Discount:

Borough: Manhattan
Section: Chelsea

The Authoritative New York City Kosher Dining Guide

Restaurant: Café 18

Phone Number: (212) 620-4182
Fax: (212) 366-9657

Address: 8 East 18ᵗʰ Street (bet. 5ᵗʰ Ave. - Broadway)

Hechsher: Star K (Cholov Yisroel, Pas Yisroel)

Proprietor/Manager: Alex Goldring / Mohmed (Manager)

Type(s) of Food: Dairy - Mexican, Italian, American

Price Range:	*Lunch*	*Dinner*	*Take out*
Entrées:	$5.95-$9.95	Same	Same
Desserts:	$2.25-$4.25		Local Delivery Only
Drinks:	$1.25-$3.50,	$3.50-$3.95 (Beer),	$3.95/gl (Wine)

Food Specialties: Stuffed Butternut Squash, Vegetarian "Chicken," Quesadillas, Enchiladas, Burritos, Curry Tuna, Salads, Tuna Melt

> *Description:* The dishes, from several continents with some health orientation. The Quesadilla, a tortilla filled with stir fried vegetables and topped w/ melted cheese & salsa, Smoked Maple "Chicken," Cajun "Chicken," and Vietnamese Peanut Noodles are among the more exotic possibilities. More familiar are the: Eggplant Parmesan, Salmon Patties, Lasagna, Quiches, Salads, pastas, sandwiches. Coffees and teas, and a large selection of tempting desserts are the finale. Three cake sample special.

> *Comments:* Light cuisine prepared unconventionally. The entrée portions are moderately sized. Best items on the menu are the large salads and the desserts. The Veggie Burrito was not authentic. The Spinach-Mushroom Quiche was apparently defrosted, having had that telltale watery taste.

Ambiance (Decor): A soft edge, modern setting that features paintings, sculptures, and a wine, pink, and gray color scheme suggesting a South Western influence. Lite background music provides a relaxed milieu for casual dining in this mid-sized café. Spacious feeling is aided by the high ceiling.

Service: Standard

General Comments: Convenient to major booksellers. A Chabad shiur is conducted here every Thursday evening. A unique place for casual and light dining.

Hours: **Sun-Thurs:** 10:30am-10pm   **Fri:** 10:30am-1 hr before Shabbos
Sat: Opens 1 hr after Shabbos till 1am

Credit Cards Accepted: MC, Visa, AmEx, Discover

Restaurant Discount: 10% OFF

Borough: Manhattan
Section: Chelsea

The Authoritative New York City Kosher Dining Guide

Restaurant: Kosher Dairy Luncheonette   *Phone Number:* (212) 645-9315
                                                       Fax: None

Address: 223 West 19th Street (bet. 5th Ave. - 6th Ave.)

Hechsher: Rabbi Josephy

Proprietor / Manager:

Type(s) of Food: Dairy - American

Price Range:	*Lunch*	*Dinner*	*Take out*
Entrées:	$3.50-$7.00	Same	Same
Desserts:	$1.25-$2.00		Delivery Available
Drinks:	$ .80-$1.40		

Food Specialties: Fresh Fish, Soups, Salads, Sandwiches, Knishes

    Description: This fast food establishment offers two freshly made soup specials daily, as well as fresh salad, kugel, knishes and a variety of sandwiches. The fresh fish is either fried or baked.

    Comments: A small but sufficient scope of options for a quick and light meal on the go. Nothing fancy, just plain, basic food.

Ambiance (Decor): Hardly a restaurant, this small establishment offers only 6 seats for eating on premises.

Service: Self-serve or they will accommodate

General Comments: However small, it serves its purpose. Handy to know about when you want a quick bite while in the neighborhood. One block away from Barnes and Noble's main store and shopping.

Hours: **Mon-Thurs:** 7:30am-6pm   **Fri:** 7:30am-2 hrs before Shabbos
      Saturday Closed   **Sunday Closed**

Credit Cards Not Accepted: CASH ONLY!

Restaurant Discount:

Midtown Manhattan
(West & East)

Borough: Manhattan
Section: Midtown West

The Authoritative New York City Kosher Dining Guide

Restaurant: Dimple   **Phone Number:** (212) 643-9464
                                 Fax: (212) 642-9468
Address: 11 West 30th Street (Broadway – 5th Ave.)

Hechsher: Rabbi Leonard Bronstein – RESTAURANT IS OPEN 7 DAYS A WEEK

Proprietor/Manager: Pankaj Parekh (Manager)

Type(s) of Food: Vegetarian, Dairy – Indian

Price Range:	Lunch	Dinner	Take out
Entrées:	$3.99-$8.99	$4.95-$8.95	Same – Free Local Delivery
Desserts:	$2.50-$2.95	**Dinner-To-Go:** $5.95	**Breakfast Specials:** $3.95
Drinks:	$1.00-$3.95	**Lunch Buffet Special:** $5.99 (M-F, 11:30am-3pm)	

Food Specialties: Chat, Idli, Dosa, Uthappam, Vada, Kofta Curry, Paneer, Jain

Description: Mostly vegetarian combinations often served with flour or rice pancakes that can be soft or crispy. A predominance of South Indian dishes, but all other areas also represented. Dairy is usually found in the shakes, Falooda, Lassi, and desserts. The menu offers a complete overview of Indian cuisine and Mr. Parekh, the manager, gladly educates the uninitiated. In the South, long grain rice is the staple and a major ingredient in cooking. Not so in the North, where wheat flour is used. Different and better quality rice called Basmati is used in the North, where there is also a preference for spicy vegetables.

Comments: Although, I have yet to taste the entrées, I sampled a number of desserts here and was very impressed. They were really good!

Ambiance (Decor): Seating on two floors: 40 seats on the 1st and 50 seats on at street level. The ground level (a step up) is split with a large display counter on one side and booth seating running parallel on the other side. The upper floor is formed as a balcony and features covered tables and chairs.

Service: Self-serve until 3pm, after that waiter service

General Comments: The Dimple in Queens is not kosher at this time.

Hours: **Sun:** 11am-8pm **Mon-Fri:** 8:30am-10pm **Sat:** 11am-10pm
         - RESTAURANT IS OPEN 7 DAYS A WEEK

Credit Cards Accepted: MC, Visa, AmEx, Discover, Diners Club

Restaurant Discount: 10% Off

Borough: Manhattan
Section: Midtown West

The Authoritative New York City Kosher Dining Guide

Restaurant: Kosher Delight *Phone Number:* (212) 563-3366
Fax: (212) 268-9352
Address: 1365 Broadway (bet. W. 36th St. - W. 37th St.)

Hechsher: Vaad Harabbanim of Flatbush

Proprietor/Manager:

Type(s) of Food: Meat - Deli, Chinese, Burgers

Price Range: *Lunch* *Dinner* *Take out*
Entrées: $8.00-$16.50 Same Same – Local Delivery Available
Desserts: $1.50-$1.95 *Chinese Entrées:* $10.95-$15.95
Drinks: $ .60-$1.30 *Sandwiches:* $5.50-$8.25 *Hero:* $20.95/ft.

Food Specialties: Burgers, Grill, Kebobs, Fried Chicken, Deli, Chinese Menu, Ribs

Description: The fast food chain store menu of burgers and fries has been extended to include Chinese and deli. Chinese dishes are made fresh to order w/o MSG. Hero by the Foot has been added to the deli sandwich selections. Fried chicken is sold by the piece in various box sizes, buckets, etc. Soups and salads are also offered.

Comments: The food tends to be greasy, but it has its devotees. Portions are scant and everything is à la carte.

Ambiance (Decor): Wood frame chairs with padded seats and wood tables with Formica inlaid in the tops distinguishes this restaurant from the molded plastic in the rest of the chain locations. Plastic, cafeteria type trays to eat on. Frequented by local workers, shoppers, and also favored by families (weekends can be somewhat noisy and chaotic at the height of mealtimes). Spacious.

Service: Self-serve

General Comments: Well situated near shopping on 34th St. and relatively close to Madison Square Garden. This restaurant is a good possibility for a fast bite. The least crowded of the chain, it caters mostly to adults working in the area.

Hours: **Sun-Thurs:** 11am-11pm **Fri:** 11am-4pm
Sat: Opens1 hr after Shabbos till 1am (Closed Summer)

Credit Cards Accepted: MC, Visa, AmEx, Discover

Restaurant Discount:

Borough: Manhattan
Section: Midtown West

The Authoritative New York City Kosher Dining Guide

Restaurant: Mr. Broadway/Me Tsu Yan   *Phone Number:* (212) 921-2152
                                                     Fax: (212) 768-2852

Address: 1372 Broadway (bet. W. 37th St. - W. 38th St.)

Hechsher: OU (Glatt Kosher, Chassidishe Shechita)

Proprietor/Manager: Jack Dock (owner)

Type(s) of Food: Meat - Chinese, Deli

Price Range: *Lunch* (11am-3pm)   *Dinner*   *Take out*
   Entrées: $8.95 (Special) $10.75-$23.75   Same - Delivery Avail ($3 Min)
   Desserts: $2.75-$ 4.75   *Sandwiches:* $5.95-$9.45, $11.75 (Hot Open)
   Drinks: $1.00-$ 2.00 $2.75-$3.75 (Beer)

Food Specialties: Deli, Chinese, Jewish-American, Mediterranean (in that order)

> *Description:* The menu is a merging of two restaurants. The Chinese menu features a nice selection of entrées including chicken, beef, veal, duck and fish. Specialty dishes include General Tso Chicken and Sesame Chicken. The emphasis in the deli menu is on sandwiches, which come in great variety and are billed as oversized. The rest of the menu includes salads and entrées with a Jewish or American theme such as BBQ Spare Ribs, Roast Vermont Turkey, or Stuffed Cabbage.

> *Comments:* Salad bar with a large variety to choose from. Hearty portions

Ambiance (Decor): Three tiered restaurant with a deli on the first tier, Mediterranean cuisine on the second, and Chinese food on the third. Casual, suitable for family, relaxed social, and business engagements. Tablecloths dress up the tables for evening dining. 150 seats.

Service: Standard

General Comments: Free street parking after 7pm. Evening reservations for large parties (5-9) are recommended. Something for everyone, it is the perfect place to go when you can't agree on what to eat. Great midtown location near Herald Square and Madison Square Garden.

Hours: **Sun-Thurs:** 10am-10pm
       Fri: 10am-1½ hrs before Shabbos (till 4pm Summer)   **Closed Saturday**

Credit Cards Accepted: MC, Visa, AmEx, Discover, Carte Blanch, Diners Club

Restaurant Discount: 10% Off. Discount Does Not Apply During Lunchtime.

Borough: Manhattan
Section: Midtown West

The Authoritative New York City Kosher Dining Guide

Restaurant: Ben's Manhattan Kosher Deli   *Phone Number:* (212) 398-2367
                                              Fax: (212) 391-6516
Address: 209 West 38th Street (bet. 7th Ave. - 8th Ave.)

Hechsher: Rabbi Israel Mayer Steinberg - RESTAURANT OPEN 7 DAYS A WEEK

Proprietor/Manager: Ronnie Dragoon / Manny (manager)

Type(s) of Food: Meat - Deli

Price Range: *Lunch*   *Dinner*   *Take out*
Entrées: $10.95-$19.95   Same   Free Local Delivery Avail.
Desserts: $2- $3.25 *Sandwiches:* $5.95-$11.95 *K id's Menu:* $5.25
Drinks: $1.25-$1.55, $3.25-$3.95 (Beer), $4-$5/gl $10-$20/btl (Wine)

Food Specialties: Sandwiches, Burgers, Homemade Soup, Stuffed Cabbage, Salads

    Description: An extensive deli menu. Tongue & corned beef are cured on
    premises. Nice selection of freshly made salads and cold platters. 3 egg
    omelets are served with potato pancakes and apple sauce or fries.
    Poultry, beef, veal, and fresh salmon entrées come with 2 vegetables.
    Traditional specialties range Hungarian Goulash, Chicken Fricassee,
    Boiled Beef In The Pot (flanken), pasta e.g. Primavera or Marinara,
    and homemade soups: mushroom barley, chicken, and soup of the day.

    Comments: Empire & Hebrew National meats served every way to satisfy
    one's deli cravings. Presentation-wise, you won't be disappointed.

Ambiance (Decor): Not your typical deli, this one year old restaurant is spacious,
    and very attractive. Modern amenities, but its character is derived from the Art
    Deco, Beaux Arts genre. Booths and tables, offer seating for 160, in a room
    outside the deli counter/take out area. Sophisticated, catering to office personnel
    as well as the theater crowd. Casual, but fine for a business lunch too.

Service: Standard

General Comments: Impressive setting for a deli, hopefully a model for others.
    Hashgacha is given by an Orthodox Rabbi. Stays open Shabbos by utilizing a
    sale of the business to a non-Jew (שטר מכירה), and cooking food beforehand.
    Shabbos meals can be prepaid. One of 7 in Ben's deli chain.

Hours: **Sun-Sat:** 9am-9pm - RESTAURANT IS OPEN 7 DAYS A WEEK

Credit Cards Accepted: MC, Visa, AmEx, Discover, Diners Club

Restaurant Discount:

⬛ 🍆 🍷 🍲 $$

The Authoritative New York City Kosher Dining Guide

Restaurant: Colbeh

Phone Number: (212) 354-8181
Fax: (212) 354-8184

Address: 43 West 39th Street (bet. 5th Ave. - 6th Ave.)

Hechsher: ⊃ - K (Glatt Kosher)

Proprietor/Manager:

Type(s) of Food: Meat - Persian

Price Range: *Lunch*   *Dinner*   *Take out*
     Entrées: $10.50-$18.50 $12.50-$20.50 $9.50-$19.50   Delivery Avail.
     Desserts: $4.50   *Sandwiches:* $5.50-$11.50 (Lunch Only)
     Drinks: $2-$2.50, $5/gl (House Wine), $18-$28/btl (Wine), $6/gl (Mix Drks)

Food Specialties: Beef, Veal, Chicken, Turkey & Fresh Fish Kabobs, Stews

> *Description:* Authentic Persian fare: Chelo Kabab Koobideh (marinated strips of ground beef char-broiled served with Persian rice & tomato), or Bademjan (fried eggplant in fresh tomato and onion sauce with cubes of beef served with Persian rice). Taboulli Salad (parsley, tomatoes, mint, wheat, onion, lemon juice, olive oil) and Ciondl (ground chicken breast, chick peas and Persian spices) are representative appetizers.

> *Comments:* Exotic sounding, but not totally unfamiliar. Chicken, beef and ground beef shish kabobs, and stews, make up the bulk of the entrées, which are usually accompanied by a grilled tomato and Persian rice. Surprisingly, to this first timer, the food is not spicy but delicious, fresh, attractively presented, and of good quality. The portions are hefty.

Ambiance (Decor): An attractive restaurant set in tones of green and salmon (seats approx. 65). The walls are punctuated with oriental recesses that house framed prints of historical Persian scenes. Candlelight, potted trees (artificial, but not disturbingly so), mirrors, linen napkins, and tablecloths. Dimmed lighting with neon accents and wall sconces, create an inviting, intimate, relaxed atmosphere.

Service: Friendly, helpful and competent

General Comments: Colbeh is a delightful find and a place for good food. Full bar.

Hours: **Sun-Thurs:** 12:30pm-11pm   **Fri:** 12pm-2 hrs before Shabbos
        Saturday Closed (may change)

Credit Cards Accepted: MC, Visa, AmEx, Discover

Restaurant Discount: 5% Off

Borough: Manhattan
Section: Midtown

The Authoritative New York City Kosher Dining Guide

Restaurant: Chabad Lubavitch Midtown Center   *Phone Number:* (212) 972-0770
Fax: (212) 697-6749

Address: 509 Fifth Avenue 2nd Floor (bet. 42nd St. - 43rd St.)

Hechsher: Bas Din of Crown Heights (Glatt Kosher)

Proprietor/Manager: David

Type(s) of Food: Meat – Deli, Jewish American

Price Range:	*Lunch*	*Dinner*	*Take out*
Entrées:	Free – Sat.	$18/pp-Friday Night	None
Desserts:		All inclusive	
Drinks:			

Food Specialties: Friday Night Shabbos Meal & Saturday Afternoon Buffet

Description: Although this is not technically a restaurant, many people staying in midtown hotels have inquired about the availability of Shabbos meals and services. The $18/pp charge includes gefilte fish, salads, chicken or roast beef entrée (not a choice, available different times), kugel, side dishes, dessert (can be either parve ice cream or cake), and tea or coffee. The Shabbos afternoon buffet is basically a free kiddush after morning prayers (about 12:30pm). It consists of cold cuts, gefilte fish, cholent, and salads. I have been assured that no one goes away hungry.

Comments: Reservations must be made by the previous Thursday by 5pm.

Ambiance (Decor): Located on the 2nd floor of the building, a flight of stairs must be climbed.

Service: Standard

General Comments: Torah classes, seminars, holiday parties and other events, as well as prayer services are also offered during the week. The meals, however, are strictly for Shabbos. RESERVATIONS A MUST. Call by 5pm, Thursday.

Hours: **Friday Night:** Dinner served after evening prayer service. Time is dependent on season. **Saturday Lunch:** After morning prayers, about 12:30 pm.

Credit Cards Not Accepted:

Restaurant Discount:

The Authoritative New York City Kosher Dining Guide

Restaurant: My Most Favorite Dessert Company   *Phone Number:* (212) 997-5130
Fax: (212) 997-5046
Address: 120 West 45th Street (bet. 6th Ave. - Broadway)

Hechsher: OU (Cholov Yisroel, Mashgiach Temidi)

Proprietor/Manager: Scott Magram

Type(s) of Food: Dairy - Continental, American

Price Range: *Lunch*   *Dinner*   *Take out*
  Entrées: $11-$18 $15-$24 $6-$7 (Daily Specials) Free Delivery
  Desserts: $5 (L)-$6(D) *Sandwiches:* $9-$12 *Café Lunch Special:* $6-$7
  Drinks: $1.50-$4.00 $5.50-$6.50/gl. (House Wine), $3.50-$4.00 (Beer)

Food Specialties: Salads, Sandwiches, Pastas, Fish, Pizza, Café Menu, Coffees

> *Description:* Fresh, high quality Italian favorites in nicely sized portions.
> Salad Entrées for lunch ($10.95) include the Niçoise, Caesar, Greek,
> and Grilled Salmon Salads. Tuna, salmon, or whitefish sandwiches are
> served on pumpernickel raisin, whole wheat or Italian baguettes with a
> choice of side salad. The fresh fish entrées such as the Grilled Salmon or
> Tuna, are served with sautéed vegetables and roasted red bliss potatoes.
> Breakfast menu. Sunday Brunch Entrées: $8-$12. Dessert menu.

> *Comments:* Menus for just about anything. Nice selection. Yummy desserts.

Ambiance (Decor): Uptown feel, suitable for larger groups and social engagements.
The restaurant can serve up to 150 people on its two floors. In an atrium, the
first floor area has a garden setting complete with palm trees and a fountain
where the atmosphere is casual and informal. There is also a cafeteria that is
accessed through the building's lobby with 2nd floor seating and takeout.

Service: Standard

General Comments: Located in the theater district, this restaurant is particularly
convenient for quick bites before shows. It offers a tranquil and pleasant oasis.

Hours: **Mon-Thurs:** 8:30am-10pm   **Fri:** 11:30am-3 hrs before Shabbos
  Sat: Opens 1 hr after Shabbos till 1am   **Sun:** 11:30am-10pm
  Cafe Hours: Mon-Thur: 7:30am-5pm   **Fri:** 7:30am-2:30pm   <u>**Sat Closed**</u>

Credit Cards Accepted: MC, Visa, AmEx, Diners Club

Restaurant Discount:

Borough: Manhattan
Section: Midtown West

The Authoritative New York City Kosher Dining Guide

Restaurant: Boychick's

Phone Number: (212) 719-5999
Fax: (212) 719-2267

Address: 19 West 45th Street (bet. 5th Ave. - 6th Ave.)

Hechsher: Rabbi Pinchus Horowitz (Chuster Rav) (Cholov & Pas Yisroel)

Proprietor/Manager: Gaddy Haymov

Type(s) of Food: Dairy - Italian, Middle Eastern, Sushi Bar

Price Range:	Lunch	Dinner	Take out
Entrées:	$6.95-$9.95	$4.95-$15.95	Same - Delivery Available
Desserts:	$1.99-$3.95	**Sandwiches:** $3.50-$6.95 soups $2.75	
Drinks:	$ 1.00-$2.95	**Breakfast Special:** $1.95-$4.95	

Food Specialties: Pizza, Grilled Tuna, Salmon, & Red Snapper, Sandwiches, Falafel

Description: Entrées include Poached Salmon, Fish & Chips, Fetuccini Alfredo, Combo Platter, and Pasta Primavera, plus standard pizza parlor fare. Heart Healthy Salads available, as well as various hot and cold items (e.g. lasagna, stuffed mushrooms, fresh mozzerella items, Chummus, or Babaganush). Traditional sushi is offered along with more original Boychick Rolls. A la carte selections complement 13 sushi entrées. Extensive beverage selection (incl. Espresso, Double Espresso, Cappuccino) and (19) homemade soups prepared fresh daily. Pizza (incl. Chicago style), new Salad Bar and hot Bar ($5.95 lb.) Low fat yogurt.

Comments: No lack of variety here!

Ambiance (Decor): Seats 90 after recent renovation. A new peach and white décor sets off a unique American fast food concept. A series of three individual food counters allow diners to "shop around" for their meals: the Sushi bar in middle of room, the Pizza bar in back and in between them hot & cold bars. Each bar area has its own menu display hanging above it. Cafeteria atmosphere.

Service: Self-serve during the day, waiter service after 5pm

General Comments: An optimal Midtown location for a quick dairy meal. The name and ownership has changed (used to be the IDT Megabite Café/Pizzaria) but the menu remains essentially the same.

Hours: Mon-Thurs: 6:30am-8pm (Summer till 9pm)
Fri: 6:30am till 2 hrs before Shabbos **Saturday Closed** **Sun:** 6:30am-6pm

Credit Cards Accepted: MC, Visa, AmEx, Discover, Diners

Restaurant Discount: 10% Off

Borough: Manhattan
Section: Midtown West

The Authoritative New York City Kosher Dining Guide

Restaurant: Mom's Bagels   *Phone Number:* (212) 764-1566
               Fax: (212) 764-1674
Address: 15 West 45th Street (bet. 5th Ave. - 6th Ave.)

Hechsher: כ - K (Cholov Yisroel, Pas Yisroel, Mashgiach Temidi)

Proprietor/Manager: Michael C. Cook

Type(s) of Food: Dairy, Vegetarian - Jewish American, Israeli

Price Range:	*Lunch*	*Dinner*	*Take out*
Entrées:	$4.50-$7.95	None	Same - Delivery Available
Desserts:	$ .90-$2.50	Breakfast Special: $2.25-$6.95	
Drinks:	$ .75-$2.25, $3.00 (Shakes)		*Sandwiches:* $3.90-$10.25

Food Specialties: Bagels, Fish, Pasta, Salads, Soups, Pastries, Muffins

 Description: Healthy portions, standard dairy fare; also some Middle Eastern
  favorites such as Babaganoush, Techina, Chummus, etc. Features a wide
  selection of salads, Vegetarian Chopped Liver, Baked Salmon, Caesar,
  and Greek Salads are some examples. The "homemade" soups are made
  fresh daily on the premises, as are all the baked goods. The cakes are a
  particular source of pride and include brownies, muffins, cheesecake,
  and carrot cake. Daily Chef's Specials include pastas and other hot
  dishes, seasonal salads, and broiled fish.

 Comments: Fast food for people on the go in midtown.

Ambiance (Decor): Can be characterized as a small luncheonette (seats 80).

Service: Self-serve

General Comments: A convenient midtown location, near the theater district and
  Rockefeller Center. Suitable for a quick dairy meal, or for dining with the
  children. This eatery mostly caters to local office workers or people attending
  matinees.

Hours: **Mon-Thurs:** 6:30am-6pm **Fri:** 6:30am-2:30pm
   Saturday Closed **Sun:** 9:30am-3:30pm

Credit Cards Accepted: MC, Visa, AmEx, Diners Club, Discover

Restaurant Discount:

Borough: Manhattan
Section: Midtown West

The Authoritative New York City Kosher Dining Guide

Restaurant: Kosher Delight *Phone Number:* (212) 869-6699
Fax: (212) 819-1139
Address: 1156 Avenue of the Americas (bet. 45th St. - 46th St.)

Hechsher: Rabbi Pinchus D. Horowitz - Chuster Rav (Glatt Kosher)

Proprietor/Manager:

Type(s) of Food: Meat - Deli, Chinese, Burgers

Price Range: *Lunch*   *Dinner*   *Take out*
    Entrées: $8.00-$16.00   Same   Same- Delivery Available
    Desserts: $1.50 Strudel   *Chinese Entrées:* $7.95-$13.95
    Drinks: $ .60-$1.19   *Sandwiches:* $3.35-$7.95

Food Specialties: Burgers, Grill, Kebobs, Fried Chicken, Deli, Chinese Menu, Ribs

Description: The fast food chain store menu of burgers and fries has been
        extended to include Chinese and deli. Chinese dishes are made fresh to
        order w/o MSG. Hero by the Foot has been added to the deli sandwich
        selections. Fried chicken is sold by the piece in boxes, buckets, etc., of
        various sizes. Soups and salads are on the menu. Everything is a la carte.

Comments: The food tends to be greasy, as it is in the other restaurants of this
        chain, but it has its devotees. Unique to this branch however, is that it
        serves a parve breakfast. The food preparation varies by the location.

Ambiance (Decor): In keeping with its midtown location, this restaurant foregoes the
        molded plastic chairs and instead offers wood tables and chairs. Situated on the
        second floor, it requires walking up a flight of stairs. Large windows overlook
        6th Avenue, allowing diners to enjoy the scene outside. The large room has a
        spacious feel and can accommodate 100 people. The casual atmosphere is
        tempered by office attire of local workers. Disposable cutlery, containers, etc.

Service: Self-serve

General Comments: Located in the heart of Manhattan, its within easy walking
        distance of the theater district, including the Disney complex.

Hours: **Mon-Thurs:** 7:30am-10pm **Fri:** 7:30am-2pm (winter) 3:30pm (summer)
        Saturday Closed **Sun:** 12pm-8:30pm

Credit Cards Accepted: MC, Visa, AmEx, Discover, Diners Club

Restaurant Discount:

The Authoritative New York City Kosher Dining Guide

Restaurant: Le Marais   *Phone Number:* (212) 869-0900
Fax: (212) 869-1016

Address: 150 West 46th Street (bet. 6th Ave. - 7th Ave.)

Hechsher: OK Labs (Glatt Kosher, Chassidishe Shechita)

Proprietor/Manager: Mr. Philip Lajeunie, Chris (Manager)

Type(s) of Food: Meat - French

Price Range: *Lunch*   *Dinner*   *Take out*
   Entrées: $15.50-$27.50 $15.75-$29.50   Same
   Desserts: $6.00-$9.00 *Brunch Entrées:* $11.00-$22.50 (Sun. 12-4pm)
   Drinks: $4-$12.50 (Beer), $6.00/gl.(House wine); $18-$45/btl.(Wines)

Food Specialties: Ravioli de Veau Provençale, Steak au poivre, l'entrecôte

> *Description:* Spit roasted or grilled meat, poultry, and fish avec une acçent
> Française. The Lunch Menu differs from the Dinner Menu only in that it
> offers a more extensive fish selection. Extensive bar.

> *Comments:* The restaurant focuses on what it does best: prepare meats. The
> menu is limited with few accommodations for non-meat eating diners.
> Food is fresh and of good quality. Send backs are accepted graciously
> when needed, so don't feel intimidated! French sized portions (small).

Ambiance (Decor): The front of the restaurant accommodates a "butcher shop" where
you can buy your meat for the week. White tablecloths and butcher paper don
the tables giving this dining room the aura of a French Bistro. There are two
levels. The second level has a more formal, private English club atmosphere
with mahogany paneling and leather chairs. Dimly lit, the setting upstairs is
more intimate. Downstairs, it can get very noisy when busy.

Service: Standard

General Comments: This popular restaurant has a reputation among the cognoscenti
of being the place to go to for a quality steak dinner. As they are often crowded,
it would be wise to make reservations.

Hours: **Sun-Thurs:** 12pm-12am **Fri:** 12pm - 3pm
    Sat: Opens 1 hr after Shabbos till 1am

Credit Cards Accepted: MC, Visa, AmEx, Diners Club

Restaurant Discount:

Borough: Manhattan
Section: Midtown West

The Authoritative New York City Kosher Dining Guide

Restaurant: Gan Eden   *Phone Number:* (212) 869-8946
                                          Fax: None
Address: 74 West 47th Street 3rd Floor (bet. 5th Ave. - 6th Ave.)

Hechsher: Rabbi Yachov Nazirov (Glatt Kosher)

Proprietor/Manager: Maya Iskhakov

Type(s) of Food: Meat – Buckharian, Middle Eastern

Price Range:	*Lunch*	*Dinner*	*Take out*
Entrées:	$5.50-$10.00	Closed	Same – Free Local Del. ($5 Min.)
Desserts:	$1.50	*Lunch Special:* $6.50-$8.00	
Drinks:	$ .50-$2.00	*Soups:* $3.75-$5.99	

Food Specialties: Shish Kebobs, Stuffed Grape Leaves, Mamtu, Fish, Sweet Breads

> *Description:* Not quite Middle Eastern and not quite European, a Bucharian luncheon menu that offers homemade cooking and baking. Everything is freshly made from scratch, even the halavah for dessert. Plov, Stuffed Peppers, Schnitzel, Stuffed Cabbage, Bakhsh (an ethnic specialty of meat chunks cooked with rice & cilantro in a bag), fried whiting (in garlic & parsley), Gosht Gishta (meat pie), Grilled Salmon, Mantu (steamed dumplings) & 7 different kebobs (beef, lamb, chicken, kofta, etc.) are a good sample of what you'll find. 2 popular soups (among 4-5) are Borscht and Lagman. Fried Eggplant, potato, & Israeli are some salads. Lunch Special includes 2 kebob skewers, bread, salad, & rice.

> *Comments:* Not your usual fast food eatery. Food is made fresh to order & can take a few extra minutes to prepare, but it's worth the wait.

Ambiance (Decor): A small restaurant with seating for 30. The décor depends on mirrors and two paintings with Jewish themes. White tablecloths and glass cover the tables. The 3rd floor location has no elevators.

Service: Standard

General Comments: New to us, but in operation for 3 years.

Hours: **Mon-Thurs:** 11:30am-4pm   **Fri:** 11:30am-2 hrs before Shabbos
Saturday Closed   Sunday Closed

Credit Cards Accepted: MC, Visa, AmEx, Discover, Diners Club ($10 Min.)

Restaurant Discount:

Borough: Manhattan
Section: Midtown West

The Authoritative New York City Kosher Dining Guide

Restaurant: Taam Tov
Phone Number: (212) 768-8001
Fax: None
Address: 46 West 47ᵗʰ Street 4th Floor (bet. 5ᵗʰ Ave. - 6ᵗʰ Ave.)

Hechsher: Rabbi Yaachov Nasirov (Glatt Kosher)

Proprietor/Manager: Shamuel

Type(s) of Food: Meat – Euro-Asian, Buckharian

Price Range: Lunch   Dinner   Take out
    Entrées: $6.00-$10.00   Same   Same – Free Local Del. ($6 Min.)
    Desserts: None   **Lunch Special:** $6.00
    Drinks: $1.00

Food Specialties: Kebobs, Baked Salmon, Beef Stroganoff, Plov, Gosht Gidja

> **Description:** A compact menu that specializes in Jewish Bucharian dishes.
> Bucharest is the capital of Romania near Russia and the Middle East so
> the food from that region has influences from each. You'll find Borsht
> and Beef Stroganoff alongside kebobs and Plov (rice & meat or
> chicken). The cuisine, however, has the region's unique stamp in the
> spices used and the preparation. Soups include Lagman, Meat Ravioli, &
> vegetable. Entrées include cooked items, kebobs, Tabaka (?), Gosht
> Gidja (meat pie), Kovurogan (?), and Salmon baked or kebobed.
> Lunch Specials offer a choice among 3 soups, and either bread & kebob
> (2 skewers) or meat dumplings.

> **Comments:** The dishes are intriguing and promise new, unfamiliar flavors.

Ambiance (Decor): Seating for 45 at table clothed tables and not much else. The
focus is all about the food rather than décor. The plain setup reveals the mostly
take-out nature of the business. Restaurant location is on the 4ᵗʰ floor.

Service: Standard

General Comments: Opened in 1998, the restaurant focuses mostly on lunchtime
business. Orders are taken from 11am. Accessible via an elevator.

Hours: **Mon-Thurs:** 8am-5pm   **Fri:** 8am-1 hr before Shabbos
    Saturday Closed   **Sunday Closed**

Credit Cards Accepted: CASH ONLY! (Cards in the future. Call to find out.)

Restaurant Discount:

The Authoritative New York City Kosher Dining Guide

Restaurant: Diamond Dairy **Phone Number:** (212) 719-2694
  Fax: (212) 398-1668
Address: 4 West 47th Street (In the Mezzanine) (bet. 5th Ave. - 6th Ave.)

Hechsher: CRC - (Cholov Yisroel, Pas Yisroel)

Proprietor/Manager: Mr. Samuel

Type(s) of Food: Dairy, Vegetarian - Jewish, American

Price Range:	Lunch	Dinner	Take out
Entrées:	$3.75-$6.75	Closed	Local Delivery
Desserts:	$1.25-$2.00		$7.50 Min.
Drinks:	$ .65-$1.25		

Food Specialties: Blintzes, Potato Perogen, Soups

> **Description:** Nothing frozen, everything is freshly made. Home style cooking "like grandma used to make." Heimishe cooking served in portions that grandma would approve of. Entrées include three side dishes.

> **Comments:** The blintzes received rave reviews in the N.Y. Times and the soups came in a close second.

> **Ambiance (Decor):** A mid-sized cafeteria style restaurant in a unique setting (no pun intended) in the Mezzanine that overlooks the Jewelry Exchange through a glass partition.

Service: Standard

General Comments: It is necessary to walk one flight up to reach this restaurant. However, if that's not a problem the location makes for a unique eating environment in the heart of Manhattan. The food is apparently good too!

Hours: Mon-Thurs: 8am-5pm **Fri:** 8am-2pm
   Saturday Closed   Sunday Closed

Credit Cards Accepted: MC, Visa, AmEx

Restaurant Discount:

Borough: Manhattan
Section: Midtown West

██ ██ ██ ██ ██ **$$**

The Authoritative New York City Kosher Dining Guide

Restaurant: Zenith Vegetarian Restaurant

Phone Number: (212) 262-8080
Fax: (212) 489-8260

Address: 888 Eighth Avenue (cor. 52nd St.)

Hechsher: United Kosher Supervision - RESTAURANT IS OPEN 7 DAYS A WEEK

Proprietor/Manager:

Type(s) of Food: Vegetarian - Oriental (Chinese, Thai, Japanese, etc.)

Price Range:

	Lunch	*Dinner*	*Take out*
Entrées:	$10.50-$13.50	$12.50-$14.50	$6-$14.50 Del.Avail.($6 Min)
Desserts:	$4.50	*Prix Fixe Dinner:* $25 (not incl. Tax & Gratuities)	
Drinks:	$1.25-$3.50	$4.75-$5.75/gl, $17-$22/btl (Wine), Mix Drinks	

Food Specialties: Zenith Blossom, Fragrant Chick, Treasure Island, Fireworks Squid

Description: Western style, Nouveau Oriental cuisine featuring organic vegetables, freshly squeezed fruit juices, low fat, and steamed dishes, seasoned and prepared to individual preferences. Special emphasis is placed on presentation. Faux shrimp, squid, and other seafood, (also veggie chicken, and duck) approximate the real thing. Interesting inclusions are the (Organic) Vegetarian Pasta Specials. These include tofu and chummus tortellini, and spinach, mushroom, or pumpkin stuffed ravioli. The Curry Maharani is another unexpected excursion.

Comments: Newly revised, this inventive and exciting menu cries out to be tried. The emphasis on health is an added bonus. Beautifully presented, delicious, and surprisingly filling portions.

Ambiance (Decor): The serene and restful setting reflects the natural foods served here. The neutral beige color scheme and use of wood serve as a backdrop. Tablecloths throughout the day, but the candles come out for dinner only. The walls feature engaging prints of vegetables. Seating capacity: 110. Casual.

Service: Standard

General Comments: Zenith offers an exciting change of pace for the kosher scene. Located near the heart of the theater district, it is an island of tranquillity in the midst of the crowded hustle and bustle just outside the door.

Hours: **Sun-Thurs:** 11:45am-11pm **Fri-Sat:** 11:45am-11:30pm
- RESTAURANT IS OPEN 7 DAYS A WEEK

Credit Cards Accepted: MC, Visa, AmEx

Restaurant Discount: 10% Off

Borough: Manhattan
Section: Midtown West

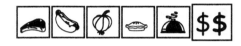

The Authoritative New York City Kosher Dining Guide

Restaurant: Café Classico   *Phone Number:* (212) 355-5411
        a.k.a. 57th Street Gourmet   *Fax:* (212) 355-5736
Address: 35 West 57th Street Upstairs (bet. 5th Ave. - 6th Ave.)

Hechsher: OK Labs - (Glatt, Chassidishe Shechita, Mashgiach Temidi, Bodek Veg)

Proprietor/Manager: Eli Cohen (Manager)

Type(s) of Food: Meat - Deli, Italian, American

Price Range: *Lunch*   *Dinner*   *Take out*
    Entrées: $5.95-$12.95+ $12.75-$17.95 $6-$10+ - Free Local Delivery
    Desserts: $2.25-$3.45 $1.25-$2.95 $1.85-$2.95
    Drinks: $ .90-$2.55 $ .70-$2.55   *Sandwiches:* $6.45-$8.95

Food Specialties: Deli Sandwiches, Pasta, Salads, Deli, Soups

    Description: Big sandwich selection, from a Burger Deluxe to double and
       triple deli combos, to a choice of eleven gourmet sandwiches such as
       Grilled Breast of Chicken (sliced chicken with arugula, sliced tomatoes,
       watercress and creamy honey-mustard), or Avocado & Grilled Chicken
       Breast (sliced avocado & chicken with arugula, watercress, grilled
       tomato with creamy honey-mustard & herb mayo). Chicken entrées
       come with a baby red potato, 2 vegetables & assorted breads & rolls.

    Comments: Their menu says it all, "designed to reflect freshness, health, and
       superb taste with a touch of the gourmet." "…generous sizes of light
       salads, soups, fine cold cuts, sandwiches, delicious entrées, healthy
       shakes and more." Food tends to be a bit dry.

Ambiance (Decor): Located one flight up, this restaurant combines a Soho loft and a
       European café. The dining area seats 135 in a casual and informal atmosphere.
       Some tables overlook 57th Street (chilly in winter), while booths lead you to the
       rear more tables are found. A service counter in the center divides the
       space. In keeping with the café style, there are no tablecloths. Large structural
       columns disguised as classical, lend character to the room, but are badly placed.

Service: Standard

General Comments: Terrific midtown location right in the middle of everything. A
       block from Carnegie Hall, and 5th Ave. Central Park is just two blocks away.

Hours: **Mon-Thurs:** 11:30am-10pm **Fri:** 10am-2pm <u>**Saturday Closed**</u>
       Sun: 11:30am-10pm (Closed Summer)

Credit Cards Accepted: MC, Visa, AmEx, Discover
       (THEY ONLY TAKE CREDIT CARDS WHEN THEY FEEL LIKE IT!)

Restaurant Discount:

Borough: Manhattan
Section: Midtown West

☐ ☐ ☐ ☐ ☐ **$ $**

The Authoritative New York City Kosher Dining Guide

Restaurant: The Great American Health   *Phone Number:* (212) 355-5177
     & Espresso Bar   *Fax:* (212) 355-5466
Address: 35 West 57th Street (bet. 5th Ave. - 6th Ave.)

Hechsher: Tablet "K" Rabbi Saffra - RESTAURANT IS OPEN 7 DAYS A WEEK

Proprietor/Manager: Steve Cohen

Type(s) of Food: Dairy, Vegetarian - American, Italian

Price Range:	*Lunch*	*Dinner*	*Take out*
Entrées:	$6.95-$12.95	Same	$5.95-$6.75
Desserts:	$2.75-$3.75		Delivery Available
Drinks:	$1.25-$3.25		

Food Specialties: Salads, Pastas, Soups, Slim Shakes, Fruit & Vegetable Juices

  Description: You'll find health salads, hot and cold vegetable entrées served
    with house salad and alfalfa sprouts, daily homemade soups, freshly
    baked breads and desserts. An array of sandwiches are served with
    salad. Freshly squeezed fruit and vegetable juices, milk shakes, lo-cal
    ice cream and frozen yogurt are what you can expect. A mostly
    American and Italian menu (e.g. 8 pasta dishes and Eggplant Parmesan)
    complemented by Fish of the Day and a Middle Eastern combination
    platter. Curried rice and veggie chili are indicative of the diversity of the
    specials that are offered.

  Comments: A health conscious, fast food dairy menu. Adequate portions.

Ambiance (Decor): This casual Edward Hopper-esque diner features a counter with
  11 stools that dominates the entry and are exposed to 57th street by the glass
  restaurant facade. Booths and tables line the wall and lead to the back. Neon
  accents reminiscent of a bygone era add a colorful touch to the incandescent
  lighting. The restaurant is a set of stairs below street level. Seats 84.

Service: Standard

General Comments: A bit of Americana in fast paced NYC. Excellent midtown
  location, a block from Carnegie Hall, art galleries, Central Park, etc. Hashgacha
  allows restaurant to be open Shabbos because of a non-Jewish business partner.

Hours: **Mon-Fri:** 8am-10pm **Sat:** 9am-10pm **Sun:** 11am-9pm
  - RESTAURANT IS OPEN 7 DAYS A WEEK

Credit Cards Not Accepted: CASH ONLY!

Restaurant Discount:

Borough: Manhattan
Section: Midtown East

The Authoritative New York City Kosher Dining Guide

Restaurant: Madras Mahal
Phone Number: (212) 684-4010
Fax: None
Address: 104 Lexington Avenue (bet. E. 27th St. - E. 28th St.)

Hechsher: Rabbi Chaim Dov-Ber Gulevsky - RESTAURANT IS OPEN 7 DAYS A WEEK

Proprietor/Manager: Nidin Vyas

Type(s) of Food: Vegetarian - Indian

Price Range:

	Lunch	*Dinner*	*Take out*
Entrees:	$6.95 Buffet (Mon-Fri)	$5.45-$8.95	10% off
Desserts:	$2.95		
Drinks:	$1.25-$2.95	$3.95 (Beer)	

Food Specialties: Dosai, Utthappam, Curries From Punjab & Gujarat

> *Description:* Dosai (various large, light crepes served with coconut chutney & sembar "hot bean sauce"), Utthappam (pancakes), and the large selection of Curries (various vegetable combinations served with plain pullav rice) are featured in this traditional Indian restaurant. Several Combination Dinners permit you to sample an array of Indian cuisine. Everything is freshly prepared, so expect a leisurely meal. Nice selection of soups, salads, appetizers, breads, and Indian desserts. Curries are hot and spicy in varying degrees. The cuisine features legumes, vegetables, fruits, rice and grains. Margarine, Fish, and eggs are completely omitted. Most dishes are parve (about 20% are dairy).

> *Comments:* Surprisingly good food and not spicy unless you want it to be. Satisfying Indian fare that is served in good sized portions.

Ambiance (Decor): The new owners have yet to transform this fairly large, plain and sparsely decorated restaurant. Tablecloths cover the tables, but the dining room is undistinguished. Informal.

Service: Standard

General Comments: A treat for your palate, especially if you're uninitiated. Owners are not Jewish so hashgacha allows them to stay open Shabbos.

Hours: **Mon-Fri: Lunch** 11:30am-3pm **Dinner** 5pm-10pm **Sun-Sat:** 12pm-10pm

Credit Cards Accepted: MC, Visa, AmEx, Discover, Diners Club

Restaurant Discount:

The Authoritative New York City Kosher Dining Guide

Restaurant: Pongal

Phone Number: (212) 696-9458
Fax: (212) 545-8092

Address: 110 Lexington Avenue (bet. E. 27th St. - E. 28th St.)

Hechsher: Rabbi Nachum Josephy - RESTAURANT IS OPEN 7 DAYS A WEEK

Proprietor/Manager: Nazeer Ahmed

Type(s) of Food: Dairy, Vegetarian - South Indian

Price Range:	*Lunch*	*Dinner*	*Take out*
Entrées:	$6.49-$9.95	Same	15% Off In-Rest. Prices-Del. Avail.
Desserts:	$2.95-$3.95	*Combo Dinner:* $13.95	*Children Special:* $2.95
Drinks:	$1.25-$2.95	*Business Special:* $6.95 (M-F: 11:30am-3pm)	
	$4-$4.95/gl, (Wine), $3.95/btl (Beer), $6.95/btl (Indian Beer)		

Food Specialties: Pongal Special, Dosai, Utthappam, Subji from Gujarat & Punjab

> *Description:* Pongal is an Indian harvest festival, as well as a dish served on
> that day. South Indian specialties from Gujarat and Punjab. Mostly
> vegetarian entrées including various Utthappam (a pancake of rice &
> lentil flour), Dosai (crepes with fillings), Rice dishes (mixed with
> assorted spices, fruits, nuts, and/or vegetables), and Gujarati or Punjabi
> Subji. The Business Lunch Special buffet: 3 curries, bread, rice,
> appetizer, 2 salads, Raita (yogurt & onion mix), and dessert (date &
> tamarin chutney). Food is served on banana leaves.

> *Comments:* Challenges preconceptions about food from that region.
> Adventurous souls will delight in unfamiliar flavors & spices.

Ambiance (Decor): The authentic Indian decor transports you. Classical Indian
music furthers the atmosphere. Romance is inspired by candlelight, linen, and
flowers. A large painting of a rising sun highlighted by neon, at the rear of the
restaurant, imparts an optimistic message. The use of stainless steel plates, cups
and cutlery, embodies an old Indian aphorism that by eating with iron one will
gain iron strength. Accommodates 48.

Service: Gracious Indian waiters who have very little or no facility with English

General Comments: Pongol offers the opportunity to experience India both through
the traditional South Indian cuisine they serve and the evocative setting they've
created. A visual and culinary sojourn not to be missed. Non-Jewish ownership.

Hours: **Mon-Fri: Lunch:** 11:30am-3pm **Dinner:** 5pm-10pm
Sat: 12pm-10:30pm **Sun:** 12pm-10pm
- RESTAURANT IS OPEN 7 DAYS A WEEK

Credit Cards Accepted: MC, Visa, AmEx, Discover, Diners Club

Restaurant Discount:

Borough: Manhattan
Section: Midtown East

The Authoritative New York City Kosher Dining Guide

Restaurant: Jasmine **Phone Number:** (212) 251-8885
(212) 251-8884
Address: 11 East 30th Street (bet. 5th Ave. - Madison Ave.) **Fax:** (212) 251-8884

Hechsher: OK Labs (Glatt Kosher)

Proprietor/Manager: Naeder Fard

Type(s) of Food: Meat - Persian, Middle Eastern

Price Range: **Lunch** (12pm-3pm) **Dinner** **Take out**
  Entrées: Daily Specials $11.50-$16.50 $9-$13.50- Del. Avail.
  Desserts: $2.50 **Dinner Special:** Free glass of wine
  Drinks: $1.00-$2.50 $3.00-$3.50 (Beer) $15.00-$24.00/Bottle (Wine)

Food Specialties: Kabobs, Soultani Stews

  Description: A small menu featuring authentic Persian cuisine.
    Predominantly, various kebobs and stews of beef, lamb, chicken and
    fish are served in fairly large portions. Everything is natural, and no
    preservatives are used.

  Comments: "The best Persian food in town" is the claim. Intriguing dining
    possibility.

Ambiance (Decor): A small restaurant (seating 54 people) with Persian hospitality
    in a casual, relaxed atmosphere. The room has beige walls that set off the pink
    and maroon tableware. Candles grace the tables to enhance the intimate setting,
    as do the wall sconces and ceiling lights. Entry is 3 steps below street level.

Service: Friendly and accommodating

General Comments: An interesting possibility if you're unfamiliar with Persian food
    and are in an adventurous mood, or for those who like Middle Eastern foods.

Hours: **Sun-Thurs:** 11:30am-8:30pm **Fri:** 11:30-2 hrs before Shabbos
    Saturday Closed

Credit Cards Accepted: MC, Visa, AmEx, Diners Club, Discover, Carte Blanche

Restaurant Discount: 10% Off (On Food Only)

Borough: Manhattan
Section: Midtown East

The Authoritative New York City Kosher Dining Guide

Restaurant: Café 1-2-3

Phone Number: (212) 685-7117
Fax: (212) 685-3059

Address: 2 Park Avenue (bet. E. 32nd St. - E. 33rd St.)

Hechsher: Vaad Harabonim of Queens (Cholov Yisroel food, but not desserts)

Proprietor/Manager: Jerry Berkowitz

Type(s) of Food: Dairy, Vegetarian - Eclectic

Price Range:

	Lunch	Dinner	Take out
Entrées:	$5.95-$12.95	Same	Same - Delivery Available
Desserts:	$1.50-$3.50	Sandwiches: $4.95-$6.25	
Drinks:	$1.00-$3.00	Breakfast Specials: $3.23-$3.93	No Alcohol

Food Specialties: Wrapped Sandwiches, Pizza, Grilled Mahi Mahi, Pea Soup

Description: They boast of having the "best soups in town" with such Soup Specials as yellow or green Split Pea, Mexican Tortilla Soup, and Portabello Mushroom Soup. A full coffee and juice bar serves "Seattle's Best Coffee." Popular entrées include the Grilled Tuna or Salmon Steaks. Entrées are served with two vegetables. Wrapped tortillas (Mexican flour pancakes), are offered with 6 different fillings: portabello mushrooms, avocado, etc.

Comments: The Minestrone was bland, but the Pea Soup, was delicious (good consistency, seasoned just right). A good lunch choice: Spinach & Mushroom Quiche served with a lettuce & tomato salad. The Penne was disappointing, (dried tomatoes w/canned artichokes). After some discussion ("no returns" policy) it was replaced w/ the better portabello.

Ambiance (Decor): Old fashioned, '50s ambiance marks the tone of this restaurant. The front area is allotted to take out/fast food while the back has seating (70) for dining in. Unadorned tables & chairs, Pea Soup green walls & kitsch lamps.

Service: Standard

General Comments: Diner class food for quick meals.

Hours: **Sun:** 10am-8:30pm **Mon-Thurs:** 7am-9pm
Fri: 7am-2 hrs before Shabbos **Saturday Closed**

Credit Cards Accepted: MC, Visa, AmEx, Diners Card

Restaurant Discount:

174

Borough: Manhattan
Section: Midtown East

The Authoritative New York City Kosher Dining Guide

Restaurant: Mendy's East

Phone Number: (212) 576-1010
Fax: (212) 889-1788

Address: 61 East 34th Street (cor. Park Ave.)

Hechsher: OU (Glatt, Chassidishe Shechita, Mashgiach Temidi, Bishul Yisroel)

Proprietor/Manager: Sammy (manager)

Type(s) of Food: Meat - Steaks, Deli

Price Range:

	Lunch	Dinner	Take out
Entrées:	$10.00-$24.00	Same	Same - Delivery Available
Desserts:	$3.95	**Sandwiches:**	$6.95-$12.95, $11.95-$12.95 (Hot)
Drinks:	$1.25-$5.00	$5.00 (Mixed Drink)	

Food Specialties: Deli Sandwiches, Grilled Steaks, etc.

Description: The extensive menu boasts an array of entrées featuring chicken, turkey, beef, duckling, lamb, veal, and fresh fish which are broiled, grilled, fried, kebobed or roasted. Mendy's Lite offers a nice selection of salads. The deli sandwich selection, likewise, has much to choose from. Appetizers and Soups round off the menu.

Comments: Their menu quotes Mayor Giuliani as saying that they have the "best pastrami in town" and credits Seinfeld as saying they have the "best pea soup anywhere in town." In fact I'm told the whole cast of Seinfeld has visited the establishment and that the restaurant has appeared on the show.

Ambiance (Decor): Smaller than its counterpart on the Upper West Side, this sports bar/restaurant accommodates 150 people. It features a small bar and is decorated in the Old New York (1900's) theme. Tablecloths cover the tables, yet the tone remains informal and casual.

Service: Standard

General Comments: Located in the heart of the midtown shopping area, it's a good dining possibility when in the neighborhood, for an informal and relaxed meal.

Hours: **Sun:** 11:30am-10:30pm **Mon-Thurs:** 11:30am-10:30pm
Fri: 11:30-3 hrs before Shabbos **Saturday Closed**

Credit Cards Accepted: MC, Visa, AmEx, Discover, Carte Blanche, Diners Club

Restaurant Discount: 10% Off All In-House Dining

The Authoritative New York City Kosher Dining Guide

Restaurant: Vege Vege II

Phone Number: (212) 679-4710
Fax: None

Address: 544 - Third Avenue (bet. E. 36th St. - E. 37th St.)

Hechsher: United Kosher Supervision - RESTAURANT IS OPEN 7 DAYS A WEEK

Proprietor/Manager: Andy

Type(s) of Food: Vegetarian - Oriental, Buddhist

Price Range:

	Lunch	Dinner	Take out
Entrées:	$5.50 - $5.95	$8.95 - $13.95	Same
Desserts:	$1.95 - $4.95		Delivery Available
Drinks:	$1.00 - $2.75	(Non alcoholic wine & beer avail.)	

Food Specialties: Crispy Prawns w/ 4 Flavor Red Wine, Phoenix Soong

Description: Everything is all natural and entirely vegetarian, no dairy, animal fat, artificial colorings, preservatives, or flavorings are used.

Comments: The menu is exotic, but the Sweet & Sour Prawns were soggy and should have been crispy. The Mongolian Beef, while interesting at first, got boring (greater vegetable variety would have broken the monotony) and the Phoenix Soong was bland. When asked if we could change this last selection, they simply added soy sauce and did not offer the option of another dish. Furthermore, tea is not included with dinner but most options do come with soup or salad. Best choice: the cold summer sampler which includes a taste of sushi, seaweed, tofu bread, and more.

Ambiance (Decor): This relatively small restaurant (seats approx. 60) has Oriental accents but is otherwise uncommitted (red walls outlined with small lights). Casual, tables covered with tablecloths and punctuated with plastic flowers.

Service: Adequate but unenthusiastic

General Comments: The menu is interesting and the food attractively presented. The restaurant is not far from Stern College, so if in the area you might want to try it, but don't go out of your way. Non Jewish owner stays open on Saturday.

Hours: **Mon-Sat:** 11:30am-11pm - RESTAURANT IS OPEN 7 DAYS A WEEK

Credit Cards Accepted: MC, Visa, AmEx, Diners Club

Restaurant Discount:

Borough: Manhattan
Section: Midtown East

The Authoritative New York City Kosher Dining Guide

Restaurant: Abigael's

Phone Number: (212) 725-0130
Fax: (212) 725-3577

Address: 9 East 37th Street (bet. Madison Ave - 5th Ave.)

Hechsher: ⊃ - K (Glatt Kosher, Chassidishe Shechita, Mashgiach Temidi)

Proprietor/Manager: Harvey Riezenman (Owner)

Type(s) of Food: Meat - American

Price Range:

	Lunch	Dinner	Take out
Entrées:	$15.95-$21.95	$17.95-$28.50	Same -
Desserts:	$5.50-$7.50		Delivery Available
Drinks:	$1.50-$2.00,	$17-$27/btl	$4.50/gl (Wine); $5-$8/gl (Mixed Drks)

Food Specialties: Marinated Rib Eye Steak, Salmon Garlic, Skillet Roasted Chicken

Description: The menu offers two parts: the eclectic "standard" one and the innovative one that changes periodically, thanks to the creative talents of master chef and co-owner Jeffrey Nathan. Remarkable for their interesting and unexpected combination of ingredients, these dishes present the diner with a culinary adventure each and every time, making this "steak house" far from ordinary. Specials on our visit: Brazilian Brisket, Egg Roll, Chicken Ballantine, Roast Long Island Duck and the Japanese Beef Terriaki. Sample the Southwestern Spiced Chicken Paillard, the Salmon Garlic or the Chargrilled Tenderloin Steak.

Comments: The James Beard 1st place Award Winning Venison Chili takes center stage. The desserts are delicious and should not be missed. Kashrus here is not a hindrance, but an inspiration and a point of departure. Kudos to the chef for his achievements!

Ambiance (Decor): A sophisticated, mid-size (seats 90) modern restaurant with some post modern details. Spacious in feel because of the high ceiling, and arranged cleverly for intimate dining. Formal, yet conducive to relaxed conversation.

Service: Professional and competent

General Comments: A unique and special place for kosher dining. Discount parking.

Hours: Mon-Thurs: Lunch 12pm-2:30pm **Dinner** 5pm-9:30pm **Friday Closed**
Sat: 1 hr after Shabbos till 11pm (aft. Oct.) **Sun:** 5pm-9pm

Credit Cards Accepted: MC, Visa, AmEx, Diners Club

Restaurant Discount: 10% Off or Bottle of Wine (4 Diners) or 1 Glass/single

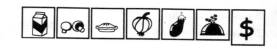

The Authoritative New York City Kosher Dining Guide

Restaurant: Vegetable Garden

Phone Number: (212) 545-7444
Fax: (212) 545-7445

Address: 15 East 40th Street (bet. 5th Ave - Madison Ave.)

Hechsher: ⊃-K (Cholov Yisroel)

Proprietor/Manager:

Type(s) of Food: Dairy, Vegetarian - Health, Eclectic: American, Italian, Mid-East

Price Range:	*Lunch*	*Dinner*	*Take out*
Entrées:	$4.43-$6.95	Same	Same - Free Local Delivery
Desserts:	$1.25-$2.60	*Sandwiches:* $4.45-$6.45	($5.00 Min.)
Drinks:	$ .70-$2.60	*Breakfast Special:* $2.36-$5.25	

Food Specialties: Homemade Soups, Pasta Specials, Fish, Salads, Juices, Shakes

Description: The focus is on health with an array of salads (e.g. Sweet Carrot, Spinach, Caesar), fish (e.g. Catch Of The Day, Poached Salmon), and vegetarian entrées (e.g. Quiches made with low-fat cheeses, Vegetarian Stuffed Cabbage, Vegetable Chili). The extensive selection of drinks include: various shakes, freshly squeezed fruit and vegetable juices. A Coffee Bar features herbal/regular teas and coffees including Espresso, Cappuccino, and Cafe Mocha. Sunday Brunch ($9.95) includes soup, fruit cup, main dish, coffee and dessert. Average sized portions.

Comments: There is a minimum charge between Noon and 3:30pm of $2.50 at the counter and $3.50 at tables. Most everything served with salad.

Ambiance (Decor): A nice sized restaurant, it accommodates 100 people, and hosts the local professional work force consisting largely of lawyers and accountants. The diners lend a formality to the ambiance, reflected in the general tone.

Service: Standard

General Comments: In the heart of Manhattan, this restaurant offers a reasonable, health conscious place to dine.

Hours: **Mon-Thurs:** 7am-7pm **Fri:** 7am-3pm **Saturday Closed**
Sun: 10am-7pm

Credit Cards Accepted: MC, Visa, AmEx, Diners Club, Discover

Restaurant Discounts:

178

The Authoritative New York City Kosher Dining Guide

Restaurant: All American Health and Café Bar *Phone Number:* (212) 370-4525
Fax: (212) 370-4249

Address: 24 East 42nd Street (bet. 5th Ave. - Madison Ave.)

Hechsher: Organized Kashruth Laboratories (Cholov Yisroel, Pas Yisroel)

Proprietor/Manager: Rachamim Cohen

Type(s) of Food: Dairy - Italian, Israeli, American

Price Range:	Lunch	Dinner	Take out
Entrées:	$5.95-$7.95	Same	Same - Delivery Available
Desserts:	$2.75-$3.95	*Sandwiches:* $5.25-$7.95	
Drinks:	$ .65-$2.95		

Food Specialties: Health food, Salads, Pastas, Vegetarian Entrées, Shakes, Muffins

Description: The portions are generous as is the selection. The sandwich
selection includes choice possibilities like the Eggplant, Garden Patch,
and Ratatouille Vegetable & Mozzarella. Entrées and sandwiches are
served with house salad and alfalfa sprouts. A coffee bar, features a nice
variety of coffees and adds to the expansive menu of herbal teas,
vegetable juices, fruit juices, and slim shakes. A plethora of desserts are
offered. The emphasis is on low fat, low cholesterol and natural foods.

Comments: The menu is large and varied and the prices are moderate.

Ambiance (Decor): Three levels in a casual setting, complete with booths and tables
adorned with candles and flowers. The first floor seats 110 people and has
waiter service. The 2nd level has a bar as well as tables and booths, but is
smaller (seats 89), informal, and self-serve. The 3rd floor is used for parties.

Service: Standard on the 1st level, self-service on the 2nd

General Comments: A healthy alternative for family dining. The menu is varied and
interesting with pizza and salads. Something to please everyone.

Hours: **Sun:** 9am-8pm **Mon-Thurs:** 7am-9pm
Fri: 7am-1½ hrs before Shabbos **Saturday Closed**

Credit Cards Accepted: MC, Visa, AmEx, Discover

Restaurant Discounts:

Borough: Manhattan
Section: Midtown East

The Authoritative New York City Kosher Dining Guide

Restaurant: The Wolf & The Lamb

Phone Number: (212) 317-1950
Fax: (212) 317-0159

Address: 10 East 48th Street (bet. 5th Ave. - Madison Ave.)

Hechsher: OK (Glatt Kosher, Mashgiach Temidi)

Proprietor/Manager: David Dery, Herschel Smith

Type(s) of Food: Meat - American

Price Range:

	Lunch	Dinner	Take out
Entrées:	$7.50-$39.50	Same	Same – Free Local Delivery
Desserts:	$4.50	Deli Sandwiches:	$7.50-$9.50
Drinks:	$1.50	$5/gl (Wine)	Soups: $3.95

Food Specialties: Rib Steaks, Grills, Burgers, Salads, Soups, Deli Sandwiches

Description: At this writing, the menu hasn't even been printed up yet, but all indications are that it will be that of an American steak house. Offered are 5-6 freshly made soups daily, including 2 Soups of the Day. Deli is available, but does not set the tenor of the menu.

Comments: Definitely a "must try" restaurant for 1999.

Ambiance (Decor): Described as elegant, the newly opened restaurant offers romantic (read dimmed) lighting, accoutered tables, and piped-in Classical music. Assorted wine bottles decorate the walls. Seats approx. 75.

Service: Formal service

General Comments: An exciting new restaurant prospect in the theatre district.

Hours: **Sun-Thurs:** 11am-11pm **Fri:** 11am- 2 hrs before Shabbos
Sat: 2 hrs after Shabbos till 11pm (May extend to 12am)

Credit Cards Accepted: MC, Visa, AmEx, Discover

Restaurant Discount: 10% Off Dinner Only

Borough: Manhattan
Section: Midtown East

The Authoritative New York City Kosher Dining Guide

Restaurant: Great American Health Bar   *Phone Number:* (212) 758-0883
                                            Fax: None
Address: 821 Third Avenue (bet. E. 50ᵗʰ St. - E. 51ˢᵗ St.)

Hechsher: Tablet K - RESTAURANT IS OPEN 7 DAYS A WEEK

Proprietor/Manager:

Type(s) of Food: Dairy, Vegetarian - International

Price Range:	Lunch	Dinner	Take out
Entrées:	$4.95-$7.95	Same	Same - Free Local Delivery
Desserts:	$1.50-$2.95	Sandwiches: $5.25-$7.95	
Drinks:	$ .65-$2.50	Breakfast: $2.25-$3.25	*

Food Specialties: Fish Of The Day, Deep Pan Pizza, Health Salads & Drinks, Soups

> *Description:* The menu claims "We start fresh everyday with love and other natural ingredients." The focus here is on health, with low calorie, freshness, and high quality food the stated aims. There is a fairly extensive salad selection (at least eight choices) and a wide variety of vegetable juices, fruit juices and shakes. Entrées include items such as Eggplant Scaloppini, Fetuccini Casserole, Curried Vegetables and Quiche Of The Day. The deep Dish Pizzas come with Tossed Salad, while the sandwiches come with House Salad & French fries.

> *Comments:* Fast food with an emphasis on health. One of several franchises.

Ambiance (Decor): Seats 75 people in a coffee shop milieu. A counter with stools is on one side, while laminate topped tables and chairs line the other, continuing to the back of the room. Renovated about 1½ years ago, it is modern & inviting.

Service: Standard

General Comments: Under the same ownership for 10 years, the restaurant caters mostly to local workers. Its proximity to sites (Museum of Modern Art, Rockefeller Center and the United Nations) makes it a possible quick stop for hungry visitors.

Hours: **Sun:** 10am-5pm   **Mon-Thurs:** 7:30am-9pm   **Fri:** 7:30am-8pm
         Sat: 10am-8pm - RESTAURANT IS OPEN 7 DAYS A WEEK

Credit Cards Accepted: MC, Visa, AmEx, Discover, Diners Club

Restaurant Discounts:

Borough: Manhattan
Section: Midtown East

| | | | | $$$ |

The Authoritative New York City Kosher Dining Guide

Restaurant: Haikara Grill

Phone Number: (212) 355-7000
Fax: (212) 759-1407

Address: 1016 Second Avenue (bet. E. 53rd St. - E. 54th St.)

Hechsher: OU (Glatt Kosher)

Proprietor/Manager: Steven Levy

Type(s) of Food: Meat - Contemporary Japanese

Price Range:

	Lunch	Dinner	Take out
Entrées:	$13.95-$17.95	$17.95-$25.95	Same as Dinner
Desserts:	$5.95		Delivery Available
Drinks:	$2.50-$3.00	$6 / glass (Wine)	$6 avg. (Mixed Drinks)

Food Specialties: Sushi, Maki Rolls, Assorted Sushi Combo, Steak, Chicken, Fish

Description: The portions are adequate and creatively presented. Daily specials, along with a large, permanent selection of Sushi/Sashimi and assorted entrées. Of the appetizers, we recommend the Tempura Moriawase which comes in a teriyaki mustard sauce. Veal Yaki is topped with mushrooms in a honey mustard marinade, and served with potatoes and fried squash. It was delicious. The veal was tender and succulent, the sauce complimentary. The Bento (Japanese Dinner Box) is a little of everything, with soup and salad.

Comments: The sushi takes top honors for presentation, quality and taste.

Ambiance (Decor): Modern, Western decor with Japanese accents. A bar, at the entry is the prelude to a dining room several steps up, (seats 100). Terrific rear bow-windowed wall overlooking garden outside. Dinnertime enhanced with candles, tablecloths and flowers. Upscale ambiance, uptown sophistication.

Service: Polite, accommodating, patient, and helpful guides to the cuisine

General Comments: Reservations one day in advance are recommended. A very good dinner choice. Each diner is <u>required</u> to order an entrée at dinnertime.

Hours: Mon-Thurs: Lunch: 12pm-2:30pm **Dinner:** 5:30pm-11pm
Fri: Lunch: 12pm-2:30pm **Sat:** 1½ hrs after Shabbos till 1am
Sun: 4:30pm-10:30pm

Credit Cards Accepted: AmEx

Restaurant Discounts:

Borough: Manhattan
Section: Midtown East

The Authoritative New York City Kosher Dining Guide

Restaurant: Glatt Dynasty

Phone Number: (212) 888-9119
Fax: (212) 888-9163

Address: 1049 Second Avenue (bet. E. 55th St. - E. 56th St.)

Hechsher: כ - K (Chassidishe Shechita - Mashgiach Tamidi)

Proprietor/Manager: Romi

Type(s) of Food: Meat - Chinese

Price Range: **Lunch** (11:15am-4pm) **Dinner** **Take out**
Entrées: $12.95 (Lunch Sp) $11.95-$23.95 $9.95-(Lunch Take Out Sp)
Desserts: $1.50-$4.25 **Peking Duck:** $48.00 (for 2) Del Avail ($20 Min.)
Drinks: $1.25-$1.75, $6/gl $22/btl (Wine), $3.50-$4.50 (Beer), $6/gl (Mix)

Food Specialties: General Tso's Chicken, Orange Flavored Beef, Fresh Fish, etc.

Description: You'll find all the standard favorites here such as Sesame Chicken, General Tso's Chicken, Sizzling Steak Kew, etc. Nice selection, respectable but not overly large portions, and fresh veggies. Diet menu as well as American favorites. Attractive presentation. The eat-in Lunch Special includes soup & egg roll.

Comments: The food is good. Sauces are restrained. Vegetables are crisp and fresh. Shabbos Super Take Out Special: Erev Shabbos DINNER menu only (with $25 min.), 20% off cash orders, 15% credit card orders. (Note: 2 discounts cannot be combined). Orders modified to taste.

Ambiance (Decor): Dim lights, mirrored walls, tablecloths, and flowers, give this room an intimate and uncrowded feel. Seating for 60 people.

Service: Pleasant and responsive. In spite of the restaurant's small size, you are not rushed through your meal. They check in periodically to make sure all is well.

General Comments: "Best Service Guaranteed" is right on the menu. If you have any comments about the food or service, you are encouraged to let them know. The food is good and the location is convenient to midtown activities. Minimum table charge of $10/pp. Easy parking after 7 pm.

Hours: **Sun:** 1pm-11pm **Mon-Thurs:** 11am-11pm (last seating 10pm)
Fri: 11am-3pm **Sat:** Opens 1 hr after Shabbos till 1am

Credit Cards Accepted: MC, Visa, AmEx, Discover, Carte Blanche, Diners Club

Restaurant Discounts: Min $20 - 15% Off With Cash, 10% Off With Credit Card

The Authoritative New York City Kosher Dining Guide

Midtown West:

Jerusalem II Pizza   *Tel:* (212) 398-1475
1375 Broadway (38th St.)
OU

Shalom Kosher Pizza   *Tel:* (212) 730-0008
1000 6th Avenue
OK Labs

Boychicks   *Tel:* (212) 719-5999
19 West 45th Street
Rabbi P. D. Horowitz (Chuster Rav)

Midtown East:

Café Roma Pizzeria   *Tel:* (212) 683-3044
459 Park Avenue South
Star-K

Upper West Side
Washington Heights

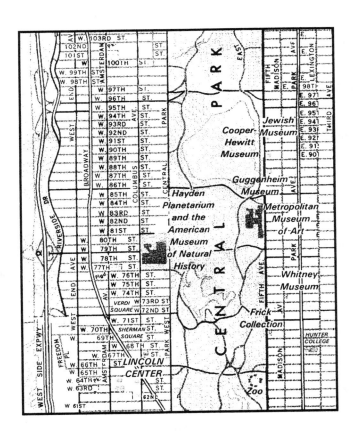

Borough: Manhattan
Section: Upper West Side

The Authoritative New York City Kosher Dining Guide

Restaurant: Levana   *Phone Number:* (212) 877-8457
                              Fax: (212) 595-7522
Address: 141 West 69ᵗʰ Street (bet. Columbus Ave. - Broadway)

Hechsher: ⊃ - K (Glatt Kosher, Pas Yisroel, Chassidishe Shechita)

Proprietor/Manager: Jan Maryann (Manager)

Type(s) of Food: Meat - American

Price Range: *Lunch*   *Dinner*
  Entrées: $17.50-$39.95 $19.95-$39.95
  Desserts: $6.50-$14.00   *Prix Fix Dinners:* $19.99/pp or $57.59/pp
  Drinks: Full Cellar: Extensive wine list and full selection of Single Malt
    Scotches ($8.00/gl.-$135.00/gl.), Mixed drinks ($4.50-$6.50)

Food Specialties: Double thick Rib Eye Steak (26oz.), Venison, Lamb

Description: Carefully prepared entrées include: Rib Eye Steak (boneless 12
  oz. prime steak with red & yellow peppers served with a Merlot and
  thyme sauce), Rack of Lamb (3 double chops with fresh basil crust and
  roast potatoes), Penne Pasta with Smoked Salmon (with arugala and
  radicchio), Breast of Chicken (grilled, marinated, served with risotto
  cakes, salsify, asparagus & oyster mushrooms) and the 26 oz. steak.

Comments: The venison, a signature dish here, is surprisingly tender and not at
  all gamy. The $19.99 dinner is by far the best value. Thumbs up for the
  Stuffed Chicken Breast, but watch out for the sharp, untrimmed string
  bean tips, "Ouch!" The Morel mushroom appetizer disappointed.

Ambiance (Decor): Upscale and formal, this restaurant offers a romantic setting with
  fully appointed tables, recorded classical music playing in the background, dim
  lighting and tasteful decoration. Eating under the stars is made possible with the
  glass enclosed extension in the rear. Private dining room as well.

Service: Formal service. For a party of 6 or more, a 17% gratuity is added to the bill.

General Comments: A restaurant convenient to Lincoln Center for before opera,
  ballet, or theater performances, however, somewhat pricey for what you get.

Hours: **Mon-Thurs:** 5:30pm-10:30pm **Friday Closed**
    Sat: 1 hr after Shabbos till 1am (Winter Only) **Sun:** 3pm-10:30pm

Credit Cards Accepted: MC, Visa, AmEx, Diners Club

Restaurant Discount:

Borough: Manhattan
Section: Upper West Side

The Authoritative New York City Kosher Dining Guide

Restaurant: Mendy's West   *Phone Number:* (212) 877-6787
                                              Fax: (212) 877-6867
Address: 208 West 70th Street (bet. Amsterdam Ave. - West End Ave.)

Hechsher: OU (Glatt Kosher)

Proprietor/Manager: Kamal Monga - Manager

Type(s) of Food: Meat – American, Deli

Price Range: *Lunch*   *Dinner*   *Take out*
  Entrées: $10.95-$26.95   Same   Same - Delivery Available
  Desserts: $3.95   *Sandwiches:* $11-$13 $6.50 Min./p.p. at table $2 Sharing
  Drinks: $1.25-$2.25, $4 (Beer) *Kids Menu:* $7.95 charge

Food Specialties: Steaks, Deli Sandwiches, Shish Kabob, Fish, Salads

  Description: Varied menu offering entrée selections of chicken, turkey, duck,
      veal, beef and fish. Large portions as in the 17oz. Prime Rib Steak, the
      1" thick Rib Eye steak, and the 24 oz. Ribsteak. Deli sandwich selection
      has all the regulars. 12 low-calorie health salads.

  Comments: The menu has become more focused. Nice selection.

Ambiance (Decor): You enter the sports bar first. There you will find a bar that
      accommodates 40 people, tables that seat 40 diners, a large screen TV with
      satellite hook up (which features sports events, in season), and game machines
      (which are very popular with the younger set). The main and semi-formal
      dining room is accessed through the bar. Here you'll find a brightly lit room
      decorated in an Old New York (1900's) motif. 99 tables (250 people max.),
      white tablecloths and napkins; flowers in season on the tables, glass showcases
      of plastic plants, and background music (usually classical) define the character.

Service: Standard

General Comments: A restaurant for family and casual dining. For groups of 6 or
      more a 17% gratuity charge is added.

Hours: **Mon-Thurs:** 5pm-12am   **Friday Closed**
      Sat: 1 hr after Shabbos till 2am   **Sun:** 12pm-1am

Credit Cards Accepted: MC, Visa, AmEx, Diners Club, Carte Blanche

Restaurant Discount: 10% Off For All In-House Dining

Borough: Manhattan
Section: Upper West Side

☒ ⊘ 🍷 🔔 **$$$$**

The Authoritative New York City Kosher Dining Guide

Restaurant: Provi Provi

Phone Number: (212) 875-9020
Fax: (212) 875-0127

Address: 228 West 72nd Street (bet. Broadway - West End Ave.)

Hechsher: OK Labs (Chalov Yisroel, Pas Yisroel)

Proprietor/Manager: Raphy (Manager)

Type(s) of Food: Dairy - Italian

Price Range:

	Lunch (Mon-Fri)	*Dinner*	*Take out*
Entrées:	$7.95-$16.95	$14.50-$25.95	Same - Delivery Available
Desserts:	$5.50	$4.50-$ 7.50	*Child Menu:* $4.50-$8.95
Drinks:	$1.50-$4.00	$4.50-$6.50/gl., $16.00-$28/botl. (Wine)	

Food Specialties: Homemade Pasta & Desserts, Fresh Fish, Ice Cream Drinks, Pizza

> *Description:* Homemade desserts, and a generous selection of homemade pasta and fresh fish daily. The large portions are well prepared.

> *Comments:* There is a special children's menu for youngsters under 12. Homemade pasta dishes and a nice variety of fresh fish offered broiled or sautéed. They also make pizza with their own "special gourmet method." Don't skip the appetizers-they're very fine and suffice as light meals. Salads are a good choice. The daily changing Dessert Menu and the Ice Cream Drink Menu offer a multitude of delicious sins. Indulge!

Ambiance (Decor): Not handicap friendly, this attractive restaurant requires descending a flight of stairs to enter. Full bar. Seats 150 people on three levels: a glass enclosed sidewalk café used year round (no street access), a basement level, main dining room (seats 75-80), and a 3rd dining area (50 seats), accessed by ascending a flight of stairs from the main dining room. This last room boasts a fireplace, tables with white tablecloths, candles, and occasionally flowers, providing greater formality and privacy for intimacy and romance.

Service: Standard, will carry handicapped customers up and down stairs if necessary!

General Comments: There is parking for $5.00 (for five hours) at Gemini Parking on West 70th bet. West End Avenue & the West Side Highway.

Hours: **Sun-Thurs:** 12am-11pm **Fri:** 12am-2:30pm
Sat: 1 hr after Shabbos till 1am

Credit Cards Accepted: MC, Visa, AmEx, Diners Club, Discover, Carte Blache

Restaurant Discount: 15% off excluding Prix Fixe Dinner & Special Dinners.

188

Borough: Manhattan
Section: Upper West Side

The Authoritative New York City Kosher Dining Guide

Restaurant: Royale (Kosher Bake Shop & Café)   **Phone Number:** (212) 874-5642
                                                    Fax: (212) 874-4701
Address: 237 West 72nd Street (bet. Broadway - West End Ave.)

Hechsher: KAJ (Cholov Yisroel)

Proprietor/Manager:

Type(s) of Food: Dairy - American

Price Range: **Lunch**   **Dinner**   **Take out**
  Entrées: $3.50-$6.00
  Desserts: $1.00-$2.00 or $8.00-$10.95/lb.
  Drinks: $ .75-$1.75

Food Specialties: Fish Sandwiches, Vegetable Liver, Pastries, Cakes, Breads

  Description: The "light meal" menu offers things like Baked Salmon,
     Eggplant Babaganoush, Herring in Cream Sauce, Sliced Nova with
     Cream Cheese, and Egg Salad. Pastries and cookies galore make the
     dessert possibilities here terrific. Nice selection of teas, coffee and other
     beverages.

  Comments: Primarily a bakery, the "restaurant" menu is minimal.

Ambiance (Decor): Essentially a bakery with a few tables that can accommodate
  9-10 people for a light repast. Mirrored wall. 7 counter stools, 1 table in front.

Service: Self-serve

General Comments: A good place to "grab a quick and light bite" when on the go, or
  to go to for dessert without the expense and bother of a regular restaurant.

Hours: **Mon-Wed:** 6am-8pm **Thurs:** 6am-9pm **Fri:** 6am-4pm
  Saturday Closed **Sun:** 7am-7pm

Credit Cards Accepted: MC, Visa

Restaurant Discount:

189

Borough: Manhattan
Section: Upper West Side

The Authoritative New York City Kosher Dining Guide

Restaurant: Dougie's BBQ & Grill
Phone Number: (212) 724-2222
Fax: (212) 724-3421
Address: 222 West 72ⁿᵈ Street (bet. Broadway - West End Ave.)

Hechsher: OU (Glatt Kosher)

Proprietor/Manager: Doug

Type(s) of Food: Meat - American; Middle Eastern

Price Range: **Lunch**   **Dinner**   **Take out**
Entrées: $5.95-$17.95 $9.95-$17.95 Same - Delivery Avail. ($10 Min.)
Desserts: $4.00   **Kid's Menu:** $5.95   **Sandwiches:** $4.95-$12.95
Drinks: $1.50-$2.00   **Lunch Special:** $5.95-$14.95 (12pm-3pm)

Food Specialties: BBQ, Steaks, Shish Kabobs, Buffalo Wings, Deli, Grills, Burgers

Description: The menu is what you would expect from a steak house, but also contains a few surprises like pizza (vegetable & also with chicken) and pasta (with grilled vegetables & also with chicken). Lunch Specials include sandwich, fries, & soda. Enormous portions nicely presented.

Comments: **What to order:** the Ribs (they *are* tender and the sauce has a nice smoky flavor), the Tenderloin Steak (actually tender), the pea soup (full bodied, flavorful), the deli sandwiches (lean and very good), the burgers (large) and the Cajun fries (good). **What to avoid:** the Chicken Soup (under all circumstances), the Rib Steak & Beef Kebob (tough) and the Buffalo Wings (the sauce is neither authentic nor hot and the wings are paltry rather than poultry). The Chili is appetizing, but could use more beans and a few jalapeños, also, fewer bell peppers. The Mushroom Barley Soup would be terrific without the added Chicken Soup. Rare/ medium orders *must be strongly emphasized* or expect them well done.

Ambiance (Decor): Simple undistinguished decor, small wooden tables and chairs crowd together in this large eatery (220 seats). Informal, noisy, and chaotic.

Service: Competent waiters, but charged with too many tables to serve

General Comments: This is a very popular restaurant and consequently usually crowded. Be prepared to wait for a table, and for a lag time in service

Hours: **Sun-Thurs:** 12am-10pm (last seating at 9:30pm)
Friday Closed   **Sat:** 1 hr after Shabbos till 12 am (Oct-Spring only)

Credit Cards Accepted: MC, Visa, AmEx

Restaurant Discount:

Borough: Manhattan
Section: Upper West Side

The Authoritative New York City Kosher Dining Guide

Restaurant: Fine & Shapiro **Phone Number:** (212) 877-2721
Fax: None

Address: 138 West 72nd Street (Columbus Ave. - Amsterdam Ave.)

Hechsher: Rabbi Leonard Bronstein - RESTAURANT IS OPEN 7 DAYS A WEEK

Proprietor/Manager:

Type(s) of Food: Meat - Deli

Price Range:

	Lunch	Dinner	Take out
Entrées:	$11.95-$19.95	Same	$10.95-$18.95
Desserts:	$1.50-$2.95	**Sandwiches:** $6.00-$14.15	**Platters:** $8.50-$15.45
Drinks:	$1.00-$2.50	$2.75-$3.00 (Beer)	

Food Specialties: Sandwiches, BBQ Ribs, Broiled Jumbo Rib Steak, Grills, Stews

Description: The menu is fairly extensive offering 29 entrées alone. A Complete Dinner which includes a choice of appetizer or soup, main course, dessert, choice of fountain soda, and coffee or tea can be had for $6.00 added to the price of an entrée. All entrées come with 2 side dishes. Standard selection of deli meats.

Comments: Standard deli fare with nice entrée selection.

Ambiance (Decor): The dining is casual and informal in this typical deli, with a take-out counter and sitting area. A 55 seat capacity restaurant, with both tables and booths. The tables, which are centrally located in the dining area, are dressed up with tablecloths for Friday night and the weekend.

Service: Standard

General Comments: New management took over last year.

Hours: **Sun-Sat:** 8am-10pm - RESTAURANT IS OPEN 7 DAYS A WEEK

Credit Cards Accepted: MC, Visa, AmEx, Discover

Restaurant Discount:

Borough: Manhattan
Section: Upper West Side

The Authoritative New York City Kosher Dining Guide

Restaurant: B.J.'s Bagels   *Phone Number:* (212) 769-3350
                                   Fax: (212) 769-3389
Address: 130 West 72nd Street (bet. Broadway - Columbus Ave.)

Hechsher: Tablet-K - RESTAURANT IS OPEN 7 DAYS A WEEK

Proprietor/Manager: Moshe

Type(s) of Food: Dairy - American

Price Range:

	Lunch	Dinner	Take out
Entrées:	$2.00-$8.50	$4.95-$8.50	Same - Free Local Delivery
Desserts:	$1.15-$1.40	*Bagel Sandwiches:* $ .80-$6.45 (**M-F**: 6am-11am)	
Drinks:	$ .85-$2.50	*Breakfast Specials:* $2.00-$3.50	

Food Specialties: Knishes, Quiche, Cheese Blintzes, 3 Egg Omelets, Pastries

> *Description:* A fast food eatery where everything is freshly made daily on the premises, including soups, entrées, cakes and pastries. The 18 varieties of bagels come with a choice of toppings, e.g. tuna, white fish, baked salmon, egg salad, etc. Breakfast Specials come with home fries, juice and bagel. Hot entrées include salad or soup and bagel. Large portions.

> *Comments:* A light menu for light eating. The freshness and homemade quality of the food is a nice touch.

Ambiance (Decor): There is a total capacity of 40 seats in this fast food/bakery establishment. A display counter occupies the wall to the right of the entry and is opposite an eating counter with 8 stools on the left. Tables extend to the back.

Service: Self-service or will serve large parties

General Comments: A convenient fast food eatery. Hashgacha allows the establishment to stay open Shabbos because of a non-Jewish business partner.

Hours: **Mon-Thurs:** 7am-8:30pm **Fri-Sun:** 7am-8pm
    - RESTAURANT IS OPEN 7 DAYS A WEEK

Credit Cards Not Accepted: CASH ONLY!

Restaurant Discount: Free Beverage With Any Hot Entrée

Borough: Manhattan
Section: Upper West Side

The Authoritative New York City Kosher Dining Guide

Restaurant: Gotham Kosher Grill *Phone Number:* (212) 787-8700
Fax: (212) 787-4848

Address: 127 West 72nd Street (bet. Columbus Ave. - Central Park West)

Hechsher: ב-K

Proprietor/Manager: Michael

Type(s) of Food: Meat – American, Deli

Price Range:	Lunch	Dinner	Take out
Entrées:	$7.99-$9.50	Same	Same – Delivery Available
Desserts:	$1.50-$3.59	*Sandwiches:* $4.99-$7.95	*Kid's Meal:* $5.50
Drinks:	$1-$3.50	*Grilled Burgers:* $2.25-$6.99	

Food Specialties: Burgers, Fried Chicken, Sandwiches, Salads, BBQ Chicken Wings

Description: Focused fast food menu summed up pretty well under "Food Specialties." The fried chicken is sold by the piece in boxes (3 pieces), buckets (5 pieces), or barrels (9, 15 or 21 pieces), as are the Chicken Nuggets (6, 9, or 20 pieces) and the BBQ Chicken Wings (5 pieces). Sandwiches include deli, grills, or fish.

Comments: A menu a kid of any age could appreciate, but especially the younger ones. A limited menu packed with popular items.

Ambiance (Decor): The red and white color scheme looks fresh and clean in this spacious eatery. Seating for 70 in booths, recalling the soda shops of a bygone, era. Tiled floors, laminate topped tables and vinyl booths invite both the younger crowd and the young at heart.

Service: Self-service

General Comments: Recently opened, this restaurant offers fast food in an attractive setting. Proximity to Central Park offers picnic possibilities.

Hours: **Sun-Thurs:** 12am-10pm
Fri: 12am-2 hrs before Shabbos (Winter Closed)
Sat: 1 hr after Shabbos till ? (Call for closing time)

Credit Cards Accepted: MC, Visa

Restaurant Discount:

Borough: Manhattan
Section: Upper West Side

The Authoritative New York City Kosher Dining Guide

Restaurant: Joseph's Café **Phone Number:** (212) 595-5004
Fax: (212) 721-1943

Address: 50 West 72nd Street (bet. Columbus Ave. - Central Park West)

Hechsher: The Midtown Board of Kashrus

Proprietor/Manager:

Type(s) of Food: Dairy, Vegetarian - Middle Eastern, Italian, American, Chinese, Mexican

Price Range:	Lunch	Dinner	Take out
Entrées:	$6.50-$16.95	Some prices higher	Same
Desserts:	$1.25-$3.85	but same range	Delivery Available
Drinks:	$ .85-$2.75	**Dinner Specials:** $12.95 Mon-Thur 3pm-Close	

Food Specialties: Brick Oven Pizza, Salads, Fish, Pasta, Sandwiches

Description: One hardly knows where to begin. A wide array of salads includes Mesclun & Endive Salad, Greek Salad, Salad Nicoise, and Grilled Blackened Tofu served over Caesar Salad, to name a few. For entrées your choices span the world from a Babaganoush Platter, Cajun Salmon, Grilled Spinach Almondine, Pepper Steak, Veggie Chicken or Veggie Beef Fajitas, Pizzas (23 toppings) and many pastas. The extensive vegetarian menu has a Rubin Sandwich (vegetarian corned beef with lettuce & tomato, sauerkraut, smothered in grilled onions, special sauce and melted cheese!) or the U.S. Grade A Vegetarian Steak. We haven't even touched on the many desserts!

Comments: A large and diverse menu with something for just about everyone. The Dinner Specials offer a 3 course meal which includes soup, entrée (19 choices), dessert (6 choices) and soft drink or coffee. $2.00 additional allows you to order fish, which is $14-$17 alone à la carte!

Ambiance (Decor): This is mid-size restaurant with seating for 70 people. Informal, relaxed atmosphere, suitable for social entertaining in a casual café setting.

Service: Friendly and responsive, the owner aims to please and actively participates in hosting his customers

General Comments: Very popular, and a good value: reasonably satisfying cuisine.

Hours: **Mon-Thurs:** 7am-10:30pm **Fri:** 7am-3pm
Sat: 8pm-1:30am **Sun:** 8am-10:30pm

Credit Cards Not Accepted: CASH ONLY!

Restaurant Discount:

Borough: Manhattan
Section: Upper West Side

The Authoritative New York City Kosher Dining Guide

Restaurant: Esti Hana Oriental Noodle Shop   *Phone Number:* (212) 501-0393
         & Sushi Bar   *Fax:* (212) 501-0458
Address: 221 West 79ᵗʰ Street (bet. Broadway - Amsterdam Ave.)

Hechsher: Ɔ-K (Glatt Kosher, Masgiach Temidi)

Proprietor/Manager:

Type(s) of Food: Meat - Japanese, Chinese

Price Range:	*Lunch*	*Dinner*	*Take out*
Entrées:	$16.00-$23.00	Same	Same - Delivery Available
Desserts:	$3.00-$5.00	*Lunch Specials:* $9.95, $13.50 (Bento Box)	
Drinks:	$1.75-$2.00		

Food Specialties: Sushi, House Specials, Chinese, Fish Dishes

> *Description:* A menu that encompasses both Japanese and Chinese favorites, often influenced by the chef's original touches. An example of this is the egg drop soup that contains corn kernels that impart an unexpected sweetness. The sushi is good. The Gomatori (boneless chicken breast with sesame seeds in a mildly sweet sauce) and the Chi Chi Chicken (with black mushrooms, bamboo shoots, green peppers, ginger scallions & honey walnuts) were flavorful, but not hot as described on the menu.

> *Comments:* The menu changes seasonally and also at the whim of the chef, who is given much latitude. Dishes that reflect western preferences and cater to an Upper West Side clientele.

Ambiance (Decor): Recently refurbished, the enhanced setting is even more attractive and pleasant to sit in than before. Oriental trappings dot the neutral, wainscoted walls. The fish tank (not inspired by feng shui) in the back has been retained. Tables: covered with tablecloths and paper. Casual.

Service: Standard

General Comments: A pleasant and comfortable restaurant for all dining purposes.

Hours: **Mon-Thurs:** 12pm-11pm   **Fri:** 12pm-2 hrs before Shabbos
       Sat: 1 hr after Shabbos till 12:30am   **Sun:** 11am-11pm

Credit Cards Accepted: MC, Visa, Diners Club

Restaurant Discount: 10% With Cash Only!

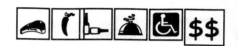

The Authoritative New York City Kosher Dining Guide

Restaurant: Polanco

Phone Number: (212) 799-1434

Fax: None

Address: 502 Amsterdam Avenue (bet. 84th St. - 85th St.)

Hechsher: OK Labs (Mashgiach Temidi, Glatt Kosher)

Proprietor/Manager: Elad Snir & Ranee Remone

Type(s) of Food: Meat - Mexican

Price Range:

	Lunch	*Dinner*	*Take out*
Entrées:	$11.96-$18.95	Same	Same – Delivery Avail. ($10 Min.)
Desserts:	$3.45-$3.95	*Combo Platters:* $10.45-$20	
Drinks:	$1.00-$2.25	Liquor License Pending	

Food Specialties: Burrito Tampico, Pollo con Mole, Pollo Guadalajara, al Mango

Description: Mexican menu featuring a variety of burritos, enchilades, tacos, tostadas, tamales, fajitas, etc. Corn tortillas, either soft or hard characterize most of these dishes. Then you have the various chicken or beef entrées accompanied by different combinations of vegetables, legumes (refried beans, black beans), and Mexican rice.

Comments: Mexican food that is toned down to accommodate Jewish palates. Food is not bad, though not always authentic. Be sure to specify desired doneness of meat, though it may not arrive as requested.

Ambiance (Decor): A nice place to eat with a pleasant attractive setting. When full, the room can get a bit cozy. Mexican terra Cotta tiles cover the floor, white washed walls decorated with rustic brick arches and Spanish lamps invoke the Mexican theme. The attractive menus likewise reflect the earth tones of the terra cotta. Seating indoors accommodates 42. Outside there is seating for 6. Casual.

Service: Quite helpful and accommodating Mexican waiters

General Comments: Finally, a kosher Mexican restaurant! Pleasant eatery.

Hours: Sun: 11am-11pm **Mon-Thurs:** 12pm-11pm **Fri:** 11am-3pm
Sat: 1 hr after Shabbos till 1am

Credit Cards Accepted: MC, Visa, AmEx, Discover ($15.00 Min. Charge)

Restaurant Discount: 10% Off

Borough: Manhattan
Section: Upper West Side

The Authoritative New York City Kosher Dining Guide

Restaurant: Deli Kasbah   **Phone Number:** (212) 496-1500
Fax: None

Address: 251 West 85th Street (bet. Broadway - West End Ave.)

Hechsher: OK Labs (Glatt Kosher, Mashgiach Temidi, Bodek Vegetables)

Proprietor/Manager: David Dery

Type(s) of Food: Meat - Israeli, Moroccan, Turkish

Price Range: **Lunch**   **Dinner**   **Take out**
  Entrées: $10.50-$24.50   Same   Same - Delivery Available
  Desserts: $2.95-$4.00   **Sandwiches:** $5.75-$11.50 (Sm) $7.50-$13.50 (Lg)
  Drinks: $1.00-$3.50   **Grilled Open Sandwiches:** $11.50-$14.50

Food Specialties: Deli, Shish Kabob, BBQ Ribs, Grill, Shawarma, Rib-Eye Steak

> **Description:** Expanded entrée selection: Texas BBQ Ribs, Deli, Char-grilled
> Steaks, Marinated and Grilled Chicken and Steak; Lamb Toledo, Breast
> of Chicken in Cream Sauce, Jerusalem Mixed Grill and Shish Kebob.
> Salads include Babaganoush, "Moroccan Knish," Falafel, Chummus and
> Moroccan Cigars, etc. Five dessert choices round off the menu.

> **Comments:** The food is unremarkable. We ordered Shish Kebob, which was
> somewhat tough and dry. The vegetable soup however was flavorful and
> appeared to be freshly made. The corned beef sandwich was fattier than
> I would have liked and came in what seems to be the standard deli
> sandwich mode: packed high in the middle and sparsely at the ends.

Ambiance (Decor): A spacious room with two levels of seating, a few steps apart.
An extinct bar is in the back and a deli counter is by the entry. Casual, for
family dining. It is hard to ignore Rabbi Schneerson z"l who appears just about
everywhere you turn: at the entry, on the walls, and on the televisions sets
giving drushas. Tables with glass tops, accommodating 80.

Service: Friendly and accommodating.

General Comments: Entry requires negotiating stairs. Despite the otherwise pleasant,
informal ambiance, there is an inescapable feeling "the Rebbe" is watching you.

Hours: **Mon-Thurs:** 12pm-10:45pm   **Friday Closed**
        Sat: 1 hr after Shabbos till 12pm (Winter Only!)   **Sun:** 12am-11pm

Credit Cards Accepted: MC, Visa, Discover, Diner's Club

Restaurant Discount: 15% Off

Borough: Manhattan
Section: Upper West Side

 **$$**

The Authoritative New York City Kosher Dining Guide

Restaurant: China Shalom II

Phone Number: (212) 662-9676
Fax: (212) 663-1321

Address: 686 Columbus Avenue (bet. W. 93rd St. - W. 94th St.)

Hechsher: ⊃-K (Glatt Kosher - Mashgiach Temidi)

Proprietor/Manager:

Type(s) of Food: Meat - Chinese

Price Range: *Lunch* (Noon-3:00pm)   *Dinner*   *Take out*
  Entrées: $8.50 (Special) $13.95-$20.95 $8(L)-$20 Free Manh Del.
  Desserts: $2.95-$5.25   *Peking Duck:* $44, $23/half *Child Menu:* $9
  Drinks: $1.25-$2.25, $3/gl (Wine), $4.50-$6 (Mix Drinks), $3-$3.50 (Beer)

Food Specialties: Peking Duck, Crispy Whole Sea Bass, Asparagus w/Rib Steak

> *Description:* Menu has a nice selection of traditional Chinese entrée favorites
> featuring: Duck (7 selections), Chicken, Veal, Steak and Beef; Fish, and
> Vegetarian (13 items). The Diet menu ($12.95-$15.75) features steamed
> entrées that are salt free made without oil or cornstarch. Child's menu
> (up to12 yrs). There are no family dinners. Add $7 to the price of an
> entrée for a full dinner. Average sized portions. Dinner minimum: $10.

> *Comments:* We ordered the White Chicken w/ Cashew Nuts in White Garlic
> Sauce and the Sizzling Garlic Steak. The food is fine, but not
> spectacular. Nothing I ate inspired me to think that I should make it a
> point to come back, but no major complaints either.

Ambiance (Decor): The decoration is minimal, but pleasant enough. White walls
offset the green carpeting and tablecloths with pink top cloths. Hand painted
Chinese prints adorn the walls. Accommodation for 72 people inside and
sidewalk dining for 28 people weather permitting. With simple elegance, it
manages to exude a comfortable atmosphere for casual & relaxed eating.

Service: Service is somewhat slow and unresponsive, but not unfriendly

General Comments: A nice place to eat if you're in the area.

Hours: **Mon-Thurs:** 12pm-11pm   **Friday Closed**
  Sat: 1 hr after Shabbos till 1am   **Sun:** 1pm-11pm

Credit Cards Accepted: MC, Visa (Minimum Charge $15.00)

Restaurant Discount: 10% Off Students Only With Minimum $100 Order

Borough: Manhattan
Section: Washington Heights

The Authoritative New York City Kosher Dining Guide

Restaurant: Deli Kasbah (Yeshiva University)   *Phone Number:* (212) 568-4600
Fax: None
Address: 2553 Amsterdam Avenue (bet. W. 186th St. - W. 187th St.)

Hechsher: ב - K (Glatt Kosher, Mashgiach Temidi)

Proprietor/Manager: David Dery

Type(s) of Food: American, Middle Eastern, Deli

Price Range:	*Lunch*	*Dinner*	*Take out*
Entrées:	$1.50-$13.50	Same	Same
Desserts:	$None		
Drinks:	$1.00-$1.25		

Food Specialties: American BBQ, Steaks, Grill, Deli

Description: Deli Sandwiches, steaks, adequate portions

Comments: Moderately priced and filling.

Ambiance (Decor): Small (about 12 tables), mostly does a take out business serving the Yeshiva's students. American contemporary decor.

Service: Self-serve

General Comments: Fast food for yeshiva students and visitors to the Yeshiva's museum, as the university is directly across the street.

Hours: **Sun-Thurs:** 11am-10pm   **Friday Closed   Saturday Closed**

Credit Cards Accepted: MC, Visa, Discover

Restaurant Discount:

The Authoritative New York City Kosher Dining Guide

Upper West Side:

Pizza Cave   · *Tel:* (212) 874-3700
218 West 72nd Street
(bet. Broadway - West End Ave.)
The Midtown Board of Kashrut

Café Roma Pizzeria   *Tel:* (212) 875-8972
175 West 90th Street
(bet. Columbus Ave. - Amsterdam Ave.)
The Midtown Board of Kashrut
also Rabbi Avraham Marmorstein

Café Viva Pizza & Pasta   *Tel:* (212) 663-8482
2578 Broadway (cor. 97th St.)
Rabbi Yacov Spivak
- RESTAURANT IS OPEN 7 DAYS A WEEK

Washington Heights:

Time Out Pizza   *Tel:* (212) 923-1180
2549 Amsterdam Avenue
(Nr. Yeshiva University)
Khal Adath Jeshurun

Upper East Side

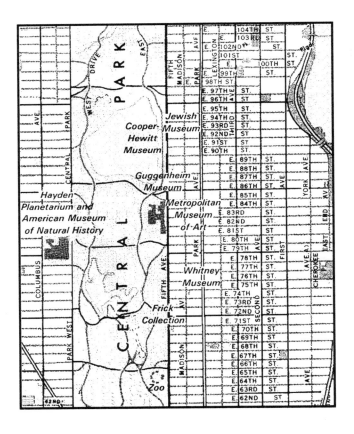

Borough: Manhattan
Section: Upper East Side

The Authoritative New York City Kosher Dining Guide

Restaurant: Glatt China

Phone Number: (212) 396-2600
Fax: (212) 570-6018

Address: 1363 First Avenue (bet. E. 73rd St. - E. 74th St.)

Hechsher: OU (Glatt Kosher, Chassidishe Shechita)

Proprietor/Manager: Yaacov, David

Type(s) of Food: Meat – Chinese, Sushi

Price Range:	*Lunch*	*Dinner*	*Take Out*
Entrées:	$6.00-$12.00	Same	Same – Free Local Delivery
Desserts:	$2.50		
Drinks:	$1.00-$1.50	MENU IS NOT COMPLETED AT THIS TIME	

Food Specialties: Mei Fun, Chow Fun, Kung Po Chicken, Sushi, Maki, Tamaki

Description: Although there is no printed menu at this time, one can infer from the menu of Glatt China Express, the precursor to this restaurant, that traditional Cantonese, Szechuan and Hunan dishes will figure into the new menu. They will diverge from the previous menu with the introduction of Sushi here. A full Sushi menu is planned.

Comments: The newest kosher Chinese/Japanese combo in NYC, will it also be the best? Will it survive its perilous first year? Check our web site during the coming year for a review or leave your impressions.

Ambiance (Decor): Handmade furniture from Thailand, woodwork and shoji fretwork, suggest an Oriental theme, but are merely backdrops for two large paintings of Israeli landscapes, one of Bethlehem and the other of Kever David. 46 seats will accommodate diners at tables covered with tablecloths, and possibly sporting candles and fresh flowers. Expect a relaxed atmosphere in the semi-formal setting. This new restaurant is, at this writing, poised to open soon.

Service: Standard

General Comments: The Upper East Side's 1st excursion into the kosher Far East!

Hours: **Sun-Thurs:** 9am-11pm **Fri:** 9am-2pm **Sat:** 1 hr after Shabbos till 1am

Credit Cards Accepted: MC, Visa, AmEx

Restaurant Discount: 10% Off

Borough: Manhattan
Section: Upper West Side

The Authoritative New York City Kosher Dining Guide

Restaurant: 1st on 1st

Phone Number: (212) 570-2800
Fax: (212) 570-6018

Address: 1363 First Avenue (bet. E. 73rd St. - E. 74th St.)

Hechsher: OU (Glatt Kosher, Chassidishe Shechita)

Proprietor/Manager: David, Yaacov

Type(s) of Food: Meat – Middle Eastern, American, Deli (soon)

Price Range:

	Lunch	*Dinner*	*Take out*
Entrées:	$5.95-$13.50	Same	Same – Free Local Delivery
Desserts:	$3.50	*Sandwiches:* $3.50 (Cold)- $7.95 (Hot)	
Drinks:	$1.00-$1.50		

Food Specialties: Shawarma, Kebobs, Shnitzel, Chirping Chicken, Salads, Falafel

Description: Chirping Chicken, you ask? It's chirping, because that's what they call the marinade. The chicken is marinated and then grilled. The rest of the menu is that of an Israeli steakia and is still evolving. I would imagine other chirping critters are on their way. Already offered are 6 soups, 11 salads, 12 appetizers and an indefinite number of fresh fish selections. Free Salad Bar. Deli sandwiches are planned in the future.

Comments: Nice to see a new, moderately priced kosher meat restaurant on the Upper East Side. As it turns out, Chirping Chicken is a West Coast chain and this is its first East Coast entré.

Ambiance (Decor): A glass partition separates the dining area from the food preparation area/ take-out display counter. This means a smoke free environment for a maximum of 60 diners. Handicapped must be able to maneuver a single step above street level to enter restaurant.

Service: Standard

General Comments: So new, this restaurant is still in the throes of becoming.

Hours: **Sun-Thurs:** 9am-11pm **Fri:** 9am-2pm **Sat:** 1 hr after Shabbos till 1am

Credit Cards Accepted: MC, Visa, AmEx

Restaurant Discount: 10% Off

Borough: Manhattan
Section: Upper East Side

The Authoritative New York City Kosher Dining Guide

Restaurant: Bisseleh Classic

Phone Number: (212) 717-2333
Fax: (212) 639-1403

Address: 1435 Second Avenue (bet. E. 74ᵗʰ St. - E. 75ᵗʰ St.)

Hechsher: Vaad Hakashrus Le'Mehadrin (Chalov Yisroel, Pas Yisroel)

Proprietor/Manager: Ovad

Type(s) of Food: Dairy - Israeli, Yemenite

Price Range:
	Lunch	*Dinner*	*Take out*
Entrées:	$8.00-$18.00	Same	Same
Desserts:	$4.75		Delivery Available
Drinks:	$1.50-$4.00		

Food Specialties: Bisseleh, Malawah, Ftuts, Borekas, Pizza, Fish, Pasta, Salads

> *Description:* Bisseleh (sesame topped dough with different fillings), Malawah (served with tomato sauce, Bissaleh shug and hard boiled egg), Ftuts (w/ shug & tomato sauce), Bissaleh Pizza (a small pie with your choice of toppings), Turkish, Greek, Yemenite, and Israeli salads; and five soups (including French Onion Soup) are offered. Choice of 7 coffees.

> *Comments:* Everything is ordered separately. The soups are good. I prefer the salads, which tend to be fresh and are served in respectable portions. The Greek Salad's feta cheese is usually very fresh and mild. The combination salads are fine. The dough preparations lose their novelty and become cumbersome. Small sizes are similar to large, save the cost.

Ambiance (Decor): Conforms to the uptown location by offering a sophisticated, semi-formal ambiance. Indoors seats 60, plus sidewalk dining when appropriate. Tables are covered with tablecloths and topped with fresh flowers. Suitable for social entertaining and family meals (especially Sunday). Relaxed.

Service: Standard

General Comments: Unique menu and attractive atmosphere are inviting. One partner from the split duo that opened the original Brooklyn Bissaleh.

Hours: **Sun-Thurs:** 10am-12am **Friday Closed** **Sat:** 1 hr after Shabbos till 2am

Credit Cards Accepted: MC, Visa

Restaurant Discount:

Borough: Manhattan
Section: Upper East Side

The Authoritative New York City Kosher Dining Guide

Restaurant: Pita Express

Phone Number: (212) 249-1300
Fax: None

Address: 1470 Second Avenue (cor. E. 77th St.)

Hechsher: Avraham Shlomo Fishelis

Proprietor/Manager: Yossi

Type(s) of Food: Meat - Middle Eastern

Price Range:

	Lunch	Dinner	Take out
Entrées:	$8.00-$15.95	Same	Same
Desserts:	$2.50		Free Local Delivery
Drinks:	$1.00-$1.50	*Sandwiches:* $3.00-$6.00	

Food Specialties: Cous-cous, Shish Kebob, Rib Steak, Moroccan Fish, Shawarma

Description: The menu consists of Middle Eastern favorites. Eleven salads are offered by the pound. Seven soups include: Vegetable, Split Pea, Lentil, Bean, Chicken Noodle, Yemenite style meat soup, as well as a soup of the day. House Specials feature Baked Chicken, Fish and Chips, Moroccan Cigars, Kibbeh, among others. Entrées feature Baby Lamb Chops, Chicken, Beef and/or Koufta Kebob, Falafel Plate, and Burgers, which can be bought as sandwiches in a pita as well.

Comments: The selections offer a nice variety of different foods, to please most palates.

Ambiance (Decor): This fast food establishment is only slightly smaller than its sister restaurant in Stuyvesant Town, seating 35. Modern, with no distinguishing decor. Casual.

Service: Standard

General Comments: The only one in the chain that opens Motzei Shabbos.

Hours: **Sun-Thurs:** 10am-12am **Fri:** 10am-1 hr before Shabbos
Sat: Opens 1 hr after Shabbos till 1am

Credit Cards Not Accepted: CASH ONLY!

Restaurant Discount: 10% off For Orders Over $10

Borough: Manhattan
Section: Upper East Side

| 🥛 | ⌀ | 🍷 | **$$$$** |

The Authoritative New York City Kosher Dining Guide

Restaurant: Va Bene
Phone Number: (212) 517-4448
Fax: (212) 517-2258
Address: 1589 Second Avenue (bet. E. 82nd St. - E. 83rd St.)

Hechsher: OU (Chalov Yisroel)

Proprietor/Manager: Giuseppe Lattanzi

Type(s) of Food: Dairy - Italian

Price Range:	Lunch	Dinner	Sunday Brunch:
Entrées:	$9.95-16.95	$15.95-$25.95	$19.95 (Prix Fix) bet. 2pm-3pm
Desserts:	$4.95	$6.95	**Take out:** Same
Drinks:	$2.75-$7.00	$6 (Mixed Drinks)	$5.95/glass (House Wine)

Food Specialties: Antipasti, Soups, Pasta, Fish, Desserts, Daily Specials

Description: The mainly homemade pasta and fish dishes are artfully prepared, well presented, and pleasing to the palate. The Crostino Romano (baked mozzarella, mushrooms, anchovies and capers between pieces of toast, topped with Marsala sauce) had just the right blend of textures and flavors. The Carpaccio caldo di tonno (thinly sliced fresh tuna topped with hot sautéed mushrooms) is delicate. The Tuna Grill, with shitaki mushrooms, scalloped potatoes, and carrots, was excellent. The Salmone alla livornese (fresh salmon sautéed with black olives, capers, onion, white wine and tomato sauce) was light, flaky, and succulent. Dessert: The Tirami-su is deliciously light and not too sweet.

Comments: A Roman by birth, the owner comes from a family of restaurateurs, and takes great pride in his restaurant. With a decidedly Italian flair, Kosher Italian dining is taken to a new and delicious level.

Ambiance (Decor): Mediterranean flavor; attractive, elegant, seats 80, with soft lighting, burgundy wood, and walls in terra cotta tones. Formal table settings enhanced with tablecloths, flowers and candle light create an atmosphere of old world charm, with a contemporary attitude. Rear alcove affords greater privacy.

Service: White jacketed waiters graciously & attentively serve you promptly

General Comments: The owner has managed to transplant a bit of Rome to New York City. A handsome and well run restaurant to enjoy without the kids. It offers fine dining equally suited for business and social entertaining.

Hours: **Mon-Thurs: Lunch:** 12pm-3pm (Winter) 11am-3pm (Summer)
Dinner: 5pm-10:30pm **Friday Closed**
Sat: 1 hr after Shabbos till 12:30am (Winter Only) **Sun:** 2pm-10pm

Credit Cards Accepted: AmEx

Restaurant Discount: One Time 10% Off Dinner on Mon., Tues., or Wed.

Borough: Manhattan
Section: Upper East Side

The Authoritative New York City Kosher Dining Guide

Restaurant: Domani *Phone Number:* (212) 717-7575
Fax: Same

Address: 1590 First Avenue (bet. 82nd St. - 83rd St.)

Hechsher: OK Labs (Glatt Kosher)

Proprietor/Manager: Alex

Type(s) of Food: Meat - Italian

Price Range: *Lunch*   *Dinner*   *Take out*
   Entrées: Closed $16.95-$31.95   None
   Desserts: $6.95
   Drinks: $2.00-$3.50, $6/gl, $18-$25/btl (Wine), $5-$5.50 (Beer)

Food Specialties: Pasta Fresca, Grills, Fresh Fish, Homemade Breads

> *Description:* An authentic Italian menu that makes up for its brevity by offering dishes that are uncommonly good (e.g. Portabella Marinati All'Italiana served warm). Variety here means not only 3-4 choices of chicken, meat, or fish, but also a menu that keeps reinventing itself.

> *Comments:* Top quality meat, fresh homemade soups, salads, desserts, etc. Heir to the La Fontana legacy and chefs, Domani offers sophisticated cuisine prepared with care. Still in the throes of its debut, the menu is being defined and refined, but, the commitment to great food is evident. The Red Snapper and Halibut served in white wine sauce was superb: moist, flaky, and very fresh. Its delicate sauce had much depth. The veal Marsala was a winner. Don't miss the tiramisu for dessert.

Ambiance (Decor): Domani is triple the size of La Fontana. The first room holds 36, and is cozy, with exposed brick, and a bar in the rear. A second, more private room is a show of Italian carpentry and has as its focal point a faux fireplace. A recent expansion has added 30 seats in a third, Roman style room with columns. Upscale and trendy. Restrooms in the basement.

Service: Accommodating and attentive, professional with warmth

General Comments: The La Fontana phoenix has risen. Reserve for 6pm-8pm.

Hours: **Mon-Thurs:** 5pm-11pm   **Friday Closed**
     Sat: 1 hr after Shabbos till 12pm (kitchen closes)   **Sun:** 3:30pm-10:30pm

Credit Cards Accepted: MC, Visa, AmEx

Restaurant Discount:

The Restaurant of the Month Club

cordially invites

*you to an evening of fine kosher dining at some of
the best kosher restaurants the world has to offer.
This is an excellent opportunity to be exposed
to new and exciting types of cuisine while
getting the benefit of a month long prise fixe special.*

Log on to

www.diningkosher.com
for details each month!

Borough: Manhattan

Section: Upper East Side

The Authoritative New York City Kosher Dining Guide

Restaurant: Tevere 84

Phone Number: (212) 744-0210

Fax: (212) 249-7504

Address: 155 East 84th Street (bet. Lexington Ave. - 3rd Ave.)

Hechsher: OU (Glatt Kosher)

Proprietor/Manager: Giuseppe Lattanzi

Type(s) of Food: Meat - Italian (Jewish Roman)

Price Range:	*Sunday Brunch* (bet. 2pm-3pm)	*Dinner*	*Take Out*
Entrées:	$19.95 (Prix Fix)	$15.95-$39.95	Available
Desserts:		$6.95	
Drinks:	$2.75-$7.00,	$6-$7/gl.(Mixed Drinks, Wine),	$16-$29/btl.(Wine)

Food Specialties: Homemade Pastas & Soups, Variety of Meats, Poultry & Fish

> *Description:* Fine dining inspired by the ancient Roman Jewish community. Chicken, turkey, veal, lamb, beef, and fish selections are meticulously prepared and attractively presented. The Boccette (Veal & chicken broth w/ rice) was full bodied and hearty, interlaced with bits of meat very effectively. The Minestrone all' Italiana, homemade vegetable soup, was thick with fresh vegetables. The Manzo alla griglia (grilled boneless rib eye beef steak w/ mushrooms) was large, thick, tender, juicy and made to exact specifications. The Vitello al Marsala was modified, at my request, to include a healthy topping of mushrooms, and was delicious!

> *Comments:* Concern and pride in the preparation is evident.

Ambiance (Decor): After a few steps down, you enter this small (seats 50), intimate, upscale restaurant that looks as if it was transplanted from Rome. Exposed brick, a pot belly stove (prop), and wood details create a provincial setting. Italian landscape paintings dot the walls and culminate in one wall-sized painting of Renaissance style. Together they provide a rich, colorful, and evocative backdrop to dine by. Dimly lit, the dining room with its formal table settings, linen, candles and flowers has all the elements for a warm, friendly, & romantic evening.

Service: Gracious, unhurried, and attentive

General Comments: Highly recommended for special occasions, for creating special occasions, or for fine dining any day. Located steps from Museum Mile.

Hours: **Mon-Thurs:** 5pm-10:30pm **Friday Closed**

Sat: Opens 1 hr after Shabbos till unspecified time **Sun:** 2pm-10pm

Credit Cards Accepted: AmEx

Restaurant Discount: One Time 10% Off Dinner on Mon., Tues., or Wed.

The Authoritative New York City Kosher Dining Guide

Restaurant: Galil

Phone Number: (212) 439-9886
Fax: (212) 327-4247

Address: 1252 Lexington Avenue (bet. E. 84th St. - E. 85th St.)

Hechsher: ⊃-K

Proprietor/Manager: Miriam, Jackie

Type(s) of Food: Meat - Moroccan, Israeli

Price Range:

	Lunch	*Dinner*	*Take out*
Entrées:	$12.95-$22.95	$12.95-$24.95	Same - Delivery Available
Desserts:	$ 2.95-$3.95	*Lunch Specials:* $7.45-$8.45 (11:30am-3:30pm)	
Drinks:	$1.00-$1.75	$3.50/gl (Wine, Beer) *Sandwiches:* $3.25-$6.95	

Food Specialties: Kebobs, Lamb Tajin, Veal Marrakech, Duck L'Orange, Fresh Fish

Description: A newly revised menu that is solidly grounded in the Middle
Eastern genre, with Shish Kebobs Shawarma, Cigars, Kuba, Mergez,
Falafel, etc., but makes forays into other realms with its Schnitzel w/
Mushroom, Moussaka, Beef Roti, Cornish Hen, Hamburger and Prime
Rib. Large variety of fish served grilled, as steaks or prepared whole.

Comments: The vegetable soup is generously served and is quite good.
Substantial portions in general. Not gourmet, but filling.

Ambiance (Decor): This Multi-level, mid-size restaurant has been spruced up. One
must walk up a few stairs to enter the restaurant where you are greeted by
wooden tables either without (lunchtime) or with (dinner) tablecloths. The
service counter that leads to the kitchen in the rear is next. Further back, a few
more stairs take you to another dining room (used as needed) which is
somewhat more formal with tablecloths, flowers at times and candles. 75 seats.

Service: The service is friendly and accommodating, very slow during lunch

General Comments: Convenient to 86th St., Central Park, and Museum Row it is a
good family restaurant possibility, and suitable as well for a casual date.

Hours: **Mon-Thurs:** 11:30am-11:30pm   **Fri:** 11:30am-2 hrs before Shabbos
Sat: Opens 2 hrs after Shabbos till 1am (Winter Only)

Credit Cards Accepted: MC, Visa, AmEx, Diners Club

Restaurant Discount: 10% Off

Borough: Manhattan
Section: Upper East Side

The Authoritative New York City Kosher Dining Guide

Restaurant: Pastrami Queen

Phone Number: (212) 828-0007
Fax: (212) 996-6658

Address: 1269 Lexington Avenue (bet. E. 85th St. - E. 86th St.)

Hechsher: Rabbi Bronstein - RESTAURANT IS OPEN SEVEN DAYS A WEEK

Proprietor/Manager: Gary

Type(s) of Food: Meat - Deli

Price Range:	*Lunch*	*Dinner*	*Take out*
Entrées:	$9.95-$18.95	Same	Same – Free Local Delivery
Desserts:	$1.95-$3.50	*Sandwiches:*	$4.50-$8.25 (Reg), $8-$11 (Combo)
Drinks:	$ .95-$1.50	$2.55-$2.95 (Beer), $3.25/gl (Wine)	

Food Specialties: Deli Sandwiches, Chicken Fricassee, Hungarian Goulash, Kebobs

> *Description:* Traditional deli menu with an occasional inclusion of items not so traditional such as Shish Kebob, Pasta Primavera, and Lemon Chicken. Breakfast Specials (9am-11am) are $2.45-$4.95 (sandwich) or $4.95-$6.95 (plate) served with French fries, coffee or tea. The Kiddie Kingdom (for children under 10 years) ranges $4.50-$5.45 including entrée, fries, and fountain soda.

> *Comments:* A menu packed with traditional favorites.

Ambiance (Decor): Dining on two floors: the first floor offers several tables in the rear while a second floor dining area in the form of a u-shaped balcony overlooks from above. Seating can accommodate 50.

Service: Standard

General Comments: Relocated from Queens and previously known as Pastami King, this new restaurant is off and running. The centerpiece is their pastrami which is still cured in house by the traditional method developed when the establishment was in Williamsburg (before Manhattan or Queens). The texture of the meat is much different from the standard Hebrew National issue, being softer and a bit saltier. Customer reaction has been good.

Hours: **Sun-Thurs:** 9am-10pm   **Fri-Sat:** 9am-12pm
-RESTAURANT IS OPEN SEVEN DAYS A WEEK

Credit Cards Accepted: MC, Visa, AmEx

Restaurant Discount:

213

Borough: Manhattan
Section: Upper East Side

The Authoritative New York City Kosher Dining Guide

Restaurant: Siegel's Kosher Delicatessen   *Phone Number:* (212) 288-3632
Fax: None

Address: 1646 Second Avenue (bet. E. 85th St. - E. 86th St.)

Hechsher: Rabbi Leonard Bronstein - RESTAURANT IS OPEN 7 DAYS A WEEK

Proprietor/Manager: Jeffrey (Manager)

Type(s) of Food: Meat - Deli

Price Range:	*Lunch*	*Dinner*	*Take out*
Entrées:	$9.95-$17.45	Same	Same - Free Local Delivery
Desserts:	$1.50-$3..95	*Sandwiches:*	$6.95-$8.95
Drinks:	$ .95-1.50		

Food Specialties: Deli Sandwiches & Platters, Prime Rib Steak

Description: All the standard sandwiches and traditional cooked Jewish fare.

Comments: What you would expect in the typical deli menu.

Ambiance (Decor): Small, with 30 seats in a standard deli set-up. Display counter up front.

Service: Standard

General Comments: Not personally familiar with this one, I can only tell you they seem constantly busy when you call them.

Hours: **Mon-Thurs:** 11am-10pm   **Fri-Sat:** 10am-10pm
- RESTAURANT IS OPEN 7 DAYS A WEEK

Credit Cards Accepted: MC, Visa, AmEx, Discover, Diners Club

Restaurant Discount:

Borough: Manhattan
Section: Upper East Side

The Authoritative New York City Kosher Dining Guide

Restaurant: Phil's Kosher Delicatessen   ***Phone Number:*** (212) 427-5000
Fax: (212) 427-5293

Address: 435 East 86ᵗʰ Street (bet. 1ˢᵗ Ave. - York Ave.)

Hechsher: Rabbi Israel Steinberg - RESTAURANT IS OPEN 7 DAYS A WEEK

Proprietor/Manager: Philip, Bob

Type(s) of Food: Meat - Deli

Price Range:	***Lunch***	***Dinner***	***Take out***
Entrées:	$6.95-$17.95	Same	Same (Some items less) Del. Avail.
Desserts:	$2.25-$3.95	***Deli Sandwiches:*** $7.25-$12.95 (Hot Open)	
Drinks:	$ .75-$1.50	***Burgers:*** $6-$8 ***Seniors Early Bird:*** $10% Off	

Food Specialties: Deli Sandwiches, Burgers, Salads, Omelets, Stuffed Cabbage

> ***Description:*** The menu proclaims "traditional cuisine of eastern European heritage...in the healthiest manner possible...fresh delicious food, prepared with 100% natural ingredients in a clean, friendly environment." This translates as deli fare that includes homemade soups (3), homemade knishes (3), the usual hot deli entrées, sandwiches, and platters; Salads (5), Omelets, and burgers (beef, turkey, and homemade veggie). The Early Bird Special is offered for seniors 65+ daily from 4pm-7pm.

> ***Comments:*** The menu offers no surprises, but looks promising.

Ambiance (Decor): A modern rendition of the typical traditional deli using a stainless steel and glass vocabulary. Seating for 50.

Service: Standard

General Comments: Newly opened during the past year, the restaurant benefits from its owners 25 years of previous deli experience.

Hours: **Sun-Sat:** 9:30am-10pm - RESTAURANT IS OPEN 7 DAYS A WEEK

Credit Cards Accepted: MC, Visa, AmEx

Restaurant Discount:

Borough: Manhattan
Section: Upper East Side

The Authoritative New York City Kosher Dining Guide

Restaurant: Café Weissman (Jewish Museum)   *Phone Number:* (212) 423-3307
                                              Fax: (212) 423-0566
Address: 1109 Fifth Avenue (cor. E. 92nd St.)

Hechsher: Star-K - (Glatt Kosher, Mashgiach Temidi)

Proprietor/Manager:

Type(s) of Food: Meat - Eclectic

Price Range: **Lunch**   **Dinner**   **Take out**
  Entrées: $7.75-$9.25   Same   None
  Desserts: $1.75-$4.85   *Sandwiches:* $6.25-$8.25
  Drinks: $1.50-$2.00   *Soups:* $4.50   *Box Lunch:* $14.00-$15.00

Food Specialties: Salmon en Croute, Grilled Chicken Breast Julienne, Salade Niçoise

> *Description:* Menus change approximately every three months and are
> coordinated with the changing museum exhibits. Currently, the museum
> is having a show of Soutine's paintings, hence the French cuisine. Some
> soups are Potage de Legumes au Vermicelle, Watercress and French
> Onion. Sandwiches vary from Turkey wrap to egg salad on croissant.
> For groups, Box Lunches must be ordered at least 4 days in advance and
> contain a sandwich, chips, pasta salad, dessert and soft drink or coffee.

> *Comments:* A small, sophisticated menu of tempting choices.

Ambiance (Decor): This museum cafe accommodates 70-75 diners. Diners enter
through glass doors that open to a modern space with Swedish wood tables and
cushioned wood chairs. A glass display showcases the café's offerings. Stained
glass "windows" add color, as do the artificial flowers that top off mirrors on
the walls. An attractive cafeteria setting that is informal.

Service: Self-serve

General Comments: Museum & good food, how better to spend an afternoon!

Hours: Sun-Mon, Wed-Thurs: 11am-5:30pm   **Tues:** 11am-7:30pm
         Friday Closed   Saturday Closed

*Credit Cards **Not** Accepted:* CASH & TRAVELER'S CHECKS ONLY!

Restaurant Discount:

The Authoritative New York City Kosher Dining Guide

Pizza Cave   *Tel:* (212) 987-9130

1376 Lexington Avenue
(bet. E. 90th St. - E. 91st St.)
The Midtown Board of Kashrut

Riverdale

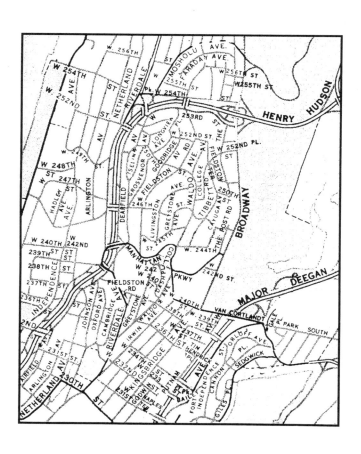

Borough: Bronx
Section: Kingsbridge

The Authoritative New York City Kosher Dining Guide

Restaurant: Loeser's Kosher Deli   *Phone Number:* (718) 601-6665
Fax: (718) 884-7015
Address: 214 West 231ˢᵗ Street (bet. Broadway - Godwin Terr.)

Hechsher: NO HECHSHER - RESTAURANT IS OPEN 7 DAYS A WEEK

Proprietor/Manager: Freddy

Type(s) of Food: Meat - Deli

Price Range: *Lunch*   *Dinner*   *Take out*
    Entrées: $8.95-$9.95   Same   Same – Delivery Available ($50 Min)
    Desserts: None   *Deli Sandwiches:* $5.10-$6.50
    Drinks: $1.00-$1.25   *Knishes:* $2.00-$3.95   *Omelets:* $6.95-$8.95

Food Specialties: Stuffed Cabbage, Homemade Knishes, Deli Sandwiches, Omelets

   Description: Homemade knishes spanning different meat and vegetable
       possibilities. Soups are homemade, with three choices offered daily.
       Sandwiches are served on a choice of Rye Bread or Club Roll.

   Comments: Typical deli menu with no surprises.

Ambiance (Decor): Hanging salamis, laminate topped tables with seating for 30
    diners, recently replaced counter. Informal.

Service: Lone waiter

General Comments: Open since 1960 and celebrating its 39ᵗʰ anniversary, it is still
    owned and operated by the original owner. Although the restaurant finds itself
    in an area that is no longer Jewish, it retains its old fashioned Jewish
    delicatessen flavor.

Hours: **Sun-Sat:** 10am-6pm - RESTAURANT IS OPEN 7 DAYS A WEEK

Credit Cards Not Accepted: CASH ONLY!

Restaurant Discount: 10% Off

Borough: Bronx
Section: Kingsbridge

The Authoritative New York City Kosher Dining Guide

Restaurant: Mr. Bagel of Broadway   **Phone Number:** (718) 549-0408
                                          Fax: None
Address: 5672 Broadway (bet. W. 233rd – W. 234th St.)

Hechsher: Vaad Harabonim of Riverdale

Proprietor/Manager: Judy (Manager)

Type(s) of Food: Dairy - American

Price Range: **Lunch**   **Dinner**   **Take out**
  Entrées: $4.50-$5.99   Same   Same
  Desserts: $1.25
  Drinks: $ .70-$1.35

Food Specialties: Bagel Sandwiches, Pastry & Cakes, Salads, Knishes, Lasagna

  Description: Fast food a la heimishe bagel plus. Bagels with different
  toppings. The "plus" refers to items like the eggplant parmigiana, the
  vegetable lasagna, tuna salads, veggie hamburgers, etc. Bagels, pastry
  and cakes are freshly baked daily.

  Comments: There is no written menu, just order what's posted for the day.

Ambiance (Decor): 19 seats maximum in this small eatery/bakery. Undistinguished
  in appearance.

Service: Self-service

General Comments: For quick bites, it serves its purpose.

Hours: Sun-Thurs: 6am-7pm   **Fri:** 6am-1 hr before Shabbos   <u>**Saturday Closed**</u>

Credit Cards _Not_ Accepted: CASH ONLY!

Restaurant Discount:

Borough: Bronx
Section: Riverdale

 **$$**

The Authoritative New York City Kosher Dining Guide

Restaurant: River Delight
Phone Number: (718) 543-4270
Fax: (718) 543-7545
Address: 3534 Johnson Avenue (bet. W. 235ᵗʰ St. - W. 236ᵗʰ St.)

Hechsher: Vaad of Riverdale (Glatt Kosher, Mashgiach Temidi, Bishul Yisroel)

Proprietor/Manager:

Type(s) of Food: Meat - Deli, Middle Eastern

Price Range: **Lunch** (11am-3pm) **Dinner** **Take out**
    Entrées: $7.95 (Specials) $9.95-$18.95 Same – Free Local Del. ($20 Min)
    Desserts: $ Changes **Complete Dinner:** $3.95 + Entrée **Kids:** $4.95
    Drinks: $1.00-$1.95 **Sandwiches:** $6-$14 **Early Bird:** $10 (3-5:30pm)

Food Specialties: Charcoal Grills, Cous-Cous, Brisket Dinner, Kabobs, Deli, Salads

    Description: A new expanded menu maintains the deli and Middle Eastern cuisine and adds a touch of the gourmet with items like Stuffed Breast of Veal, Stuffed Capon, Turkey Medallion, London Broil, and Prime Rib Eye Steak. A new Middle Eastern brine meat marinade made with olive oil, garlic, white vinegar and a host of secret ingredients, not only improves flavor, but purportedly reduces the carcinogen threat of charbroiled meat. Everything is homemade and the portions are large. Entrées come with choice of potato, rice, vegetables or fresh salad.

    Comments: Their corned beef and pastrami sandwiches are on par with the best we've had: no fat, good texture and not stringy. The Cobb Salad (sliced, grilled chicken breast on salad) was tender, juicy, light, and flavorful, while the salad was fresh and crispy.

    Ambiance (Decor): The take out counter has been expanded usurping the space formally occupied by several tables. To the left, a narrow dining room (seats 70) is revealed through arched openings in the wall. Mahogany stained paneling and trim surround the coral colored walls, which are decorated with photos of Israel and lighted by sconces. Although the tables are covered with white tablecloths, and sometimes candles and flowers, the mood is relaxed.

Service: Pleasant, friendly, and accommodating

General Comments: The setting is casual and excellent for family dining.

Hours: **Sun-Wed:** 10am-10pm **Thurs:** 8am-10pm **Fri:** 8am-1 hr before Shabbos
    Sat: Currently closed, but when open: 1 hr after Shabbos till 1am (CALL)

Credit Cards Accepted: MC, Visa, AmEx, Diners Club

Restaurant Discount: 10% Off Dinner Excluding Sundays, Holidays, or Specials
                     when paying by cash, MC, or Visa.

The Authoritative New York City Kosher Dining Guide

Restaurant: Corner Café & Bakery

Phone Number: (718) 601-2861
Fax: (718) 548-0985

Address: 3552 Johnson Avenue (cor. W. 236th St.)

Hechsher: Vaad Harabonim of Riverdale (Cholov Yisroel in MAIN DISHES ONLY)

Proprietor/Manager: Ken & Cohava Dubin

Type(s) of Food: Dairy - Continental, Mediterranean, Eclectic

Price Range:
	Lunch	Dinner	Take out
Entrées:	$6.95-$8.95	$12.50-$19.95	Same - No Delivery Available
Desserts:	$3.00-$4.95	**Sandwiches:** $2.95-$6.95	**Salads:** $6.95-$8.95
Drinks:	$1.50-$3.00	**Breakfast:** $1.50-$5.95	**Dinner Min.:** $5 (Sun-Th)

Food Specialties: Bagel Sandwiches, Waffles, Pasta, Salads, Fish, Foccocia, Cakes

Description: A menu of light dishes, heavily Italian, but not exclusively. Nice selection of salads. The pasta dishes are homemade, fresh, and served with mixed garden vegetables. The 3 fish selections ($16.95-$19.95) come with soup or salad. The 4 Kid Korner choices ($4.95) include main course with fries, soda, and cookie. The menu selections are modified seasonally. Ice cream, desserts, and select coffees make this restaurant a good after dinner stop, as well.

Comments: The two slices of cake we sampled were not large in size, but very good. The entrées looked tempting but were not on our agenda that day.

Ambiance (Decor): This small (34 indoor seats, 24 outdoor in season), narrow black and white café has a charming arty atmosphere. Small "marble" topped tables, classic bent wood chairs and banquet seating on a black and white checkered tile floor. Potted trees at the entry guard passage to the back dining area. An exposed brick wall contrasts with an opposing white wall where framed posters of photos by Ansel Adams hang. Wall sconces provide soft, indirect lighting. Music provides the finishing touches. Casual.

Service: Standard

General Comments: There is a $5.00 Saturday night minimum per person.

Hours: Mon-Thurs: 7am-9pm **Fri:** 7am-2 or 3pm
Sat: 1 hr after Shabbos till 12am **Sun:** 8am-9pm

Credit Cards Accepted: MC, Visa, AmEx, Diners Club, Carte Blanche

Restaurant Discount:

The Authoritative New York City Kosher Dining Guide

Restaurant: Liebman's Kosher Deli   *Phone Number:* (718) 548-4534
                                                        Fax: None
Address: 552 West 235th Street (cor. Johnson Ave.)

Hechsher: NO HECHSHER - RESTAURANT IS OPEN 7 DAYS A WEEK

Proprietor/Manager:

Type(s) of Food: Meat- Deli

Price Range:	*Lunch*	*Dinner*	*Take out*
Entrées:	$5.95 (Special)	$8.95-$17.95	Same - Free Local Del. ($15 Min)
Desserts:	$2.95	*Sandwiches:* $4.95-$8.95, $12.95 (Hot Open)	
Drinks:	$ .75-$1.35	$2.50-$3.50 (Beer)	

Food Specialties: Deli, Rib Steak, Roast Turkey and Beef, Southern Fried Chicken

> *Description:* Deli sandwiches and traditional Jewish favorites such as Stuffed
> Pepper, Stuffed Cabbage, and Hungarian Goulash. The Lunch Special
> includes either Tuna or Chicken Salad with a cup of soup.

> *Comments:* A fairly complete deli menu. Some departures like Liebman's
> Mixed Grill and the Middle Eastern Specialties (falafel in a pita or
> platter, or in a combination platter consisting of falafel, techina,
> chummus, salad, & pita). Liebman's Lite selections culminate in a
> Weight Watcher's Special (roast turkey on one slice of whole wheat
> bread, health salad and cole slaw).

Ambiance (Decor): On the small side, with seating for 40-50 people, the setting is
both traditional and familiar with no distinguishing characteristics. A large
display counter dominates the front area and tables are situated in the back.

Service: Standard

General Comments: Judging by the people standing on line to get in on the Thursday
we visited, this restaurant appears to be very popular. Take-out orders were
flying out the door.

Hours: **Sun-Tues:** 8am-10pm **Wed-Sat:** 8:30am-10pm
RESTAURANT IS OPEN 7 DAYS A WEEK

Credit Cards Accepted: MC, Visa, AmEx, Diners Club, Discover, Carte Blanche

Restaurant Discount:

Borough: Bronx
Section: Riverdale

The Authoritative New York City Kosher Dining Guide

Restaurant: The Main Event   ***Phone Number:*** (718) 601-Main
                                                          Fax: (718) 601-0008
Address: 3708 Riverdale Avenue (bet. Fieldston Rd. - W. 236th St.)

Hechsher: Vaad of Riverdale (Chalov Yisroel except for the yogurt & waffles)

Proprietor/Manager: Joey Bodner / Eddie Izso

Type(s) of Food: Dairy, Vegetarian - Italian, Middle Eastern

Price Range: ***Lunch***   ***Dinner***   ***Take out***
    Entrées: $3.25-$8.00   Same   Same – Free Local Delivery
    Desserts: $1.25-$3.00   ($20 Min.)
    Drinks: $ 1.00-$1.25   ***Pita Sandwiches:*** $3.00-$4.25

Food Specialties: Pizza, Falafel, Italian, Middle Eastern

> ***Description:*** Large selection of salads, pizzas, and entrées including fish
> dishes, calzones, vegetarian and tofu entrées.

> ***Comments:*** A small restaurant with a sizable selection.

Ambiance (Decor): Seating 50-55 people, this restaurant is a modern, bright and
child proof environment. With laminated table tops, plastic molded bench
seating, and ceramic tiles (pink and blue) on walls and floor, it offers a casual
and worry free choice for family dining.

Service: Self-serve

General Comments: Bring the kids and relax.

Hours: **Mon:** 9am-8pm   **Sun, Tues-Thurs:** 11am-9pm
    Fri: 9am-2 ½ hrs before Shabbos   **Sat:** ¾ hr after Shabbos till 1am

Credit Cards Not Accepted: CASH ONLY!

Restaurant Discount:

Borough: Bronx
Section: Riverdale

The Authoritative New York City Kosher Dining Guide

Restaurant: Szechuan Garden Chinese Restaurant *Phone Number:* (718) 601-7763
Fax: None

Address: 3717 Riverdale Avenue (bet. 236th St. - 238th St.)

Hechsher: Vaad of Riverdale (Glatt Kosher)

Proprietor/Manager: Billy

Type(s) of Food: Meat - Chinese

Price Range: *Lunch* (12pm-3pm) *Dinner* *Take out*
  Entrées: $9.95 (Special) $13.00-$18.75 $12.50-$18.25- Free Local Del.
  Desserts: $2.75 *Dinner Special:* $16.95 $44 Peking Duck (for 2)
  Drinks: $1.00-$1.25 *Lunch Take-out Special* : $7.75

Food Specialties: Peacock Nest Chicken, Double Tinkling Bells, Lovers In The Star

> *Description:* An extensive menu that has just about everything you would
> want running the gamut of veal, beef, chicken, and fish (Sea Bass or
> Flounder served whole) dishes. Besides the usual favorites, however, are
> dishes that are unfamiliar, such as the Double Tinkling Bells and Lovers
> in the Star. There are five selections under "Chef's Special Diet Food"
> that features steamed selections, and six American staples for those not
> in the Chinese mood. The dinner and lunch specials include soup.

> *Comments:* The menu invites those who are familiar with Chinese food to try
> something new. I really am curious about those bells.

Ambiance (Decor): This mid-size (seats 80) pink, gray, and white restaurant has a
modern decor that is casual and family oriented. Potted trees, mirrored walls,
and gray carpeting work together to create an agreeable setting. Subdued
lighting imparts an intimate feel and helps create an atmosphere that is
conducive to conversation.

Service: Standard

General Comments: Kosher restaurants in the Bronx are few are far between, so its
especially nice to find one with so much to offer.

Hours: **Sun-Thurs:** 11:30am-9:30pm **Fri:** 12pm-3pm (till Oct. 31st ONLY)
  Sat: Opens ½ hr after Shabbos till around 10pm (After Nov.)

Credit Cards Accepted: MC, Visa

Restaurant Discount: 10% Off

Five Towns

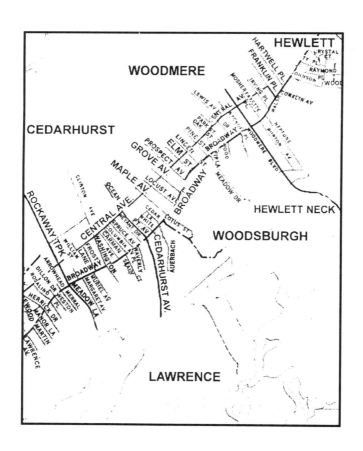

County: Nassau **(Long Island)**
Town: Lawrence

The Authoritative New York City Kosher Dining Guide

Restaurant: Epstein Bros. *Phone Number:* (516) 239-1103
Fax: (516) 239-1199
Address: 274 Burnside Avenue (bet. Rockaway Tpk. - Lawrence Ave.)

Hechsher: NO HECHSHER- RESTAURANT IS OPEN 7 DAYS A WEEK

Proprietor/Manager: Seymore Epstein

Type(s) of Food: Meat - Deli

Price Range: *Lunch*   *Dinner*   *Take out*
    Entrées: $8.75-$12.95   Same   Same – Delivery Available
    Desserts: $1.10-$1.95   *Deli Sandwiches:* $5.25-$9   *Dinners:* $11-$12.50
    Drinks: $ .85-$2.50, $2.25/Domestic $2.40-$2.50/Importrd (Beer)

Food Specialties: Deli Sandwiches, Eat-A-Pita, Omelets, Grills, Burgers, Knishes

    Description: For the most part, a typical deli menu. A complete dinner
       includes soup, entrée, dessert, and coffee or tea. All food is fried in
       cholesterol free vegetable oil. Sandwiches come in a large assortment of
       possibilities: on bread, club, rolls, pita, or bagels. 9 salads include a
       Chef's Salad, Chopped Liver, Tuna, Egg and Salmon.

    Comments: No great surprises here, except maybe for the lone deviant Chili.

Ambiance (Decor): Over 30 years at this location. Booths, as well as regular
       laminate topped tables, provide seating for 140. The proverbial glass
       display/take-out counter dominates the entry area. Informal.

Service: Standard

General Comments: This is one of three Epstein family owned and operated
       restaurants. In business for over 30 years, they apparently know their deli.

Hours: **Sun-Fri:** 9am-9pm   **Sat:** 9am-10pm – RESTAURANT IS OPEN 7 DAYS
A WEEK
Credit Cards Accepted: MC, Visa, AmEx

Restaurant Discount:

County: Nassau **(Long Island)**
Town: Lawrence

The Authoritative New York City Kosher Dining Guide

Restaurant: Traditions Restaurant   *Phone Number:* (516) 295-3630
                                        Fax: (516) 295-3834

Address: 302 Central Avenue (bet. Rockaway Pwy. - Frost Ln.)

Hechsher: Vaad Hakashrus of the 5 Towns (Glatt Kosher)

Proprietor/Manager: Kenny Jerome

Type(s) of Food: Meat - Continental

Price Range: *Lunch* (12pm-2:30pm) *Dinner*   *Take out*
   Entrées: $6.95 (Special) $10.95-$16.95   Free Local Delivery ($20 Min.)
   Desserts: $2.95   *Early Bird Special:* $9.95 (3pm-5:30pm Weekdays)
   Drinks: $ .95-$1.35 *Monday Night All You Can Eat Buffet:* $15.95

Food Specialties: Deli, Grills, BBQ Chicken & Ribs, Roast Veal, Chicken In A Pot

   Description: A wide deli menu with occasional departures from its base.
      Pasta dishes, as well as Chicken Cacciatore, Chicken Cutlet Marinara,
      Chicken Marsala, and Veal w/ Peppers. The Diet-Lite Entrées feature
      chicken or veal (grilled or broiled) and a choice of several salads.
      Jewish traditional favorites include goulash, brisket, and flanken. Rib
      steaks, burgers, and veal chops, are also served. Broiled salmon or sole
      fillet are the seafood selections. Eggs and omelets round off the menu.
      Ethan's Kiddie Menu, for children under 10 years, ranges $6-$6.50.

   Comments: Portions are very large. Enough variety to meet most demands.

Ambiance (Decor): A deli display counter dominates the initial area. To the right are
   two dining rooms, each with its own distinctive personality. Together they
   accommodate a total of 140 diners (70 each). The first room, is informal with
   seating at booths and unadorned tables. Stained wood paneling accented with
   neon lights lines the walls and imparts a timeless quality. The second, more
   formal room, functions as the party room. Here covered tables, dimmed
   lighting, and mirrored walls lend greater elegance.

Service: Standard

General Comments: We have yet to try it. Reservations not required

Hours: **Sun-Thurs:** 12pm-10pm   **Fri:** 8am-2 hrs before Shabbos
   <u>**Saturday Closed**</u>

Credit Cards Accepted: MC, Visa, AmEx, Diners Club, Carte Blanche

Restaurant Discounts: 15% Off – Invalid With Any Other Coupon or Discount

County: Nassau **(Long Island)**
Town: Lawrence

The Authoritative New York City Kosher Dining Guide

Restaurant: Cho-sen Island

Phone Number: (516) 374-1199
Fax: (516) 374-1459

Address: 367 Central Avenue (cor. Frost Ln.)

Hechsher: 5 Towns Vaad (Glatt Kosher, Mashgiach Temidi, Chassidishe Shechita)

Proprietor/Manager: Normond Wong, Neil J. Wallin

Type(s) of Food: Meat - Chinese/Japanese

Price Range: *Lunch* (Special) *Dinner* *Take out*
  Entrées: $10.50-$10.95 $13.50-$19.95 20% off Dinner Menu Del. Avail.
  Desserts: $2.95 $45.00/2 (Peking Duck) *Sushi:* $2-$3/ea.
  Drinks: $1.50 (Soda), $3.50-$3.95 (Beer), $4.00-$4.95 (Mixed Drinks)
  $3.50/glass (House Wine), $12.00-$17.00/bottle (Wine)

Food Specialties: Szechuan, Hunan, and Mandarin Chinese favorites, Sushi

> *Description:* A complete Chinese menu showcasing popular dishes and chef specialties. Entrées center around veal, chicken, beef, duck and vegetables. Special offerings include lo-cal Light Gourmet Delights, and From the Garden (100% vegetarian dishes). Sushi has been added to the menu in answer to popular demand. Dinner comes with complementary dessert, fortune cookies or melon in season.

> *Comments:* The food rivals the best of the Chinese restaurants in the city. It is generally well prepared and attractively presented.

Ambiance (Decor): This is a large (120 seats) and attractive restaurant. A party room in the back, several steps up, can serve to accommodate an overflow crowd. Modern in design, the room is light and airy. Except for some fretwork reminiscent of Chinese screens, there is no reference to the oriental nature of the menu. The carpeted dining area is sectioned off from the entry and bar traffic, providing a calm and ordered environment. Semi-formal.

Service: Standard

General Comments: This is the sister of Cho-sen Gardens in Queens, of the same ownership. A nice restaurant to visit when you're in the neighborhood.

Hours: **Sun-Thurs:** 12pm-10pm **Friday Closed** **Sat:** 1 hr aft Shabbos till 12am

Credit Cards Accepted: MC, Visa, AmEx

Restaurant Discount:

County: Nassau **(Long Island)**
Town: Lawrence

The Authoritative New York City Kosher Dining Guide

Restaurant: Dairy Revue   *Phone Number:* (516) 295-7417
                                          Fax: None
Address: 143 Washington Avenue (bet. Central Ave. - Railroad)

Hechsher: Vaad Hakashrus of the 5 Towns (Cholov Yisroel, Pas Yisroel)

Proprietor/Manager: Abe Orzel

Type(s) of Food: Dairy - American

Price Range:	*Lunch*	*Dinner*	*Take out*
Entrées:	$8.95-$15.50	Same	Same – Delivery Not Available
Desserts:	$2.00-$3.00	*Open Salad Bar*	
Drinks:	$ .90-$3.50		

Food Specialties: Pasta, Soups, Fish, Salads, Blintzes, Omelets

> *Description:* Large selection of fresh fish offered. Homemade soups and salads are made fresh daily. Generous portions.

> *Comments:* Nothing fancy, just familiar homemade cuisine.

Ambiance (Decor): Newly opened, this transplanted remake of the previous Delicious Kosher Dairy now seats 80-90 diners. This informal family restaurant is described as modern and is characterized by a liberal use of wood accents and trim, mirrored walls and its tiled floor. Spotlights provide the lighting. A separate party room seats 35.

Service: Self-serve

General Comments: Open just 5 months at this writing, this transformation of the now defunct Delicious Kosher Dairy is off and running.

Hours: **Sun-Thurs:** 11am-9pm   **Friday Closed**
        Sat: 8pm-1am (November-March Only)

Credit Cards Accepted: AmEx

Restaurant Discount:

County: Nassau **(Long Island)**
Town: Cedarhurst

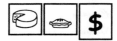

The Authoritative New York City Kosher Dining Guide

Restaurant: Toddy's Appetizers   *Phone Number:* (516) 295-1999
                                          Fax: (516) 295-1627

Address: 436 Central Avenue (bet. Spruce St. - Cedarhurst Ave.)

Hechsher: Vaad Hakashrus of the 5 Towns

Proprietor/Manager:

Type(s) of Food: Dairy, Parve - American

Price Range:	*Lunch*	*Dinner*	*Take out*
Entrées:	$3.00-$5.00	Same	Same
Desserts:	$1.75-$2.00		
Drinks:	$ .75-$2.50		

Food Specialties: Sandwiches, Salads, Soup, Lasagna, Pasta, Omelets

> *Description:* The standard sandwich selection: tuna, egg salad, smoked white fish, etc. Eggs are available cooked every which way. Soup is served during the winter season only. Kugel, macaroni and cheese, and cake are some other menu items.

> *Comments:* Basically a lunch-time menu for quick meals. Primarily, services local workers or shoppers wanting a quick bite.

Ambiance (Decor): Small (11 seats) café style eatery, dominated by the take out counter. Undistinguished in appearance. Casual.

Service: Self-serve

General Comments: Good for when you're in the neighborhood, time is short, and you want a quick bite.

Hours: **Sun-Thurs:** 7am-5:30pm   **Fri:** 7am-2 hrs before Shabbos
Saturday Closed

Credit Cards Accepted: MC, Visa, AmEx

Restaurant Discount:

County: Nassau **(Long Island)**
Town: Cedarhurst

The Authoritative New York City Kosher Dining Guide

Restaurant: The Natural Gourmet &   *Phone Number:* (516) 569-7609
        The Gourmet Grill   *Fax:* None
Address: 546 Central Avenue (bet. Cedarhurst Ave. - Maple Ave.)

Hechsher: Vaad Hakashrus of the 5 Towns

Proprietor/Manager: Kim, the Rosses

Type(s) of Food: Vegetarian, Meat - Eclectic

Price Range: *Lunch & Dinner*   *Take out*
    Entrées: Veg: $5.50-$7.95   *Grill:* $8.95-$14.95   Same - Free Local Delivery
    Desserts: $1.75-$3.00   Bklyn/Manhattan $15 Charge
    Drinks: $1.25-$4.25   *Sandwiches:* $2.50-$7.95

Food Specialties: Stuffed Cabbage, Terriyaki Beef, Chili, Pepper "Steak," Chulent

     Description: Truly eclectic, the menu travels to China, Japan, the Middle East,
       Italy, North America, traditional Jewish, and back again. Food is "home
       cooked," organic, dairy free, oil free, and made fresh daily. The newly
       expanded selection includes soups (eight), salads, cooked entrées,
       desserts, etc. The grill menu focuses on chicken or fresh fish kebobs
       (salmon, tuna or halibut), shawarma, and assorted salads. Freshly
       squeezed fruit and vegetable juices are prepared at the juice bar.

     Comments: The food is prepared under the guidelines of Dr. Dean Ornish's
       Healthy Heart Food Line, which is geared to prevent heart attacks and
       reduce cholesterol, through a low fat, vegetarian diet. This is a restaurant
       for the nineties. Health conscious eating made pleasurable, and sensible.

Ambiance (Decor): Small but charming café-like decor with seven booths (can seat
       42), and a few café tables. Hanging plants and assorted nik-naks adorn the
       walls. A small counter in the back. Separate juice bar by the entry.

Service: Self-serve, or will accommodate if not busy at counter

General Comments: An interesting and healthy idea housed in a pleasant and
       palatable surroundings.

Hours: **Sun-Thurs:** 11:30am-9pm   **Fri:** 8:30am-3 hrs before Shabbos
       Saturday Closed

Credit Cards Not Accepted: CASH or LOCAL CHECK ONLY!

Restaurant Discounts:

County: Nassau **(Long Island)**

Town: Cedarhurst

The Authoritative New York City Kosher Dining Guide

Restaurant: King David Delicatessen

Phone Number: (516) 569-2920
Fax: Same

Address: 550 Central Avenue (bet. Cedarhurst Ave. - Maple Ave.)

Hechsher: Vaad Hakashrus of the 5 Towns (Chassidishe Shechita)

Proprietor/Manager: Robert Ross

Type(s) of Food: Meat - Deli, Mexican

Price Range:	*Lunch*	*Dinner*	*Take out*
Entrées:	$9.95-$ 18.95	Same	Same ($5/Local Delivery)
Desserts:	$1.90-$4.95	*Dinner Special:* (M-Th)$9.95, (Sun)$11.95-$13.95	
Drinks:	$ .95-$1.75	*Children's Menu:* $6.25-$7.95	

Food Specialties: Grills, Deli Sandwiches, Fajitas (Steak or Chicken), Rotisserie

> *Description:* A deli menu that occasionally meanders south of the border. All the deli standards are here, but if you suddenly develop a yen for Beef Tacos or Burritos, don't worry, they're offered too! An omelet selection provides breakfast or brunch. Special lo-cal selections cater to dieters' needs. The Children's Menu (10 years or younger) offers five choices and includes a fountain soda.

> *Comments:* The food looked fresh and was served in heaping portions.

Ambiance (Decor): The large dining room is spacious, but lacks atmosphere. Seating of 107 is divided between booths and tables. Could double as a dimly lit dining room at a hotel in the Catskills. Family dining easily accommodated.

Service: Standard

General Comments: Open for 13 years, this restaurant apparently satisfies with its food. Though not visually exciting, it is a place to go to for good hearty eating. Patrons dining here gave it their thumbs up. More in our next edition.

Hours: **Sun-Thurs:** 10:30am-10pm
Fri: 8am-5pm (Summer) till 3pm (Winter)   **Saturday Closed**

Credit Cards Accepted: MC, Visa AmEx

Restaurant Discount: 10% Off Cash Payment For One Time Only

234

County: Nassau **(Long Island)**
Town: Cedarhurst

The Authoritative New York City Kosher Dining Guide

Restaurant: Ruthie's Kosher Desserts   *Phone Number:* (516) 569-1818
                                          Fax: None
Address: 560A Central Avenue (bet. Cedarhurst Ave. - Maple Ave.)

Hechsher: Vaad Hakashrus of the 5 Towns (Cholov Yisroel)

Proprietor/Manager: Ruthie Barnes

Type(s) of Food: Dairy - American

Price Range:	Lunch	Dinner	Take out
Entrées:	$2.50-$2.95	Same	Same (No Delivery Available)
Desserts:	$1.50-$4.75	*Yogurt, Ice Cream:* $1.65-$3.50	
Drinks:	$1.25-$2.50		

Food Specialties: Cakes, Blintzes, Belgium waffles, Fresh Juice Bar, Lo-cal shakes

> *Description:* Noshers delight! Beautiful and delicious cakes, cookies, freshly made blintzes and waffles, freshly squeezed juices, shakes, ice cream, yogurts, sorbét and coffees make this establishment a dessert heaven.

> *Comments:* The cake masterpieces created by pastry chefs Judy Pallach (well known on "The Island") and Ruth Barnes (owner) must be seen to be believed. The cheese cake I indulged in was pure heaven with its blend of different, but harmonious flavors. The caramel cake was unparalleled. The cakes are so pretty, it is almost a shame to have to cut them up.

Ambiance (Decor): The interior, of this new eatery, is a confection in itself. Well lit, and squeaky clean. Newly decorated in fresh green and white with some mauve accents, this restaurant is a pleasure to sit in. A showcase filled with cakes lines one side of the room, while on the opposite wall there are booths with seating for 16. Outdoor tables can accommodate another 18. A glass blintz and waffle counter in the back allows you to watch your orders as they are being made.

Service: Self-serve

General Comments: If you are anywhere within a 50 mile radius, go and enjoy!

Hours: **Mon-Wed:** 11am-10pm   **Thus , Sun:** 11am-11pm
         Fri: 11am-3 or 4pm   **Sat:** Opens 1 hr after Shabbos till 2am

Credit Cards Not Accepted: CASH ONLY (& Local Checks)

Restaurant Discount:

County: Nassau **(Long Island)**
Town: Cedarhurst

The Authoritative New York City Kosher Dining Guide

Restaurant: The Cedar Club   *Phone Number:* (516) 374-1714
                                             Fax: Same
Address: 564 Central Avenue (bet. Cedarhurst Ave. - Maple Ave.)

Hechsher: Vaad Hakashurus of the 5 Towns

Proprietor/Manager: David Baker, Lew Levine/ David Elphant (Manager)

Type(s) of Food: Meat - American

Price Range:	*Lunch*	*Dinner*	*Take out*
Entrées:	Closed	$14.95-$24.95	10% off (No Delivery Available)
Desserts:		$3.95-$6.95	*Early Bird Specials:* $10-$14
Drinks:	$1.75-$3.75	$3.75/gl. (House Wine),	$5.00/gl. (Mixed Drinks)
	$14-$40/bottle (Wine)		$10-$150/glass (Single Malt Scotch

Food Specialties: Grilled Rib Eye, Chicago Pan Seared Steak, Bourbon St. Chicken

Description: The quintessential American steakhouse menu, a carnivore's
delight. Taking top billing is a host of steaks, ribs, and chops. Diners can
choose the Marinated Grilled Rib Eye, the Chicago Pan-Seared Steak,
BBQ Veal Ribs or Chicken; Honey Mustard Chicken, or Tenderloin.
Blackened Salmon & Red Snapper are among 4 fish selections. The
Early Bird Special (4pm-5:30pm) consists of soup, selected entrées, tea
or coffee, & cookies or sorbet. The Kids Menu ($6) includes a drink.

Comments: A sophisticated menu that offers something for everyone. The
restaurant was bustling and diners seemed content with their meals.

Ambiance (Decor): An exclusive, private club atmosphere pervades this large and
attractive restaurant. The entry is dominated by a well stocked bar. On the right,
a room with 70 seats has leather backed chairs, white tablecloths, curtained
windows, carpeting, and French doors. Another room seating 50 has hunter
green walls set off by cedar wood and white tablecloths.

Service: Formal service

General Comments: An attractive setting for any occasion. Reservations
recommended. 18% gratuity added to parties of 8 or more.

Hours: **Sun-Thurs:** 4pm-9:30pm   **Friday Closed**
       Sat: 1 hr after Shabbos till 12am (Winter only)

Credit Cards Accepted: MC, Visa, AmEx, Discover, Diners Club

Restaurant Discount:

County: Nassau **(Long Island)**
Town: Cedarhurst

The Authoritative New York City Kosher Dining Guide

Restaurant: Wok Tov   *Phone Number:* (516) 295-3843
                              Fax: (516) 295-3865
Address: 594 Central Avenue (bet. Cedarhurst Ave. - Maple Ave.)

Hechsher: Vaad Hakashrus of the 5 Towns (Glatt Kosher, Chassidishe Shechita)

Proprietor/Manager:

Type(s) of Food: Meat - Chinese

Price Range: *Lunch*   *Dinner*   *Take out*
  Entrées: $9.70-$13.95   Same   Same - Free Local Del. ($18 Min.)
  Desserts: $ None *Lunch Special:* $5.25 *Diet Entrées:* $ 7.00-$9.70
  Drinks: $ .90-$1.50 *Combination Platters:* $7.25-$7.25

Food Specialties: General Tso's Chicken, Crispy Chicken w/ Plum Sauce, Tea
          Smoked Duck, Chinese Braised Tongue, Champagne Chicken

Description: Entrées encompass chicken, beef, veal, vegetable and fish.
          Seafood selections include "mock shrimp" in a number of different
          combinations. The number of "American Specials" has been expanded.
          Now you can order burgers, franks and chicken nuggets for a change of
          pace. A Diet Gourmet menu for the health conscious offers twelve
          steamed chicken or vegetable choices. The Luncheon Special is served
          with fried rice and choice of 3 soups.

Comments: A fast food Chinese restaurant serving both Szechuan and Hunan
          dishes, but they will spice to taste. Average sized portions.

Ambiance (Decor): This very small restaurant is bright and noisy. Outdoor seating
          extends capacity of 12 to a total of 18 weather permitting. Take-out atmosphere.

Service: Self-serve

General Comments: Dinnertime was busy and crowded with people ordering take-
          out. The families we observed eating appeared content.

Hours: **Mon-Thurs:** 11am-10pm   **Fri:** 11am-2 hrs before Shabbos
          Sat: 1 hr after Shabbos till 1am (Winter Only)   **Sun:** 12pm-10pm

Credit Cards Accepted: MC, Visa, AmEx, Discover ($15 Min.)

Restaurant Discounts:

The Authoritative New York City Kosher Dining Guide

Restaurant: Bagel Delight *Phone Number:* (516) 374-7644
Fax: (516) 374-7643

Address: 598 Central Avenue (bet. Cedarhurst Ave. - Maple Ave.)

Hechsher: Vaad Hakashrus of the 5 Towns (Cholov Yisroel)

Proprietor/Manager:

Type(s) of Food: Dairy, Parve - American, Eclectic

Price Range: *Lunch* *Dinner* *Take out*
 Entrées: $2.30-$4.50 (Bagels & Ass'ted toppings)
 Desserts: $ 5.99/lb. (Bakery Cookies) *Omelets:* $2.00-$5.95
 Drinks: $ .75-$1.25 *Salads:* $3.00-$3.50 *Breakfast Special:* $2.50

Food Specialties: Bagels, Salads, Omelets, Pasta, Baked Potato

   Description: Bagels offered every-which-way, from bagel with butter (80¢) to bagel with white fish ($4.50). The freshly made salads include tuna, egg, Israeli, Greek, and Caesar. Omelets are made as-you-like-it. Two pasta choices and baked potatoes are available. Coffees, soda, and juices to quench your thirst.

   Comments: A limited menu for light eating. Best for breakfast, lunches, or light suppers.

Ambiance (Decor): With seating for 70, this casual eatery is spacious and like its menu, unpretentious. Ceramic floor, bright florescent lighting, and unadorned laminate tables characterize the room. The seating area in the front, near the large glass windows, provides diners with a view of the street. Could be described as a fast food eatery, or a café without attitude.

Service: Self-serve

General Comments: What could be bad? Open for only 1½ years, the restaurant is playing it safe. No surprises here, its exactly as it sounds.

Hours: **Mon-Thurs:** 6am-8pm **Fri:** 6am-2 hrs before Shabbos
 Sat: 1 hr after Shabbos till 1am **Sun:** 6am-5pm

Credit Cards Not Accepted: CASH & LOCAL CHECKS ONLY!

Restaurant Discount:

County: Nassau **(Long Island)**
Town: Cedarhurst

The Authoritative New York City Kosher Dining Guide

Restaurant: Anise

Phone Number: (516) 569-2922
Fax: (516) 569-2169

Address: 600 Central Avenue (cor. Maple Ave.)

Hechsher: Vaad Hakashrus of the 5 Towns (Glatt Kosher)

Proprietor/Manager: Mayer

Type(s) of Food: Meat – Middle Eastern

Price Range:

	Lunch	*Dinner*	*Take out*
Entrées:	$7.95 (12pm-3pm)	$12.95-$22	$10.95-$22 - Local Delivery Avail
Desserts:	$3.00	Same	*Daily Specials:* $11.00-$15.00
Drinks:	$1.50-$2.50	*Children's Menu:* $6.95	*Early Bird:* $11.95

Food Specialties: Marinated Grilled Chicken, Rib Steak, Grilled Salmon, Siniya

Description: Middle Eastern favorites such as grills, salads, soups, kabobs, Moroccan Cigars, Kibbeh and Siniya (a mixed grill of chicken, turkey and beef with mushrooms & onions served on a chummus platter). The Early Bird Special is offered 3pm-5pm, Mon-Thurs. 12 salads. Entrées served with grilled onions, rice or fries, and okra or beans.

Comments: Note that only the first basket of homemade tandoori bread comes free, additional ones cost $1/each.

Ambiance (Decor): Conceived of with a good sense of proportion and design, this spacious, attractive, modern restaurant offers dining on several levels: a main dining room (40 seats), a raised tier (20 seats), and a basement level party room (40 seats). Crisp hunter green tablecloths and white walls, create a pleasantly fresh, and serene setting. Ongoing renovations while the restaurant remains open, will carve out a separate and independent deli take-out area with eat-in counter & stools.

Service: Standard

General Comments: Suitable for family dining and informal social occasions.

Hours: **Sun-Thurs:** 3pm-11pm (Take-out: 9am-11pm)
Friday Closed (Take out: 8am-3pm)
Sat: 1 hr after Shabbos till 12am (Winter Only) (Take out: Not Determined)

Credit Cards Accepted: MC, Visa, AmEx, Diners Club

Restaurant Discount: 10% Off In Restaurant Only

County: Nassau **(Long Island)**
Town: Hewlet

The Authoritative New York City Kosher Dining Guide

Restaurant: Dave's Glatt Kosher Deli   *Phone Number:* (516) 374-3296
                                          Fax: (516) 374-9019

Address: 1508 Broadway (bet. Avalon Rd. - Yale St.)

Hechsher: Vaad Hakashrus of the 5 Towns

Proprietor/Manager: Sheila (Manager)

Type(s) of Food: Meat - Deli

Price Range: *Lunch*   *Dinner*   *Take out*
  Entrées: $9.95-$16.95   Same   Same - Delivery Available
  Desserts: $2.00   *Sandwiches:* $5.95-$12.95 *Sandwich Special:* $6.95
  Drinks: $ .85-$1.35 *Children's Menu:* $3.95-$5.95 (10 yrs. & Under)

Food Specialties: Sandwiches, Rib Steak, Veal/Lamb Chops, Grills, Burgers, BBQ

> *Description:* Standard deli menu. The Sandwich Special includes a cup of
> soup with any deli sandwich, or salad served with grilled chicken in a
> pita. Homemade soups include Soup du Jour and Chicken Noodle /
> Matzoh Ball. Flame Broiled Veal Chops, Lamb Chops, Rib Steak, and
> Rumanian Tenderloin are served with two side dishes and salad, as are
> the Hot Chicken Platters. Large portions.

> *Comments:* The menu is not extensive, but manages to cover all the necessary
> bases.

Ambiance (Decor): A typical deli with the display counter running along one wall
and laminate topped tables with 25 seats along the other. Casual and familiar.

Service: Standard

General Comments: A family friendly restaurant and take out establishment.

Hours: **Sun-Thurs:** 9am-8pm **Fri:** 9am-3pm <u>**Saturday Closed**</u>

Credit Cards Accepted: MC, Visa, AmEx

Restaurant Discount: Free Can of Soda or Cup of Soup With Dinner Only.
                       5% Off With Take Out, ($20 Minimum)

County: Nassau **(Long Island)**
Town: Hewlet

The Authoritative New York City Kosher Dining Guide

Restaurant: Woodro Kosher Restaurant　　　*Phone Number:* (516) 791-4033
　　　　　　　　　　　　　　　　　　　　　　　Fax: None
Address: 1342 Peninsula Boulevard (in the Peninsula Shopping Center)

Hechsher: Rabbi Israel Mayer Steinberg - RESTAURANT IS OPEN 7 DAYS A
　　　　　　　　　　　　　　　　　　　　　　　　　　　　WEEK
Proprietor/Manager: Norman (Owner), George (Manager)

Type(s) of Food: Meat - Deli, American, Eclectic

Price Range:　　　*Lunch*　　　*Dinner*　　　*Take out*
　　Entrées: $9.45-$14.25　　$12.00-$16.00　　Same - Deliveries Arranged
　　Desserts: $1.75-$2.50 *Sandwiches:* $5.25-$6.95, $7.15-$13.80 (Combo)
　　Drinks: $1.25-$1.45　$2.50 (Beer) *Tues/Thurs Dinner Special:* $13.95

Food Specialties: Deli, Chili Con Carne, Chicken Pot Pie, Spinach Log, Fish Filet

　　Description: Predominately a deli menu, with the expected sandwiches,
　　　　platters, and traditional Jewish cooked favorites. But, dishes like Chili
　　　　Con Carne, Hawaiian Chicken, Polynesian Chicken, Sesame Chicken,
　　　　Lemon Chicken, BBQ Chicken, and Pasta Primavera are also served.
　　　　The daily seafood special ($13.95) features broiled Norwegian Salmon
　　　　Filet, served with potato and steamed vegetable. Several take-out
　　　　specials $12.75-$23.95. The 4 regular soup selections are augmented
　　　　with a daily changing soup. 4 diet choices consist of various salads,
　　　　some with optional chicken or meat, such as the Hawaiian Chicken
　　　　Salad or the Chef's Salad. The grill offers turkey or beef burgers.

　　Comments: An embellished deli menu that has some chicken and other stuff
　　　　for everyone.

Ambiance (Decor): Spacious, with 125-130 seats, otherwise a typical deli setting.

Service: Standard

General Comments: Without compunction, the owner declared his deli to be the best
　　anywhere and invited us to taste for ourselves. Check our next edition.

Hours: **Sat-Sun:** 8am-8pm (Closed during Major Jewish Holidays)
　　 - RESTAURANT IS OPEN 7 DAYS A WEEK

Credit Cards Accepted: MC, Visa, AmEx, Discover Diners Club

Restaurant Discount:

The Authoritative New York City Kosher Dining Guide

Lawrence:

Jerusalem Kosher Pizzeria   *Tel:* (516) 569-0074
(a.k.a Pizza Plus)
344 Central Avenue
Vaad Hakashrus of the 5 Towns

La Piazza   *Tel:* (516) 295-1700
357 Central Avenue
Vaad Hakashrus of the 5 Towns

Cedarhurst:

Sabra Kosher Pizza   *Tel:* (516) 569-1563
560C Central Avenue
Vaad Hakashrus of the 5 Towns

Pizza Cave   *Tel:* (516) 295-6925
580 Central Avenue
Vaad Hakashrus of the 5 Towns

Shula's Pizza & Catering   *Tel:* (516) 569-7408
608 Central Avenue
Vaad Hakashrus of the 5 Towns
(Cholov Yisroel)

Woodmere:

Pizza Pious   *Tel:* (516) 295-2050
1063 Broadway
Vaad Hakashrus of the 5 Towns
(Cholov Yisroel)

The Authoritative New York City Kosher Dining Guide

Lawrence:

Dunkin' Donuts *Tel:* (516) 239-2052
299 Burnside Avenue
Vaad Hakashrus of the 5 Towns

Hungry Harbor Bakery *Tel:* (516) 374-1131
311 Central Avenue
Vaad Hakashrus of the 5 Towns

Cedarhurst:

Donut Delight *Tel:* (516) 295-5005
125 Cedarhurst Avenue
Vaad Hakashrus of the 5 Towns

Ruthie's Kosher Desserts *Tel:* (516) 569-1818
560A Central Avenue
Vaad Hakashrus of the 5 Towns

Ultimate Yogurt Shop *Tel:* (516) 569-7821
602 Central Avenue
Vaad Hakashrus of the 5 Towns

Zomick's Bake Shop *Tel:* (516) 569-5520
444 Central Avenue
Vaad Hakashrus of the 5 Towns

Häagen Das *Tel:* (516) 374-6107
116 Cedarhurst Avenue
OU - IS OPEN 7 DAYS A WEEK

County: Nassau **(Long Island)**
Section: 5 Towns Bagel Shops

The Authoritative New York City Kosher Dining Guide

Cedarhurst:

Bagel Delight   *Tel:* (516) 374-7644
598 Central Avenue
Vaad Hakashrus of the 5 Towns

Woodmere:

Gotta Getta Bagel   *Tel:* (516) 374-5245
1033 Broadway
Vaad Hakashrus of the 5 Towns

Central
Nassau County

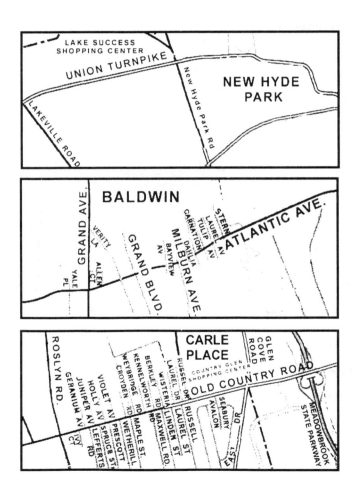

County: Nassau **(Long Island)**
Town: Long Beach

The Authoritative New York City Kosher Dining Guide

Restaurant: Lido Kosher Delicatessen   *Phone Number:* (516) 431-4411
                                          Fax: None
Address: 641½ East Park Avenue (bet. Neptune Blvd. - Dalton St.)

Hechsher: Rabbi Israel Steinberg – RESTAURANT IS OPEN 7 DAYS A WEEK

Proprietor/Manager: Walter Getz

Type(s) of Food: Meat - Deli

Price Range: *Lunch*   *Dinner*   *Take out*
Entrées: $4.99-$5.49 (Sp) $7.95-$14.95 Same – Local Free Delivery
Desserts: $2.50
Drinks: $1.50, $3.22-$3.95 (Beer), $3.99/gl (Wine)

Food Specialties: Deli, Turkey, London Broil, Omelets, Weight Watcher's Dishes

> *Description:* Typical deli menu with some dishes accommodating weight
> watchers. The Lunch Special offers a cup of soup, sandwich and coffee
> or tea. Rugalech and other baked goods are homemade, as are the
> knishes.

> *Comments:* Traditional deli made and served the old-fashioned way.

Ambiance (Decor): An informal traditional deli in a modern setting. Laminate tables
seat 60. Walls are punctuated by landscape paintings.

Service: Standard

General Comments: A lone kosher meat outpost in Long Beach that's been in
business for over 45 years.

Hours: **Sun-Sat:** 9am-10pm – RESTAURANT IS OPEN 7 DAYS A WEEK

Credit Cards Accepted: MC, Visa, AmEx, Diners Club

Restaurant Discount:

County: Nassau **(Long Island)**
Town: Oceanside

The Authoritative New York City Kosher Dining Guide

Restaurant: Top Notch Appetizering   *Phone Number:* (516) 764-3121
Fax: Same
Address: 2933 Long Beach Road (bet. Bellevue Ave.- E. Atlantic Ave.)

Hechsher: Rabbi Israel Steinberg – RESTAURANT IS OPEN SATURDAY

Proprietor/Manager: Jeff, Stan

Type(s) of Food: Dairy -

Price Range: *Lunch*   *Dinner*   *Take out*
Entrées: $Changes   Closed   Same – Delivery Available
Desserts: $8/lb   *Sandwiches:* $3-$6   ($50 Min)
Drinks: $1.00-$1.35

Food Specialties: Sandwiches, Smoked Fish, Salads, Quiche, Pirogen, Caviar

Description: An appetizing menu to whet your appetite. The printed menu is geared more for larger orders and many prices are by the dozen or by the pound. However, eating-in is accommodated, with an emphasis on sandwiches and salads. Fish figure prominently with assorted choice that include Whitefish, Baked Salmon, Poached Salmon, Tuna, Chopped Herring, Sable, etc. The homemade salads range from Whitefish, Eggplant, Egg w/ Mushrooms or Spinach, Vegetable Farmer Cheese to Raison & Nut Baked Farmer Cheese.

Comments: Not strictly "a restaurant," but they do service diners.

Ambiance (Decor): 6-7 tables add up to approximately 25 seats. If having the sights and smells of an appetizing store makes you drool, you could argue that's all the décor you need! Dining is á la papier, but that's no surprise. Dress down.

Service: Self-serve or counterman will serve

General Comments: Note the early closing time. No public bathrooms, but can accommodate.

Hours: **Sun:** 8am-6:30pm **Monday Closed** **Tues-Sat:** 7am-4pm – RESTAURANT IS OPEN SATURDAY

Credit Cards Accepted: MC, Visa, AmEx, Discover

Restaurant Discount:

County: Nassau **(Long Island)**
Town: Baldwin

The Authoritative New York City Kosher Dining Guide

Restaurant: Ben's Kosher Delicatessen   *Phone Number:* (516) 868-2072
                                                        Fax: (516) 868-2062
Address: 933 Atlantic Avenue (bet. Milburn Ave. - Grand Blvd.)

Hechsher: Rabbi Israel Mayer Steinberg - RESTAURANT IS OPEN 7 DAYS A
                                                                      WEEK
Proprietor/Manager: Ronnie Dragoon / Scott Dragoon (Manager)

Type(s) of Food: Meat - Deli

Price Range: *Lunch*   *Dinner*   *Take out*
    Entrées: $10.95-$19.95   Same   Delivery via Delivery Service only
    Desserts: $2- $3.25   *Sandwiches:* $5.95-$11.95   *Kid's Menu:* $5.25
    Drinks: $1.25-$1.55, $3.25-$3.95 (Beer), $4-$5/gl $10-$20/btl (Wine)

Food Specialties: Sandwiches, Burgers, Homemade Soup, Stuffed Cabbage, Salads

> *Description:* A complete deli menu with all the expected favorites (tongues
> & corned beef are cured on premises), and then some. Nice selection of
> freshly made salads and cold platters. 3 egg omelets are served with
> choice of potato pancake and apple sauce or fries. Poultry, beef, veal,
> and fresh salmon entrées come with 2 vegetables. Traditional specialties
> e.g. Hungarian Goulash, Chicken Fricassee, Boiled Beef In The Pot
> (flanken) are offered, as well as pasta dishes e.g. Primavera or
> Marinara. 3 homemade soups, include mushroom barley, chicken and
> soup of the day. Selection of side dishes and appetizers.

> *Comments:* Empire and Hebrew National meats are featured. The menu has
> everything to satisfy anyone's deli cravings. The restaurant is one of
> seven in Ben's deli chain. We haven't eaten here, but if their
> presentation indicates the quality of their food, it won't disappointed.

Ambiance (Decor): A capacity of 150 seats, in a modern, attractive setting. I'm told
that each of the restaurants in this chain has its own individual character and
reflects its location and clientele. Unlike other chains, which use their stamped
out decor as signatures. The word "posh" was offered as a general description.

Service: Standard

General Comments: A slick organization with all aspects of marketability down pat.

Hours: **Sun-Sat:** 9am-9pm - RESTAURANT IS OPEN 7 DAYS A WEEK

Credit Cards Accepted: MC, Visa, AmEx, Discover, Diners Club

Restaurant Discount:

County: Nassau **(Long Island)**
Town: Bellmore

The Authoritative New York City Kosher Dining Guide

Restaurant: Bellcrest Kosher Deli   *Phone Number:* (516) 785-8691
                                             Fax: (516) 785-8710
Address: 2793 Merrick Road

Hechsher: Rabbi Israel Mayer Steinberg - RESTAURANT IS OPEN 7 DAYS A
                                                                 WEEK
Proprietor/Manager: Jodi (Manager)

Type(s) of Food: Meat - Deli

Price Range: *Lunch*   *Dinner*   *Take out*
    Entrées: $9.00-$12.50   Same   Same -
    Desserts: $1.50-$2.50   *Deli Sandwiches:* $5.25 (Reg)-$9.25 (Hot)
    Drinks: $ .90-$1.35, $2.25-$2.75 (Beer) *Complete Dinners:* $11-$14.50

Food Specialties: Deli Sandwiches & Platters, Pastrami Burger, Eggs, & Omelets

  Description: Entrées contain dishes such as: Grilled Chicken Breast, Chicken
  Fricassee Deluxe, Southern Fried Chicken, Roast Beef, Rib Steak,
  Hungarian Goulash, and Corned Beef. A Children's Menu for $5.50
  includes a selection of entrées served with a cup of soup, vegetable,
  small fountain soda, and choice of dessert. The Diet Delights consist of
  4 salad choices for $6.50-$9.25.

  Comments: No major surprises here, the menu is limited to the usual deli
  selections with two exceptions: the Pepper Steak and the Chicken Stir
  Fry. Deli Combos, a category which for some reason seems to inspire a
  modicum of deli owner originality, are named after Long Island towns.

Ambiance (Decor): Usual deli setting.

Service: Standard

General Comments: Apparently popular, too busy to speak on the phone.

Hours: **Mon-Wed:** 10am-8pm   **Fri-Sun:** 10am-9pm
        RESTAURANT IS OPEN 7 DAYS A WEEK

Credit Cards Accepted: MC, Visa, AmEx, Discover
                        (Gratuities are NOT accepted on cards.)
Restaurant Discount:

County: Nassau **(Long Island)**
Town: Wantagh

The Authoritative New York City Kosher Dining Guide

Restaurant: Causeway Bagels

Phone Number: (516) 783-8956
Fax: None

Address: 3056 Merrick Road (at Woodland Ave. - King Rd.)

Hechsher: Rabbi Israel Steinberg – RESTAURANT IS OPEN 7 DAYS A WEEK

Proprietor/Manager: Dennis, Gino

Type(s) of Food: Dairy - Appetizing

Price Range:

	Lunch	Dinner	Take out
Entrées:	NONE	Same	Same – Free Local Delivery
Desserts:	$1.00-$1.30	**Sandwiches:**	$1.84-$5.99
Drinks:	$1.00-$1.50		

Food Specialties: Bagel Sandwiches, Salads, Smoked Fish

Description: A sandwich shop menu that basically offers various appetizers on a bagel. Cream cheese spreads, vegetable salads, fish salads (white fish, tuna, etc.), and other appetizers. Desserts take the form of Danishes.

Comments: An appetizer menu that is limited in scope.

Ambiance (Decor): A bagel/appetizing store with an area designated for eating in. There are 8 laminated tables in all, accommodating 32 diners for casual dining.

Service: Self-serve

General Comments: The only kosher dairy eatery in town, for quick and light bites.

Hours: **Sun:** 4:30am-4pm **Mon-Fri:** 4:30am-7pm **Sat:** 4:30am-6pm
RESTAURANT IS OPEN 7 DAYS A WEEK

Credit Cards _Not_ Accepted: CASH ONLY!

Restaurant Discount:

County: Nassau **(Long Island)**
Town: Seaford

The Authoritative New York City Kosher Dining Guide

Restaurant: Bellcrest 3 Kosher Deli

Phone Number: (516) 797-0600
Fax: (516) 797-2200

Address: 1282 Hicksville Road (off Jerusalem Ave.)

Hechsher: Rabbi Israel Steinberg – RESTAURANT IS OPEN 7 DAYS A WEEK

Proprietor/Manager: Rob

Type(s) of Food: Meat - Deli

Price Range:

	Lunch	*Dinner*	*Take out*
Entrées:	$11.00-$14.50	Same	Same – Delivery Avail. ($15 Min.)
Desserts:	$1.50-$2.50	*Dinner Specials:* $18 (2 Dinners M-Th) ($22 F-Sun)	
Drinks:	$ .90-$1.25, $2.25-$2.75 (Beer)	*Lunch Specials:* $5.25-$7.25	
	Sandwiches: $5-$9.25	*Children's Menu:* $5.50	

Food Specialties: Deli Sandwiches, Southern Fried Chicken, Smorgasbord

Description: Typical deli menu that doesn't stray from the traditional. Deli sandwiches and platters make up the bulk of the menu, while the usual cooked favorites include Roast Beef, London Broil, Broiled Liver Steaks, Hungarian Goulash, Tongue Polonaise, etc., etc. Combo sandwiches are named for Long Island towns in an expression of local pride of place. Diet salads.

Comments: Not original or extensive, but also not lacking in the most popular dishes,

Ambiance (Decor): A traditional old fashion deli wit approximately 50 seats, usually in the form of booths, but some tables, too. Casual.

Service: Standard

General Comments: As the name indicates, this is one of three with the same name. However, ownership of the three is no longer under one family.

Hours: **Mon-Wed:** 10am-8pm **Thurs -Sun:** 10am-9pm -
RESTAURANT IS OPEN 7 DAYS A WEEK

Credit Cards Accepted: Mc, Visa, AmEx, Discover

Restaurant Discount:

County: Nassau **(Long Island)**
Town: West Hempstead

The Authoritative New York City Kosher Dining Guide

Restaurant: Wing Wan

Phone Number: (516) 292-9309
Fax: (516) 292-9320

Address: 506 Hempstead Avenue

Hechsher: Rabbi Y. Kellemer, Rabbi Y. Pearl (Glatt Kosher, Mashgiach Temidi)

Proprietor/Manager: Richie Austein

Type(s) of Food: Meat – Chinese, Deli

Price Range:

	Lunch	*Dinner*	*Take out*
Entrees:	$5.25 (Combo)	$9.75 (Combo)-$12.50	Same
Desserts:	None	*Deli Sandwiches:* $3.50-$5.50	*Steak:* $12.95
Drinks:	$1.00-$1.50	*Combination Plates:* $5.25 (11am-3pm), $9.75	

Food Specialties: Szechuan Dishes, Chop Suey, Chow Fun, Deli Sandwiches, BBQ

> *Description:* A standard Chinese menu with no particular Chef Specialties listed. Veal, Beef, Poultry, Vegetable and Noodle entrées include all the favorites. 28 selections of Szechuan dishes can burn your palate to the degree of your choice. The American menu will soon be expanded to include steaks. Currently, deli sandwiches, Roast Chicken, Southern Fried Chicken and BBQ Chicken are available as are the homemade Kugels (Sweet Noodle & Potato). Combo Plates served with fried rice.

> *Comments:* A respectable selection of usual favorites Chinese and deli. The news here is the fairly large number of Szechuan dishes.

Ambiance (Decor): A typical fast food restaurant with laminate tables and seating for 50. Casual, child proof surfaces and bright fluorescent lighting. Reflective surfaces abound, so expect it to be noisy at mealtimes.

Service: Self-serve

General Comments: Inspired by the now defunct Shmulka Burnstein's of Manhattan's Lower East Side, Chinese and deli are once again a shidduch!

Hours: **Sun-Thurs:** 11am-10pm **Fri:** 10am-2 hrs before Shabbos
  Sat: 1 hr after Shabbos till 1am

Credit Cards Not Accepted: CASH OR CHECKS ONLY

Restaurant Discount:

County: Nassau **(Long Island)**
Town: New Hyde Park

The Authoritative New York City Kosher Dining Guide

Restaurant: Dairy King   *Phone Number:* (516) 437-7100
         Fax: (516) 437-8930
Address: 1564 Union Turnpike (Lake Success Shopping Center)

Hechsher: Rabbi Eckstein (Little Neck JCC) - RESTAURANT IS OPEN 7 DAYS A
         WEEK
Proprietor/Manager:

Type(s) of Food: Dairy - Jewish American

Price Range:	*Lunch*	*Dinner*	*Take out*
Entrées:	$9.95-$13.95	Same	Same - Free Local Delivery
Desserts:	$1.75-$3.95	*Luncheon Special:* $6.95-10.95	
Drinks:	$ .95-$2.50	*Fish Dinner Special:* $9.95	

Food Specialties: Blintzes, Fish Kebob, Perogen, Salads, Vegetable Cutlet, Omelets

     Description: The menu offers a complete selection of dairy favorites. The
         blintzes have made their mark as the signature dish of the restaurant,
         with the perogen a close second. The Fish Dinner Specials offer a choice
         of halibut, salmon, white fish, or sole; and come with soup, salad, and
         dessert. A selection of 6-7 soups and various salads are offered daily.
         Omelets made to order, every which way. Generous portions.

     Comments: A fairly complete American menu with a Jewish accent.

Ambiance (Decor): The contemporary café styled interior is highlighted by celebrity
         caricatures on the walls. Laminated tables with seating for 75. Casual.

Service: Standard

General Comments: Open less than a year at this printing, Dairy King is apparently
         doing well, and that speaks volumes.

Hours: **Sun-Sat:** 8am-8:30pm - RESTAURANT IS OPEN 7 DAYS A WEEK

Credit Cards Accepted: MC, Visa, AmEx

Restaurant Discount:

County: Nassau **(Long Island)**
Town: New Hyde Park

The Authoritative New York City Kosher Dining Guide

Restaurant: Deli King   Phone Number: (516) 437-8420
                                          Fax: (516) 775-3369
Address: 1570 Union Turnpike (Lake Success Shopping Center)

Hechsher: NO RABBINICAL HECHSHER - RESTAURANT IS OPEN 7 DAYS A
                                                              WEEK
Proprietor/Manager:

Type(s) of Food: Meat - Deli

Price Range:	Lunch	Dinner	Take out
Entrées:	$11.95-15.95	Same	Same - Free Local Delivery
Desserts:	$1.75-$3.95	Turkey Dinner Special:	$12.95 (Mon & Tues)
Drinks:	$ 1.25-$1.35	$2.95-$3.50 (Beer) Dinner Specials:	$12.95-$13.95

Food Specialties: Gedempted Chicken, Stuffed Cabbage, Turkey Pot Pie, Soups

Description: This is a complete deli menu with all the standard sandwiches
and then some. All entrées come with soup, salad, a vegetable and
potato, including the Daily Dinner Specials. The Turkey Dinner Special
features soup, turkey stuffed cabbage as an appetizer, freshly carved
turkey with stuffing, potato, vegetable, plus dessert. Their "famous"
stuffed cabbage comes wrapped in a crust of mashed potatoes and is
quickly becoming the signature dish. Selection of 7 soups and freshly
made salads. Generous portions.

Comments: No major surprises here.

Ambiance (Decor): Newly opened, this restaurant is a traditional deli with a modern,
contemporary appearance. Wooden tables, stone floors, high ceilings, a beige
and hunter green color scheme, and a modern display counter, all lend a new
sophistication to this familiar restaurant genre. Casual.

Service: Standard

General Comments: Family owned and operated, this new establishment is a sister to
the Dairy King next door.

Hours: **Sun-Sat:** 9am-9pm - RESTAURANT IS OPEN 7 DAYS A WEEK

Credit Cards Accepted: MC, Visa, AmEx

Restaurant Discount:

County: Nassau **(Long Island)**
Town: Albertson

The Authoritative New York City Kosher Dining Guide

Restaurant: Daphil Kosher Delicatessen   *Phone Number:* (516) 621-1818
Fax: None
Address: 1008 Willis Avenue (bet. In Wellets Road - Park Lane Dr.)
(Walbaum's Shopping Center)
Hechsher: NO HECHSHER – RESTAURANT IS OPEN 7 DAYS A WEEK

Proprietor/Manager: Joe (Manager)

Type(s) of Food: Meat - Deli

Price Range: *Lunch*   *Dinner*   *Take out*
Entrées: $5.69 (Special) $9.80-$10.80   Same – Free Local Delivery
Desserts: $1.50-$2.75   *Dinner Special:* $9-$12.88   *Seniors:* 10% Off
Drinks: $1.25-$1.50, $2.50/btl (Beer)   *Sandwiches:* $6.75-$9.50

Food Specialties: Deli Sandwiches, Stuffed Cabbage, Corned Beef & Cabbage

> *Description:* Typical deli, the menu offers no surprises. The Lunch Special
> (11:30am-2:30pm) soup or salad, entrée, dessert and coffee or tea, as
> does the Dinner Special. Some cooked favorites include, Chicken
> Fricasee, Chicken Cutlet, and Hungarian Goulash.

> *Comments:* How many ways can you say deli sandwiches? Any way you slice
> it… it's Corned Beef, Pastrami, Roast Beef, etc. wedged between layers
> of bread, roll or pita. Traditional Jewish cooked dishes … the works!

Ambiance (Decor): Seating takes the form of booths and chairs accommodating 70
diners in an informal, casual deli which has been described as being "more of a
lunch place." Brightly lit with flourescent light that bounces off the mirrors on
the walls. The walls also display paintings of Jewish themes.

Service: Standard

General Comments: A traditional Jewish deli.

Hours: **Sun-Sat:** 9am-9pm - RESTAURANT IS OPEN 7 DAYS A WEEK

Credit Cards Accepted: MC, Visa, AmEx

Restaurant Discount:

County: Nassau **(Long Island)**
Town: Roslyn Heights

The Authoritative New York City Kosher Dining Guide

Restaurant: Andel's   *Phone Number:* (516) 621-9858
                          Fax: (516) 621-5966
Address: 350 Roslyn Road (bet. Long Island Exwy – Northern Pwy.)

Hechsher: Rabbi Israel Steinberg – RESTAURANT IS OPEN 7 DAYS A WEEK

Proprietor/Manager: Jonathan Geschwind

Type(s) of Food: Meat – Deli, & Dairy – Appetizing

Price Range: **Lunch**   **Dinner**   **Take out**
  Entrées: $7.99   Closed   Same – Delivery Available
  Desserts: $1.25-$1.50 **Deli Sandwiches:** $ 5-$8.75, **Bagel:** $1.25-$12.50
  Drinks: $1.25-$2.50, $1.50-$1.95 (Beer)

Food Specialties: Soups, Salads, Smoked Fish, Deli Sandwiches, Roast Chicken

Description: The menu, of 7 soups, 20 salads, 11 dairy spreads, 8 different smoked fish, 6 specialty salmons (Vodka Dill, Bourbon, & Scotch Salmon, etc.), Deli & Bagel Sandwiches, Finger Foods (Mini Egg Rolls, Mini Knishes, Chicken Nuggets, homemade Blintzes, Pirogen, Latkes, etc.) Had few entrée dishes which included chicken either roasted or grilled. New entrées are Oriental Chicken, Chicken Cutlets, Eggplant Rollatini, as well as a selection of pasta dishes like Eggplant or Baked Ziti, Vegetable Lasagna, & Bowties (w/ scallion , tomato & Feta Cheese). Greek, Mesculin, & Tossed Green salads join Diet, fish, egg & pasta salads and are served in a wrap or by the pound.

Comments: A mouthwatering selection of the popular dishes.

Ambiance (Decor): Paper plates and plastic cutlery to eat with in very casual surroundings. Dairy and meat items are separate with totally separate kitchens, counters, etc. Not a restaurant per se, but 4 tables are provided for eat-ins.

Service: Self-serve

General Comments: In the words of the owner, "they don't come for the décor, they come for the food. " That pretty well sums it up.

Hours: **Mon-Sat:** 7:30am-6:30pm **Sun:** till 6pm – REST. IS OPEN 7 DAYS / WEEK

Credit Cards Accepted: MC, Visa, AmEx

Restaurant Discount:

County: Nassau **(Long Island)**
Town: Carle Place

The Authoritative New York City Kosher Dining Guide

Restaurant: Ben's Kosher Delicatessen   ***Phone Number:*** (516) 742-3354
                                                   Fax: (516) 742-3296
Address: 95 Old Country Road (at Cove Rd., Country Glen Shopping Center)

Hechsher: Rabbi Israel Mayer Steinberg - RESTAURANT IS OPEN 7 DAYS A
                                                                    WEEK

Proprietor/Manager: Ronnie Dragoon / Michael Barcham (Manager)

Type(s) of Food: Meat - Deli

Price Range: ***Lunch***   ***Dinner***   ***Take out***
    Entrées: $10.95-$19.95   Same   Delivery via Delivery Service only
    Desserts: $2- $3.25   ***Sandwiches:*** $5.95-$11.95   ***Kid's Menu:*** $5.25
    Drinks: $1.25-$1.55, $3.25-$3.95 (Beer), $4-$5/gl $10-$20/btl (Wine)

Food Specialties: Sandwiches, Burgers, Homemade Soup, Stuffed Cabbage, Salads

Description: An extensive deli menu with all the expected favorites (tongues
        & corned beef are cured on premises), and then some. Nice selection of
        freshly made salads and cold platters. 3 egg omelets are served with
        choice of potato pancake and apple sauce or fries. Poultry, beef, veal,
        and fresh salmon entrées come with 2 vegetables. Traditional specialties
        e.g. Hungarian Goulash, Chicken Fricassee, Boiled Beef In The Pot
        (flanken) are offered, as well as pasta dishes e.g. Primavera or Marinara.
        3 homemade soups, include mushroom barley, chicken, and of the day.

Comments: Empire and Hebrew National meats are featured. The menu has
        everything to satisfy anyone's deli cravings. The restaurant is one of 7 in
        Ben's deli chain. We haven't eaten here, but if their presentation is
        indicative of the quality of their food, you won't be disappointed.

Ambiance (Decor): A capacity of 118 seats, in a modern, attractive setting. I'm told
        that each of the restaurants in this chain reflects its location and clientele, and
        none could be described as typical, unlike other chains, which use their stamped
        out decor as signatures. The word "posh" was offered as a general description.

Service: Standard

General Comments: A slick organization with all aspects of marketability down pat.

Hours: **Sun-Thurs:** 9am-9pm **Fri-Sat:** 9am-10pm
        - RESTAURANT IS OPEN 7 DAYS A WEEK

Credit Cards Accepted: MC, Visa, AmEx, Discover, Diners Club

Restaurant Discount:

County: Nassau **(Long Island)**
Town: Greenvale

The Authoritative New York City Kosher Dining Guide

Restaurant: Ben's Kosher Deli   *Phone Number:* (516) 621-3340
                                              Fax: (516) 621-2178

Address: 140 Wheatley Plaza (Wheatly Plaza Shopping Center,
                                              at Northern Blvd. & Glen Cove Rd.)

Hechsher: Rabbi Israel Mayer Steinberg - RESTAURANT IS OPEN 7 DAYS A
                                                                                                    WEEK

Proprietor/Manager: Ronnie Dragoon / Todd Silverstein (Manager)

Type(s) of Food: Meat - Deli

Price Range: *Lunch*   *Dinner*   *Take out*
    Entrées: $10.95-$19.95   Same   Delivery via Delivery Service only
    Desserts: $2- $3.25   *Sandwiches:* $5.95-$11.95   *Kid's Menu:* $5.25
    Drinks: $1.25-$1.55, $3.25-$3.95 (Beer), $4-$5/gl $10-$20/btl (Wine)

Food Specialties: Sandwiches, Burgers, Homemade Soup, Stuffed Cabbage, Salads

> *Description:* An extensive, complete deli menu with all the expected favorites
> (tongues & corned beef are cured on premises), and then some. Nice
> selection of freshly made salads and cold platters. 3 egg omelets are
> served with choice of potato pancake and apple sauce or fries. Poultry,
> beef, veal, and fresh salmon entrées come with 2 vegetables. Traditional
> specialties e.g. Hungarian Goulash, Chicken Fricassee, Boiled Beef In
> The Pot (flanken) are offered, as well as pasta dishes e.g. Primavera or
> Marinara. 3 homemade soups, include mushroom barley, chicken and
> soup of the day. Selection of side dishes and appetizers.

> *Comments:* Empire poultry and Hebrew National meats are featured. The
> menu has just about everything to satisfy anyone's deli cravings.

Ambiance (Decor): A capacity of 160 seats, in a modern, attractive setting. I'm told
that each of the restaurants in this chain reflects its location and clientele, and
none could be described as typical, unlike other chains, which use their stamped
out decor as signatures. The word "posh" was offered as a general description.

Service: Standard

General Comments: A slick organization with all aspects of marketability down pat.

Hours: **Sun-Thus:** 9am-9pm **Fri:** 9am-10pm
            Sat: 9am-11pm - RESTAURANT IS OPEN 7 DAYS A WEEK

Credit Cards Accepted: MC, Visa, AmEx, Discover, Diners Club

Restaurant Discount:

County: Nassau **(Long Island)**
Town: Jericho

The Authoritative New York City Kosher Dining Guide

Restaurant: Ben's Kosher Delicatessen   *Phone Number:* (516) 939-2367
                                          Fax: (516) 939-2294
Address: 437 North Broadway (Birchwood Shopping Center)

Hechsher: Rabbi Israel Mayer Steinberg - RESTAURANT IS OPEN 7 DAYS A
                                                                    WEEK
Proprietor/Manager: Ronnie Dragoon / Scott Dragoon (Manager)

Type(s) of Food: Meat - Deli

Price Range: *Lunch*   *Dinner*   *Take out*
   Entrées: $10.95-$19.95   Same   Delivery via Delivery Service only
   Desserts: $2- $3.25   *Sandwiches:* $5.95-$11.95   *Kid's Menu:* $5.25
   Drinks: $1.25-$1.55, $3.25-$3.95 (Beer), $4-$5/gl $10-$20/btl (Wine)

Food Specialties: Sandwiches, Burgers, Homemade Soup, Stuffed Cabbage, Salads

   Description: An extensive deli menu with all the expected favorites and then
      some. The tongue & corned beef are cured on premises. Nice selection
      of freshly made salads and cold platters. 3 egg omelets are served with
      choice of potato pancake and apple sauce or fries. Poultry, beef, veal,
      and fresh salmon entrées come with 2 vegetables. Traditional specialties
      e.g. Hungarian Goulash, Chicken Fricassee, Boiled Beef In The Pot
      (flanken) are offered, as well as pasta e.g. Primavera or Marinara. 3
      homemade soups, include: mushroom barley, chicken, and of the day.

   Comments: Empire poultry and Hebrew National meats are featured. The
      menu has just about everything to satisfy anyone's deli cravings. The
      restaurant is one of seven in Ben's deli chain. We haven't eaten here, but
      if their presentation is indicative of the quality of their food, you won't
      be disappointed.

Ambiance (Decor): A capacity of 118 seats, in a modern, attractive setting. I'm told
   that each of the restaurants in this chain reflects its location and clientele, and
   none could be described as typical, unlike other chains, which use their stamped
   out decor as signatures. The word "posh" was offered as a general description.

Service: Standard

General Comments: A slick organization with all aspects of marketability down pat.

Hours: **Sun-Sat:** 9am-10pm - RESTAURANT IS OPEN 7 DAYS A WEEK

Credit Cards Accepted: MC, Visa, AmEx, Discover, Diners Club

Restaurant Discount:

County: Nassau **(Long Island)**
Town: Plainview

The Authoritative New York City Kosher Dining Guide

Restaurant: Boomy's Kosher Deli   *Phone Number:* (516) 433-6565
                                                                                              Fax: None
Address: 437 South Oyster Bay Road (cor. S. Oyster Bay Rd. - Woodbury Plaza)

Hechsher: NO HECHSHER – RESTAURANT IS OPEN 7 DAYS A WEEK

Proprietor/Manager:

Type(s) of Food: Meat - Deli

Price Range: *Lunch* (11am-3pm)   *Dinner*   *Take out*
   Entrées: $5.95-$8.95 (SP) $9.95-$13.95   Same
   Desserts: $1.95-$2.50   *Deli Sandwiches:* $6.25-$10.95 (Hot Open)
   Drinks: $ .80-$1.65, $2.50-$2.95 (Beer) *Children's Menu:* $ 4.95

Food Specialties: Deli, Greek Style Chicken. BBQ Beef Ribs, Rib Steak

   Description: Along with the Brisket, the Flanken, the Roast Beef and the
Tongue Polonaise, you'll find Teriyaki Chicken Breast, Honey Mustard
Chicken and Southern Fried Chicken. The selection of sandwiches is
more than adequate. There is a calorie counter's corner for the weight
conscious as well as salad platters for everyone. Omelets are served with
potatoes or vegetable, bread and relish. The luncheon Special includes
soup with any sandwich or entrée. The Children's Menu offers choice
between hot dog, jr. hamburger and chicken fingers served with fries,
fountain soda and Jello or apple sauce, but is not available for take-out.

   Comments: There's something for everyone.

Ambiance (Decor): This traditional deli sports a modern setting. Mirrors and modern
prints line the walls, but the general feel is informal. Seating (75), mostly
booths.

Service: Standard

General Comments: Sounds like a nice place. Folksy looking menu with a caricature
drawing on the front cover, no doubt of the owner, and assorted cartoon figures
interspersed throughout. Check our next edition to find out if we ever made it
out there during the upcoming year.

Hours: **Sun-Sat:** 9am-9pm Daily - RESTAURANT IS OPEN 7 DAYS A WEEK

Credit Cards Accepted: MC, Visa, AmEx, Discover, Diners Club

Restaurant Discount:

County: Nassau **(Long Island)**
Town: Plainview

The Authoritative New York City Kosher Dining Guide

Restaurant: Regal Kosher Deli *Phone Number:* (516) 938-3588
Fax: (516) 938-3591
Address: 1110 Old Country Road (bet. Old Country Rd. - Manetto Hill Rd.)

Hechsher: Kashrus Supervision Union, Rabbi Lax – RESTAURANT IS OPEN 7
DAYS A WEEK

Proprietor/Manager: Steven Weiss

Type(s) of Food: Meat - Deli

Price Range:	*Lunch*	*Dinner*	*Take out*
Entrées:	$10.95-$14.50	Same	Same – No Delivery Available
Desserts:	$1.50-$2.76	*Sandwiches:* $6.00-$9.75	
Drinks:	$ .95-$2.75, $2.60-$3.00 (Beer)		

Food Specialties: Stuffed Chicken, Grills, Deli Sandwiches, Rib Steak, Omelets

> *Description:* A typical deli menu, grounded in assorted deli sandwiches and traditional cooked dishes. Home-style cooking.

> *Comments:* Unremarkable menu except that it contains all the popular deli specialties.

Ambiance (Decor): A Rubber Tree is the centerpiece of this otherwise traditional deli. The 14'H ceiling, however, is no match for the 40'H or 50'H tree, causing the tree to spread out across the ceiling. Wood planking on the walls lends the modern restaurant rustic charm. Seating for 70.

Service: Standard

General Comments: Owned and operated continuously for 32 years by the original owners. Parking lot available for diners.

Hours: **Sun-Sat:** 9am-9pm – RESTAURANT IS OPEN 7 DAYS A WEEK

Credit Cards Accepted: MC, Visa, Diners Club

Restaurant Discount:

County: Nassau (**Long Island**)
Town: Woodbury

The Authoritative New York City Kosher Dining Guide

Restaurant: Ben's Kosher Deli & Restaurant   *Phone Number:* (516) 933-9200
                                                Fax: (516) 496-4354
Address: 7971 Jericho Turnpike . (Shop. Ctr. cor. of Southwood Rd. & Jericho Tpk.)

Hechsher: Rabbi Israel Mayer Steinberg - RESTAURANT IS OPEN 7 DAYS
                                                A WEEK
Proprietor/Manager: Ronnie Dragoon

Type(s) of Food: Meat - Deli

Price Range: *Lunch*   *Dinner*   *Take out*
  Entrées: $10.95-$19.95   Same   Delivery via Delivery Service only
  Desserts: $2- $3.50   *Sandwiches:* $5.95-$11.95   *Kid's Menu:* $5.25
  Drinks: $1.25-$1.55, $3.25-$3.95 (Beer), $4-$5/gl $10-$20/btl (Wine)

Food Specialties: Sandwiches, Burgers, Homemade Soup, Stuffed Cabbage, Salads

  Description: A complete deli menu with all the expected favorites (tongues
    & corned beef are cured on premises), and then some. Nice selection of
    freshly made salads and cold platters. 3 egg omelets are served with
    choice of potato pancake and apple sauce or fries. Poultry, beef, veal,
    and fresh salmon entrées come with 2 vegetables. Traditional specialties
    e.g. Hungarian Goulash, Chicken Fricassee, Boiled Beef In The Pot
    (flanken) are offered, as well as pasta dishes e.g. Primavera or
    Marinara. 3 homemade soups, include mushroom barley, chicken and
    soup of the day. Selection of side dishes and appetizers.

  Comments: Empire and Hebrew National meats are featured. The menu has
    everything to satisfy anyone's deli cravings. You won't be disappointed.

Ambiance (Decor): The décor harkens back to 1940's NY with devices like exposed
    steel beams, old subway-styled ceramic tiles and murals. You won't find
    tablecloths on the tables in this casual eatery, but you will find booths and chair
    seating to accommodate 160 diners. A new addition to Ben's growing chain.

Service: Standard

General Comments: Debut opening is in 1st week of Jan.'99. 7th of Ben's deli chain.

Hours: **Sun-Thurs:** 11am-9:30pm **Fri-Sat:** 11am-10pm

Credit Cards Accepted: MC, Visa, AmEx, Discover, Diners Club

Restaurant Discount:

County: Nassau **(Long Island)**
Town: Commack

The Authoritative New York City Kosher Dining Guide

Restaurant: Pastrami 'n Friends   **Phone Number:** (516) 499-9537
                                          Fax: (516) 499-6083
Address: 110A Commack Road

Hechsher: Rabbi Berman (Commack Jewish Center) - RESTAURANT IS OPEN 7
                                          DAYS A WEEK
Proprietor/Manager: Don

Type(s) of Food: Meat - Deli

Price Range: **Lunch**   **Dinner**   **Take out**
  Entrées: $8.25-$12.50   Same   Free Local Delivery
  Desserts: $1.10-$2.75 **Sandwiches:** $4.95-$8.95
  Drinks: $ .75-$2.50, $2.50-$3.00 (Beer) **Dinner Special:** $3.95 + Entrée

Food Specialties: Corned Beef, Pastrami, Stuffed Cabbage, Brisket, Fried Chicken

> **Description:** The limited menu centers around sandwiches: deli (regular and
> hot open) and char broiled burgers. Burger selection includes Deluxe,
> BBQ, Pastrami, Mushroom, Slim or plain.Cooked entrées (11) include
> roast beef, chicken, Hungarian Goulash, Homemade meat loaf, and
> Chicken In A Pot (boiled chicken). For an additional $3.95, you get a
> full dinner of soup, entrée, dessert, and tea or coffee. 3 egg omelets are
> served with cole slaw & Derma or fries and 4 salads round of the menu.
> Portions are large we're told.

> **Comments:** Not an ambitious menu, but covers all the important bases.

Ambiance (Decor): Open since 1975, this restaurant is constantly evolving.
Currently, sports memorabilia featuring mostly baseball, imparts a sports bar
feel. In what has become a frequently changing gallery, autographed baseball
pictures now hang. Casual, modern, mid sized family restaurant (70 seats).

Service: Self-serve

General Comments: Family owned for several generations, they must be doing
something right!

Hours: **Sun-Thurs:** 11am-8pm **Fri-Sat:** 11am-9pm
  - RESTAURANT IS OPEN 7 DAYS A WEEK

Credit Cards Accepted: MC, Visa, AmEx

Restaurant Discount: 10% Off On All Cash Purchases

County: Nassau **(Long Island)**
Town: Central Nassau Pizzerias

The Authoritative New York City Kosher Dining Guide

West Hempstead:

Hunki's Pizza   *Tel:* (516) 538-6655
338 Hempstead Avenue
Vaad Harabonim of Queens

Great Neck

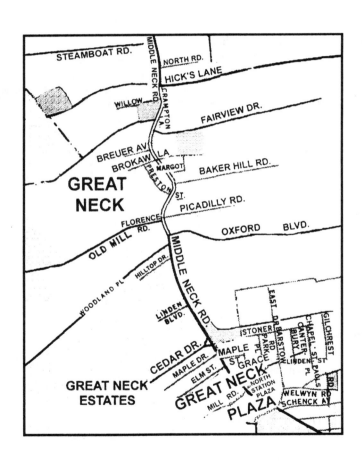

County: Nassau **(Long Island)**
Town: Great Neck

The Authoritative New York City Kosher Dining Guide

Restaurant: Empire Kosher Roasters   *Phone Number:* (516) 487-3573
                                          Fax: Same
Address: 9 Cutter Mill Road (bet. Middle Neck Rd. - Gussack Plz.)

Hechsher: Vaad Harabonim of Queens

Proprietor/Manager: Nissim Douek

Type(s) of Food: Meat - American

Price Range: *Lunch*   *Dinner*   *Take out*
   Entrées: $5.69-$13.99   Same   Free Local Delivery ($10 Min.)
   Desserts: $1.15-$2.45   *Sandwiches:* $2.99-$5.95, $4.99-$7.95 (Platter)
   Drinks: $ .60-$1.25   *Children's Menu:* $2.99-$3.49

Food Specialties: BBQ Chicken, Chicken Shish Kebob, Broiled Fish, Deli

> *Description:* Poultry served every which way (no surprise here), but fish and
> deli meat, as well. The kid's menu includes French fries & soda.
> Sandwich platters come with two side dishes and a roll or muffin.

> *Comments:* Fast food with the emphasis on poultry and fish, instead of beef.
> Many side dishes to choose from. For the coming year, plans are on the
> drawing board to extend the menu to include Chinese food.

Ambiance (Decor): Opened in 1998, this newest member of the chain is already
planning to improve upon their already winning formula. At this printing, it
remains a family friendly, cafeteria style, fast food restaurant (similar to the
Kenny Rogers / Boston Market restaurant chains). Colorful, modern, well-lit,
child oriented eatery. But no paper or Styrofoam here, you eat on regular dishes.
Seats 40 people.

Service: Self-serve

General Comments: Answers the question of where to take young children for a
meal, where they will be welcome and can dine in a relatively tension free
environment which grownups can enjoy, as well. Expect a large crowd at
lunchtime.

Hours: **Sun-Thurs:** 11am-9:00pm
     Fri: 10am-2pm (Winter) or 4pm (Summer) **<u>Saturday Closed</u>**

Credit Cards Accepted: MC, Visa, Discover

Restaurant Discount: 10% Off Platters Only Excluding Lunch Specials & Buffets

County: Nassau (**Long Island**)
Town: Great Neck

The Authoritative New York City Kosher Dining Guide

Restaurant: Colbeh

Phone Number: (516) 466-8181
Fax: (212) 354-8184

Address: 75 North Station Plaza

Hechsher: ב-K (Glatt Kosher, Masgiach Temidi)

Proprietor/Manager: Pejman (Manager)

Type(s) of Food: Meat - Persian

Price Range:

	Lunch	Dinner	Take out
Entrées:	$10.50-$18.50	$12.50-20.50	$9.50-$19.50 Delivery Avail.
Desserts:	$4.50	**Sandwiches:**	$5.50-$11.50 (Lunch Only)
Drinks:	$2-$2.50, $5/gl (House Wine), $18-$28/btl (Wine), $6/gl (Mix Drks)		

Food Specialties: Beef, Veal, Chicken, Turkey & Fresh Fish Kabobs, Stews

Description: A large assortment of appetizers, consisting of various salads, are prepared with a Persian slant. The standard variety of kabobs is expanded to include fresh salmon and white fish. Persian rice (chelo) and tomato accompany the entrées, which are most often marinated and char-broiled. The three stews all feature beef, cubed or in chunks, combined with vegetables uniquely seasoned Persian style and served with chelo (rice). Full bar.

Comments: Review to follow. Refer to Manhattan Colbeh for comments.

Ambiance (Decor): Anchored in the base of the Great Neck Hotel (also accessible through the lobby), this attractive restaurant offers a separate lounge area with a full bar (6 stools), banquettes, tables, and chairs. Both areas are decorated in a pink and green color scheme. Dimly lit and accented by neon lights, wall mirrors, hanging plants, and carpeting, the rooms have a sophisticated informality that would suit most occasions, though tables are dressed up a bit with white tablecloths, linen napkins, and candles. Both rooms seat 180.

Service: Standard

General Comments: Situated across the street from the LIRR station and in a hotel, the restaurant caters to residents and visitors alike. Attractive mealtime setting.

Hours: **Sun-Thurs:** 12pm-10:30pm   **Friday Closed**
 Sat: Opens 1 hr after Shabbos till 12am

Credit Cards Accepted: MC, Visa, AmEx, Discover, Diners Club

Restaurant Discount: 5% Off

County: Nassau **(Long Island)**
Town: Great Neck

The Authoritative New York City Kosher Dining Guide

Restaurant: Kensington Kosher Delicatessen   **Phone Number:** (516) 487-2410
Fax: None
Address: 27A Middle Neck Road (bet. Cutter Mill Rd. - Grace Ave.)

Hechsher: NO HECHSHER - RESTAURANT IS OPEN 7 DAYS A WEEK

Proprietor/Manager: Paul

Type(s) of Food: Meat - Deli

Price Range: **Lunch**   **Dinner**   **Take out**
    Entrées: $11 (Platters)   Same   Same – Delivery Min. $75.00
    Desserts: $1.75-$2.00   **Sandwiches:** $5-$10
    Drinks: $1.10-$1.40   **Soups:** $1.50-$2.50

Food Specialties: Deli Sandwiches, Soups, Deli Platters

    Description: A menu limited to deli sandwiches, platters and homemade soups. The deli meats, corned beef and tongue are home pickled. Everything is à la carte.

    Comments: The menu is short and to the point.

Ambiance (Decor): A sandwich shop described as warm and cozy. Wood plank paneling lends a countrified air. Seating for 22 is divided between booths and counter.

Service: Self-serve

General Comments: Small and unassuming sandwich shop.

Hours: **Sun-Sat:** 9am-6pm - RESTAURANT IS OPEN 7 DAYS A WEEK

Credit Cards Accepted: MC, Visa, AmEx, Diners Club

Restaurant Discount:

County: Nassau **(Long Island)**
Town: Great Neck

The Authoritative New York City Kosher Dining Guide

Restaurant: Shish-Kabob Palace

Phone Number: (516) 487-2228
Fax: (516) 466-1414

Address: 90 Middle Neck Road

Hechsher: Vaad Harabonim of Queens (Mashgiach Temidi, Glatt Kosher)

Proprietor/Manager: Gil, Avi

Type(s) of Food: Meat - Middle Eastern

Price Range:	*Lunch*	*Dinner*	*Take out*
Entrées:	$13.95-$17.95	Same	Same - Delivery Available
Desserts:	$2.00-$2.50	*Deli Sandwiches:* $6.95	
Drinks:	$ 1.00-2.50	$2.50-$3.00 (Beer)	*In A Pita:* $2.50-$6.95

Food Specialties: Shish Kabob, Shawarma, Grills, BBQ Chicken, Salads, Falafel

Description: Chicken, turkey, veal, and beef kabobs, BBQ Chicken, Sweetbread, Shawarma, Schnitzel, Romanian Steak, Lamb Chops, Rib Steak, Broiled Filet of Flounder, and a Vegetarian Special make up the entrées, which come with rice, salad and fries or are served in a pita with Israeli salad and techina. Appetizers (14) consist mostly of Mid Eastern salads. 5 soups reflect more universal Jewish tastes. The 7 sides include knishes, latkes, and rice pilaf. 5 desserts include Baklava & Napoleons.

Comments: A respectable array of Middle Eastern specialties that include enough variety to cater to a range of tastes.

Ambiance (Decor): Renovation is ongoing, though the restaurant remains open for business. Seating will increase from the current 20 to 40. The existing counter in the rear, will soon find itself in the middle of the restaurant, surrounded by tables. Minimal decor with laminate tables and chrome backed chairs. Mirrored walls and fluorescent lighting result in a brightly lit room.

Service: Standard

General Comments: Open for nine years and soon to double its capacity, this restaurant is apparently doing something right. On our list for a future visit.

Hours: **Sun-Thurs:** 11am-11pm **Fri:** 11am-2 hrs before Shabbos
Sat: 1 hr after Shabbos till 1am

Credit Cards Accepted: MC, Visa

Restaurant Discounts: 10% Off With Minimum $20 Order

County: Nassau **(Long Island)**
Town: Great Neck

The Authoritative New York City Kosher Dining Guide

Restaurant: La Pizzeria / Sushi Metsuyan

Phone Number: (516) 466-5114
Fax: (516) 466-3248

Address: 114 Middle Neck Road

Hechsher: Vaad Hakashrus of Queens

Proprietor/Manager: Ofer

Type(s) of Food: Dairy - Italian , Japanese

Price Range: *Italian*   *Japanese*   *Take out*
   Entrées: $5.50-$7.75 **Combo:** $9.95-$16.95   Same- Delivery Available
   Desserts: $1.75 **Sumanki:** $3.25-$4.75 (6 pc) **Temaki:** $2.75-$3.75/ea
   Drinks: $ .80-$2.50 **Specialty Rolls:** $4.75-$7.50 (6 pc)

Food Specialties: Pizza, Italian, Israeli Salad, Sushi, Maki, Temaki, Nigiri, Sumanki

Description: A odd marriage of two distinct and very different menus. The
pizzeria menu has the standard Italian specialties. Includes the addition
of falafel, chummus, techina Israeli and Greek salads. Along with the
calzones, you'll also find pastas, panini, burekas, home made soup, etc.
18", Stuffed and Midget Pan Pizzas present options. The "Japanese"
Specialty rolls are named after Israeli cities and offer original
combinations of salmon or tuna served raw, smoked, or grilled with a
variety of vegetables. Miso soup and Japanese salad are also available.

Comments: Untried by us, but, judging by the crowd of satisfied customers the
food appears to please. An odd combination of food, but no one is
complaining.

Ambiance (Decor): With its terra cotta, gray and white color scheme, mirrors, tiled
floor and marble topped tables, this attractive eatery looks more like a café than
a pizzeria. The lighting is bright, but without the glare. A pleasant and
apparently clean setting for casual dining. Accommodates 40.

Service: Self-serve

General Comments: This 7 year old eatery apparently caters to its clientele.

Hours: **Sun-Thurs:** 10am-10pm **Fri:** 10am-2½ hrs before Shabbos
   Sat: ¼ hr after Shabbos till 1:30am

Credit Cards Not Accepted: CASH ONLY!

Restaurant Discounts:

County: Nassau **(Long Island)**
Town: Great Neck

The Authoritative New York City Kosher Dining Guide

Restaurant: Darband

Phone Number: (516) 829-0030
Fax: (516) 829-0064

Address: 158 Middle Neck Road

Hechsher: OK Labs (Glatt Kosher, Mashgiach Temidi)

Proprietor/Manager: Zareh (Manager)

Type(s) of Food: Meat - Persian

Price Range: Lunch(Specials)   Dinner   Take out
Entrées: $9.95-$10.95 $11.95-$36.95   Same - Delivery Available
Desserts: $4.00   Lunch Sandwich Specials: $7   ($15 Min)
Drinks: $1.50-$3.50 $4/gl, $25/btl (House Wine), $5-$6/gl (Mix Drink)

Food Specialties: Chelo Kebab Sultani, Joojeh Kebab, Khoresht Gormeh Sabzi

Description: Entrées consist of assorted kebobs, usually beef (sometimes
ground), fowl, in the form of Cornish hens or chicken breasts; and Catch
of the Day. The standard sides are Chelo (Persian style rice) with a
grilled tomato. Other sides are additional and feature interesting
combinations of beans, vegetables, and occasionally fruit. The two soup
choices change seasonally. Appetizers (5) include favorites like
Babaganoush, Chummus, and Dolmeh (stuffed grape leaves.) Salads (4)
range from a simple tossed green salad (Salad Fasi) to Salad Olivieh, a
potato salad prepared with chicken and eggs. Desserts tend to be sweet.

Comments: The dishes and rice have very interesting combinations of spices.

Ambiance (Decor): The spacious, modern, and elegant interior gives no hint of the
ethnicity of the food served. Its 240 seats are divided into two rooms, so that
private parties can be accommodated, even while the restaurant is open to the
public. Semi-formal/formal attire depends on the occasion. Fully stocked bar.

Service: Standard

General Comments: Open for seven years, this restaurant enjoys such popularity that
it necessitates making advance Sunday reservations for groups of 6 or more.

Hours: Sun: 11am-11:30pm   Mon-Thurs: L: 12pm-3:30pm D: 5pm-11pm
Fri: 11am-3pm/4pm   Sat: 1 hr hour after Shabbos till 1am

Credit Cards Accepted: MC, Visa, AmEx, Discover

Restaurant Discount: 15% Off Excluding Specials

County: Nassau **(Long Island)**
Town: Great Neck

The Authoritative New York City Kosher Dining Guide

Restaurant: Hunan of Great Neck

Phone Number: (516) 482-7912
Fax: Same

Address: 507 Middle Neck Road

Hechsher: Vaad Harabonim of Queens

Proprietor/Manager: Charlie

Type(s) of Food: Meat - Chinese

Price Range: *Lunch*   *Dinner*   *Take out*
   Entrées: $8.50-21.95 $12.95-$21.95   Same- Free Local Delivery Avail.
   Desserts: $3.50-$4.00   *Luncheon Special:* $8.50 (Mon-Fri)
   Drinks: $1.50   *Peking Duck (For 2):* $46.00

Food Specialties: General Tso's Chicken, Happy Couple, Beef & Chicken Imperial

Description: A standard offering of chicken, beef, veal, duck and fish Chinese favorites. 6 health dishes feature "diet" chicken or vegetarian selections. To appease American palates, New York Rib Steak can be ordered as well as the oriental frank, or French fries. For those with a yen for Japanese, teriyaki chicken or steak is available as is beef negi maki. The Luncheon Special (not served on holidays or Sundays) includes an egg roll, soup (choice of 3) and entrée (choice of 12).

Comments: A well rounded menu with plenty to choose from.

Ambiance (Decor): A modern, American styled decor characterizes this family oriented restaurant. With its 140 seat capacity it can be sectioned off to allow for parties. Described as "expensive looking," which I expect means upscale in nature, it provides a formal table setting and service, in an attractive surroundings suitable for most occasions. Casual/semi-formal.

Service: Standard

General Comments: Check our next edition.

Hours: **Mon-Thurs:** 12pm-10:30pm   **Friday Closed**
     Sat: 1 hr after Shabbos till 1am   **Sun:** 12pm-11pm

Credit Cards Accepted: MC, Visa, AmEx

Restaurant Discount:

The Authoritative New York City Kosher Dining Guide

La Pizzeria   *Tel:* (516) 466-5114
114 Middle Neck Road
Vaad Harabonim of Queens

Great Neck / Roya Kosher Pizza   *Tel:* (516) 829-2660
770 Middle Neck Road
Vaad Harabonim of Queens

The Authoritative New York City Kosher Dining Guide

your key to unlocking
the world of fine
kosher dining in
New York City
Long Island, & Westchester.
You enjoy using it...
your friend, loved one,
associate, or client
would love it too!

Yonkers
New Rochelle

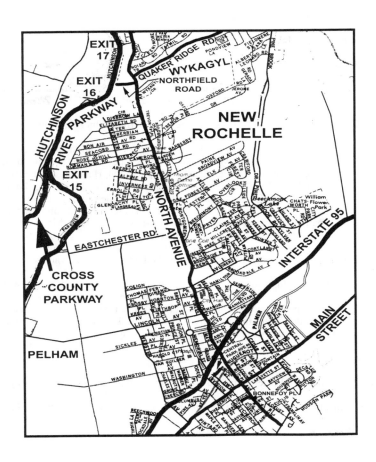

The Authoritative New York City Kosher Dining Guide

Restaurant: Epstein Bros.   *Phone Number:* (914) 793-3131
   Fax: (914) 793-1787
Address: 2574 Central Park Avenue (Off North Ave., opp. Pathmark Super Center)

Hechsher: NO HECHSHER - RESTAURANT IS OPEN 7 DAYS A WEEK

Proprietor/Manager: Seymore Epstein

Type(s) of Food: Meat - Deli

Price Range: *Lunch*   *Dinner*   *Take out*
   Entrées: $4.75-$4.95 (Special) $8.50-$12.50   Same – Delivery Available
   Desserts: $ .95-$1.95   *Sandwiches:* $5.95-$8.95   *Dinners:* $11-$14.45
   Drinks: $ .85-$1.75, $2.25-$2.50 (Beer), $2/gl (Wine) *Kids Menu:* $5-$6

Food Specialties: Deli Sandwiches, Shepherd Pie, Grilled Chicken, Blintzes

   Description: A fairly comprehensive menu that covers all the bases. Beyond the
      traditional Jewish favorites are American specialties including Southern
      Fried Chicken, Chicken Pot Pie, Shepherd Pie, Hamburgers, and BBQ
      Chicken. The Middle East is not neglected either with falafel, chummus,
      and pita sandwiches. Complete Dinners include soup, entrée, dessert, and
      coffee or tea. The Luncheon Specials change daily and come with soup,
      entrée, hot coffee or tea, but no dessert. The Children's Menu is for kids
      up to 10 years old. Early Bird Specials, too!

   Comments: A menu with much to offer, both in specials and variety.

Ambiance (Decor): Just moved across the street a year ago, from where they were in
      business for 26 years, so everything is new. Red and gray booths and regular
      laminate topped tables, provide seating for 90. The proverbial glass display/take-
      out counter dominates the entry area. The red, black, and gray color scheme sets
      off the pictures that hang above each table that lines a wall. Informal.

Service: Standard

General Comments: Epstein family owned & operated restaurants for over 30 years.

Hours: Sun- Fri: 9am-9pm   Sat: 9am-10pm - RESTAURANT IS OPEN 7 DAYS
   A WEEK
Credit Cards Accepted: MC, Visa, AmEx

Restaurant Discount:

County: Westchester
Town: New Rochelle

The Authoritative New York City Kosher Dining Guide

Restaurant: Sammy's New York Bagels   *Phone Number:* (914) 235-7800
                                               Fax: (914) 472-9618
Address: 134 North Avenue (bet. Bonnefoy Pl. - Union St.)
                          (2 blocks South of Main Street)
Hechsher: Vaad Hakashruth of the Westchester Rabbinical Council
                          - RESTAURANT IS OPEN 7 DAYS A WEEK
Proprietor/Manager: Arthur Turkel

Type(s) of Food: Dairy, Parve - American

Price Range: *Lunch*   *Dinner*   *Take out*
    Entrées: $4.00-$6.00   None   Same – Local Delivery Avail. ($15 Min.)
    Desserts: $1.00-$1.50   *Bagel Sandwiches:* $4-$6   *Soups:* $2.99
    Drinks: $1.80   *Muffins:* $1.45-$1.75

Food Specialties: Bagel Sandwiches, Soups, Muffins, Fish, Crepes, Veggie Burgers

   Description: A diverse fast food/take-out menu centered around the bagel. It
      seems that these bagels are a whopping 5½ oz and when coupled with
      either a veggie burger, fried fish, salad, or one of 11 different toppings,
      they make a hardy meal. There is a selection of cholov Yisroel cheeses, 20
      different muffins, and assorted pastry. All baked goods, including challah,
      are homemade and parve. Some salads are, tuna, babaganoush, pasta &
      white fish. Beverages include fresh squeezed orange juice & 4 coffees.

   Comments: A light lunchtime menu.

Ambiance (Decor): Black & white tiles provide the backdrop for the eating area. 10
      seats and an additional 6 outside during warm weather. **NOTE:** Establishment
      does not have a bathroom for customer use.

Service: Self-service

General Comments: Everything on a bagel plus! Not a huge menu, but enough to keep
      you munching happily. For a light mid-day meal.

Hours: Sun: 6am-3pm **Mon-Fri:** 6am-5pm **Sat:** 6am-4pm
      - RESTAURANT IS OPEN 7 DAYS A WEEK

Credit Cards Not Accepted: CASH ONLY!

Restaurant Discount:

277

County: Westchester
Town: New Rochelle

The Authoritative New York City Kosher Dining Guide

Restaurant: Wykagyl Glatt Kosher Delicatessen   *Phone Number:* (914) 636-4381
                                                  Fax: (914) 636-6251
Address: 1305 North Avenue (off Northfield Rd.)

Hechsher: Vaad Harabonim of Westchester (Glatt Kosher, Mashgiach Temidi)

Proprietor/Manager: Michael

Type(s) of Food: Meat – Deli, Chinese, Middle Eastern

Price Range: *Lunch*   *Dinner*   *Take out*
   Entrées: $10.95-$17.95   Same   Same
   Desserts: $1.95-$3.50   *Deli Sandwiches:* $6.45-$14 *Kid's Menu:* $6
   Drinks: $ .75-$1.50 $2.50 (Beer), $3.50/gl (Wine)

Food Specialties: Deli, Rumanian Steak, Shish Kebabs, Prime Rib, Chopped Liver

   Description: 3 menus in one. Complete deli menu brings you homemade
      pastrami, corned beef, and "Old Fashioned Favorites" like Hungarian
      Goulash, Grand Street Brisket, and Boiled Beef Flanken in a Pot. The
      Chinese menu offers a respectable variety of Chicken (14), Beef (15),
      and Veal (11) favorites. From the Grill harbors the Middle Eastern dishes
      with selections such as Beef Cous-cous, Kabobs, and the Shawarma
      Platter, along with the burgers, steaks, and BBQ Spare Ribs. Dieters are
      accommodated with the Wykagyl Lite selections offering: falafel,
      chummus, and techina, along with various salads and vegetarian meats.
      Soups, Appetizers, Omelets, Fish Platters complete the picture.

   Comments: Something for everyone.

Ambiance (Decor): Traditional deli in a modern setting. The obligatory hanging
   salamis share space with hanging plants. It is light, bright and casual for family
   dining with seating for 60. Washable surfaces make for child friendly milieu.

Service: Standard

General Comments: A Glatt Kosher deli in Westchester, a rare commodity!

Hours: **Sun-Thurs:** 10am-9pm **Fri:** 10am-3pm **Saturday Closed**

Credit Cards Accepted: MC, Visa, AmEx

Restaurant Discount: 10% Off Only For Dining In

278

County: Westchester
Town: New Rochelle

The Authoritative New York City Kosher Dining Guide

Restaurant: Prime Time Kosher Cafe   **Phone Number:** (914) 654-1646
                                         Fax: None

Address: 1315 North Avenue (off Quaker Mill Rd.)

Hechsher: Vaad Hakashruth of the Westchester Rabbinical Council

Proprietor/Manager: Paul

Type(s) of Food: Dairy – Italian, Middle Eastern

Price Range: **Lunch**   **Dinner**   **Take out**
    Entrées: $6.25-$12.95   Same   Same – Delivery Avail. At Times
    Desserts: $2.25   **Dinner Specials:** $9.95   **Kids:** $2.45-$4.95
    Drinks: $1.00-$1.75, $2 (Espresso), $2.75 (Cappuccino)

Food Specialties: Eggplant Parmegian, Primavera, Pizza, Falafel, Penne alla Vodka

> **Description:** Fresh fish (fillet of Sole, Salmon Steak, etc.) have been off the
> menu for a while, but will soon be making a comeback. Eggplant dishes
> are very popular with local regulars. Currently, there are 4 homemade
> soups which are made only with fresh vegetables. The French Onion
> Soup, another popular choice, comes gratinée. Pasta has a large presence
> with items like ravioli, lasagna, fettuccini, etc. Veggie burgers and salads
> offer low fat, low cholesterol choices. Only filtered water is used. Cholov
> Yisroel cheeses are used in most of the dishes (pizzas, parmigian, etc.) but
> not in all.

> **Comments:** A varied menu with a concern for freshness and health.

Ambiance (Decor): The eatery is on the small side with 3 booths and 3 tables, with
    combined seating of 18. Contemporary, in blue and gray, the emphasis is on clean
    lines as well as cleanliness. Tiffany lamps over each table provide lighting in
    tandem with incandescent high hats. Art work, often of landscapes or animals
    from a local artist, is displayed on the walls and is for sale. Informal.

Service: Standard

General Comments: There is no bathroom here, but one is accessible next door.

Hours: Sun-Thurs: 12pm-8pm   **Fri:** 12pm-3pm   **Sat:** 1 hr after Shabbos till 10pm

Credit Cards Accepted: MC, Visa

Restaurant Discount:

County: Westchester
Town: New Rochelle

The Authoritative New York City Kosher Dining Guide

Restaurant: Eden Wok

Phone Number: (914) 637-9363
Fax: (914) 637-9371

Address: 1327 North Avenue (Off Quaker Ridge Rd.)

Hechsher: Vaad Hakashrus of Westchester (Glatt Kosher, Mashgiach Temidi)

Proprietor/Manager: Kevin

Type(s) of Food: Meat – Chinese, Sushi

Price Range: | *Lunch* (11am-3pm) *Dinner* *Take out*
Entrées: $5.95 (Special) $10.95-$16.95 Same – Free Local Del ($18 Min)
Desserts: None *Lunch Specials:* $5.95 *Sushi:* $6 (3 pcs.)
Drinks: $1.00-$1.25 *Sushi or Temaki Rolls:* $ 3-$4/ea.

Food Specialties: General Tso's Chicken, Sesame Chicken, Fong Wong Gai, Sushi

Description: There are the usual selections of beef, chicken, and veal, as well as Chow Mein, Chow Fun, Combination Platters, and 17 Chef Specialties like Beef & Chicken Imperial, Champagne Chicken, and Tea Smoked Duck. You'll find Mock Shrimp dishes and 12 choices of Diet Gourmet (steamed food, no salt, oil or corn starch served w/ white rice). Most dishes are served with white rice. For fried or brown rice add $ .50. The Japanese Salads (e.g. mock shrimp, crab) Sushi, Rolls, Temaki and the large Specialty Rolls (cut in pieces) make up a respectable presentation of Japanese favorites. The Lunch Special includes fried rice, a choice of 3 soups or egg roll, and entrée selection.

Comments: Nicely stocked menu with enough variety to satisfy most.

Ambiance (Decor): This new restaurant makes its Oriental statement in brick and wood. Faux windows, wood tables contribute to the final effect. 30 seats.

Service: Standard

General Comments: A new addition to the thin but growing ranks of Westchester Glatt eateries.

Hours: **Sun-Thurs:** 11am-10pm **Fri:** 11am-2 hrs before Shabbos
Sat: 1 hr after Shabbos till 12pm

Credit Cards Accepted: MC, Visa, AmEx

Restaurant Discount:

Scarsdale
Ardsley
Hartsdale
White Plains

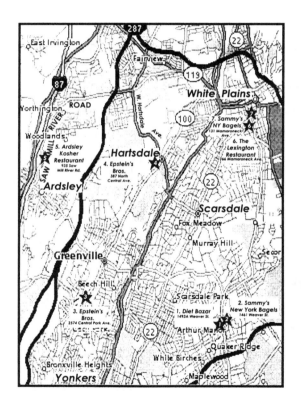

County: Westchester
Town: Scarsdale

The Authoritative New York City Kosher Dining Guide

Restaurant: Sammy's New York Bagels

Phone Number: (914) 472-0500
Fax: (914) 472-6918

Address: 1461 Weaver Street

Hechsher: Vaad Hakashruth of the Westchester Rabbinical Council
– RESTAURANT IS OPEN 7 DAYS A WEEK

Proprietor/Manager: Arthur Turker

Type(s) of Food: Dairy, Parve - American

Price Range:

	Lunch	Dinner	Take out	
Entrées:	$4.00-$6.00	None	Same – Local Delivery ($15 Min.)	
Desserts:	$1.00-$1.50	Bagel Sandwiches: $4-$6	Soups: $2.99	
Drinks:	$1.80	Muffins: $1.45-$1.75		

Food Specialties: Bagel Sandwiches, Soups, Fish Salads, Babaganoush

   Description: A diverse fast food/take-out menu centered around the bagel. It
      seems that these bagels are a whopping 5½ oz., and when coupled with
      one of 11 different toppings and salads, they make a hardy meal. There are
      also a selection of Cholov Yisroel cheeses, 20 different muffins, and
      assorted pastries offered. All baked goods including challah are
      homemade and parve. Up to 4 varieties of hot soup offered. Some salads
      are, tuna, babaganoush, pasta & white fish. Beverages include fresh
      squeezed orange juice & 4 coffees.

   Comments: Everything on a bagel plus! Not a huge menu, but enough to keep
      you munching happily for some time.

Ambiance (Decor): One could argue convincingly that this eatery is not strictly a
   restaurant, if that designation is reserved for sit-down establishments only. Eating
   here is done solely at counters. Accommodation is for 5 or 6 people.

Service: Self-serve

General Comments: Take-out is the focus here, good for lunch or a quick bite.

Hours: Sun: 6am-3pm   Mon-Fri: 6am-5pm   Sat: 6am-4pm
            – RESTAURANT IS OPEN 7 DAYS A WEEK
Credit Cards Not Accepted: CASH ONLY!

Restaurant Discount:

County: Westchester

Town: Scarsdale

The Authoritative New York City Kosher Dining Guide

Restaurant: Diet Bazaar Kosher Chicken Store   *Phone Number:* (914) 472-2888
                                                  Fax: (914) 472-2878

Address: 1493A Weaver Street (bet. Heathcote - Grossway)

Hechsher: NO HECHSHER

Proprietor/Manager: Barbara

Type(s) of Food: Meat – Jewish American

Price Range: *Lunch*   *Dinner*   *Take out*
    Entrées: $5.00-$7.00   Same   Same – Delivery Available
    Desserts: $2.00   *Dinner Special for 4:* $12.99
    Drinks: None

Food Specialties: Roast & Rotisserie Chicken, BBQ Chicken, Hot Wings, Turkey

   Description: Poultry is the mainstay, but occasionally items like brisket are
   offered. Typical chicken dishes include Lemon & Herb, Chicken Nuggets,
   Chicken Tenders, Cornish Hens (made to order), etc. Desserts include
   baked apple and packaged cookies and pastry. Empire poultry is used
   exclusively.

   Comments: More of a takeout menu than anything else. Beverages are sold in a
   neighboring establishment. Food is sold by the pound.

Ambiance (Decor): 15 seats are available between the counter seating and the tables
   and chairs located in the enclosed arcade of the Colonial Village Shopping
   Center. Informal dining is assured.

Service: Self-serve

General Comments: Calling Diet Bazaar a restaurant is a stretch, but still eating on the
   premises is an option.

Hours: Sun: 11am-5pm   **Mon-Thurs:** 10am-7pm   **Fri:** 10am-2 hrs before Shabbos
   Saturday Closed

Credit Cards Accepted: MC, Visa

Restaurant Discount:

County: Westchester
Town: Ardsley

The Authoritative New York City Kosher Dining Guide

Restaurant: Ardsley Kosher Restaurant

Phone Number: (914) 693-2232
Fax: None

Address: 935 Saw Mill River Road

Hechsher: NO HECHSHER – RESTAURANT IS OPEN 7 DAYS A WEEK

Proprietor/Manager: Mick

Type(s) of Food: Meat – Deli, Middle Eastern

Price Range: **Lunch** (12pm-4pm)   **Dinner**   **Take out**
  Entrées: $4.99-$5.95 (Special) $9.95-$11.95   Same – Free Local Delivery
  Desserts: $1.95   **Dinner Specials:** $7.95-$9.95   **Early Bird:** 10% Off
  Drinks: $ .85-$1.30   **Kids Menu:** $5-$6   **Sandwiches:** $6.35-$9.95

Food Specialties: Deli Sandwiches, Stuffed Cabbage, Chicken Piccata, Grills, Steaks

> **Description:** As you would expect, deli sandwiches are the tour de force, but they share stage time with the homemade knishes, Babaganosh, Shish Kabob, Falafel, Koufta, Chummus, Tabulah Salad, Flanken in a Pot, etc. All baked goods are homemade, as are the soups and cooked dishes.

> **Comments:** An old fashioned, traditional deli plays host to Middle Eastern specialties and finds culinary happiness.

Ambiance (Decor): The split nature of the menu is evident in the décor. On one hand a typical deli, while on the other hand, Middle Eastern vases and other artifacts hint at a Middle Eastern character. Informal for family dining with laminate tables and 90 seats.

Service: Standard

General Comments: A lone outpost for kosher dining in Ardsley.

Hours: **Sun-Sat:** 9:30am-9pm - RESTAURANT IS OPEN 7 DAYS A WEEK

Credit Cards Accepted: MC, Visa, Discover

Restaurant Discount:

County: Westchester
Town: Hartsdale

The Authoritative New York City Kosher Dining Guide

Restaurant: Epstein Bros.   *Phone Number:* (914) 428-5320
                                     Fax: (914) 428-9668
Address: 387 North Central Avenue (bet. Alexander Ave. - Dalewood Dr.)

Hechsher: NO HECHSHER - RESTAURANT IS OPEN 7 DAYS A WEEK

Proprietor/Manager: Seymore Epstein

Type(s) of Food: Meat - Deli

Price Range: *Lunch*   *Dinner*   *Take out*
  Entrées: $4.75-$4.95 (Special) $8.50-$12.50   Same – Delivery Available
  Desserts: $ .95-$1.95 *Sandwiches:* $5.95-$8.95   *Dinners:* $11-$14.45
  Drinks: $ .85-$1.75, $2.25-$2.50 (Beer), $2/gl (Wine) *Kids Menu:* $5-$6

Food Specialties: Deli Sandwiches, Shepherd Pie, Grilled Chicken, Blintzes

> *Description:* A fairly comprehensive menu that covers all the bases. Beyond the
> traditional Jewish favorites, however, American specialties include
> Southern Fried Chicken, Chicken Pot Pie, Shepherd Pie, Hamburgers, and
> BBQ Chicken. The Middle East is not neglected either with falafel,
> chummus and pita sandwiches. Complete Dinners include soup, entrée,
> dessert, and coffee or tea. The Luncheon Specials changes daily and come
> with soup, entrée, hot coffee or tea, but no dessert. The Children's Menu is
> for kids up to 10 years old. Early Bird Specials, too!

> *Comments:* A menu with much to offer both in specials and in variety.

Ambiance (Decor): At this location for over 30 years. Booths, and laminate topped
  tables, provide seating for 140. The proverbial glass display/take-out counter
  dominates the entry area. Informal.

Service: Standard

General Comments: This is one of three Epstein family owned and operated restaurants
  in Westchester and Long Island. In business for over 30 years, they apparently
  know what they are doing.

Hours: **Sun-Fri:** 9am-9pm **Sat:** 9am-10pm - RESTAURANT IS OPEN 7 DAYS
                                                   A WEEK
Credit Cards Accepted: MC, Visa, AmEx

Restaurant Discount:

285

County: Westchester
City: White Plains

The Authoritative New York City Kosher Dining Guide

Restaurant: The New Lexington Restaurant   *Phone Number:* (914) 682-7400
                                              Fax: (914) 682-0739
Address: 166 Mamaroneck Avenue (bet. Post Rd. - Maple Ave.)

Hechsher: Rabbis Reuven Flamer/Chaim Lebowitz (Glatt, Mashg Temi, Pas/Bishul Yis)

Proprietor/Manager: Paul

Type(s) of Food: Meat – Deli, Middle Eastern

Price Range:	*Lunch*	*Dinner*	*Take out*
Entrées:	$9.95-$14.95	$10.95-$22.95	Same – Delivery Available
Desserts:	$1.95-$3.95	*Deli Sandwiches:* $5.95-$12.95 (Hot Open)	
Drinks:	$1.00-$1.95	*Kids Menu:* $ 1.95-$4.95 + $2 (incl. Soda & Fries)	

Food Specialties: Deli Sandwiches, Knishes, Grills, Falafel, Salads, Soups, Burgers

Description: The Deli Sandwiches are featured, but the Entrées and Grills are
just as tempting. Entrées include diverse items such as poached or broiled
Salmon, Hungarian goulash, and pepper steak. From the grill one can
choose the PLT (roast beef or turkey w/ grilled pastrami, lettuce, tomato
on toast) BBQ Chicken or Southern Fried Chicken. Omelets are served
with fries and toast. Burgers (beef, turkey or veggie), with NYC Lower
East Side street names, are made to order and served in 7 different ways.
Middle Eastern salads and platters include falafel, Chummus,
Babaganoush, Turkish Eggplant Salad, and Israeli Salad.

Comments: A nice varied menu with all the usual favorites and then some.

Ambiance (Decor): The green and beige modern background is provided as a backdro
for Judaic paintings (for sale by Jewish Quarter) in this deli capable of
accommodating 100 diners at booths and tables. Typically, the deli display
counter dominates the entry. A second floor party room seats 40 –50 people.

Service: Standard

General Comments: Mincha Minyan: Mon-Thurs 1:30pm

Hours: Sun-Thurs: 10am-9pm **Fri:** 10am-2 or 4pm **Saturday Closed**

Credit Cards Accepted: MC, Visa, AmEx

Restaurant Discount: Full Dinner For The Price Of Any Entrée (+Tax+Tip)

The Authoritative New York City Kosher Dining Guide

Restaurant: Sammy's New York Bagels

Phone Number: (914) 683-1200
Fax: (914) 472-9618

Address: 131 Mamroneck Avenue

Hechsher: Vaad Hakashruth of the Westchester Rabbinical Council

Proprietor/Manager: Arthur Turker

Type(s) of Food: Dairy, Parve - American

Price Range:

	Lunch	Dinner	Take out	
Entrées:	$4.00-$6.00	None	Same – Local Delivery Avail. ($15 Min.)	
Desserts:	$1.00-$1.50	*Bagel Sandwiches:* $4-$6	*Soups:* $2.99	
Drinks:	$1.80	*Muffins:* $ 1.45-$1.75		

Food Specialties: Bagel Sandwiches, Soups, Muffins, Fish, Crepes, Veggie Burgers

> *Description:* A diverse fast food/take-out menu centered around the bagel. It
> seems that these bagels are a whopping 5½ oz. and when coupled with
> either a veggie burger, fried fish, salad or one of 11 different toppings,
> they make a hardy meal. There is a selection of cholov Yisroel cheeses, 20
> different muffins, 4 varieties of veggie burgers, 3 parve soups, and
> assorted pastry are offered. All baked goods including challah are
> homemade and parve. Some salads are, tuna, babaganoush, pasta, & white
> fish. Beverages include fresh squeezed orange juice & 4 coffees.

> *Comments:* Everything on a bagel plus! Not a huge menu, but enough to keep
> you munching happily for some time.

Ambiance (Decor): A designated dining area accommodates 20 people in this
combination take-out and eat-in sandwich shop. **NOTE:** There is no bathroom on
the premises.

Service: Self-serve

General Comments: Take-out is the focus here, good for lunch or a quick bite. The
only dairy eatery in town that closes on Shabbos.

Hours: **Sun:** 6am-3pm **Mon-Thurs:** 6am-5pm **Fri:** 5am- 2 hrs before Shabbos
Saturday Closed

Credit Cards Not Accepted: CASH ONLY!

Restaurant Discount:

Why take chances?

Have the all the information you need before you dine out!
Make informed decisions.

Mount Kisco

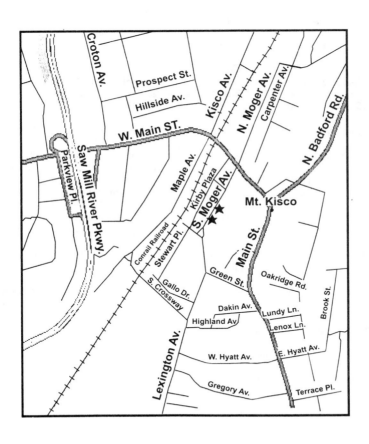

County: Westchester

Town: Mount Kisco

The Authoritative New York City Kosher Dining Guide

Restaurant: Sammy's New York Bagels

Phone Number: (914) 244-3456
Fax: (914) 472-9618

Address: 29½ South Moger Avenue (bet. West Main St. - Lexington Ave.)
(opposite train station)

Hechsher: Vaad Hakashruth of the Westchester Rabbinical Council
- RESTAURANT IS OPEN 7 DAYS A WEEK

Proprietor/Manager: Arthur Turkel

Type(s) of Food: Dairy, Parve - American

Price Range:

	Lunch	Dinner	Take out
Entrées:	$4.00-$6.00	None	Same – Local Delivery ($15 Min.)
Desserts:	$1.00-$1.50	*Bagel Sandwiches:* $4-$6	*Soups:* $2.99
Drinks:	$1.80	*Muffins:* $1.45-$1.75	

Food Specialties: Bagel Sandwiches, Soups, Fish Salads, Babaganoush

> *Description:* A diverse fast food/take-out menu centered around the bagel. It seems that these bagels are a whopping 5½ oz. and when coupled with one of 11 different toppings and salads, they make a hardy meal. There is also a selection of cholov Yisroel cheeses, 20 different muffins, and assorted pastry. All baked goods including challah are homemade and parve. Up to 4 varieties of hot soup offered. Some salads are: tuna, babaganoush, pasta, & white fish. Beverages include fresh squeezed orange juice & 4 coffees.

> *Comments:* Everything on a bagel plus! Not a huge menu, but enough to keep you munching happily for some time.

Ambiance (Decor): An appetizing store with mainly a take-out business with seating for 10 people who wish to eat in. **NOTE:** There is no bathroom on the premises.

Service: Self-serve

General Comments: Not another kosher dairy eatery for miles!

Hours: **Sun:** 6am-3pm **Mon-Fri:** 6am-5pm **Sat:** 6am-4pm
- RESTAURANT IS OPEN 7 DAYS A WEEK

Credit Cards Not Accepted: CASH ONLY!

Restaurant Discount:

The Authoritative New York City Kosher Dining Guide

Restaurant: Mt. Kisco Kosher Delicatessen *Phone Number:* (914) 666-6600
                                              Fax: (914) 666-6695
Address: 41 South Moger Avenue (bet. West Main St. - Lexington Ave.)
                                              (opposite train station)
Hechsher: NO HECHSHER - RESTAURANT IS OPEN 7 DAYS A WEEK

Proprietor/Manager: Zeev Bain

Type(s) of Food: Meat - Deli, some Middle Eastern

Price Range:	*Lunch*	*Dinner*	*Take out*
Entrées:	$10.95-$16.45	Same	Same
Desserts:	$1.95-$2.75	*Deli Sandwiches:*	$6.90-$11.75 (Hot Open)
Drinks:	$ .95-$2.50, $2.50-$3 (Beer), $3/gl, $10/½ $15/carafe (Wine)		

Food Specialties: Deli Sandwiches, Romanian Strip Steak, Roast Beef, Omelets

> *Description:* The traditional deli menu is expanded here to include a few Middle
> Eastern delicacies such as falafel, Techina, Babaganoush, Chummus,
> Eggplant and Israeli Salads. Dinners ($15-$20.45) include: appetizer or
> soup, entrée, dessert, and tea or coffee. Kisco signatures: The Kisco
> Dandy (eggs w/ corned beef, pastrami, & salami served with fries), The
> Kisco King (corned beef, pastrami, turkey, & roast beef topped with
> Russian dressing & coleslaw on club) and Kisco Nuggets (fried chicken
> nuggets with duck or BBQ sauce and lettuce, tomato & fries). Everything
> is homemade including the baked goods. Portions purported to be large.

> *Comments:* Complete assortment of deli favorites and then some.

Ambiance (Decor): Casual as you'd expect, this deli has the obligatory hanging
salamis and deli counter. Inviting atmosphere with child friendly surfaces:
laminate tables, tiled floor, and seating at booths or tables (for 96 people).

Service: Standard

General Comments: An old fashioned deli, which owner maintains is strictly kosher.

Hours: **Sun**: 9am-9pm **Mon-Thurs:** 10am-9pm **Fri-Sat:** 9am-10pm
        - RESTAURANT IS OPEN 7 DAYS A WEEK
        - CLOSED MAJOR JEWISH HOLIDAYS

Credit Cards Accepted: MC, Visa, AmEx, Discover, Diners Club

Restaurant Discount:

ORDER COUPON

COMPLETE YOUR SET OR ORDER ADDITIONAL COPIES

The Authoritative New York City Kosher Dining Guide

$19.95 per book.
Where applicable **add $1.60
New York State Sales Tax
($21.60 per book total).**
For Multiple Books to the
same address enclose
$18.00 per book. Where tax
applies **add $1.50 sales tax for a
total of $19.50 per book.**

The Authoritative Mid-Atlantic States Kosher Dining Guide

$14.95 per book.
Where applicable **add $1.23
New York State Sales Tax
($16.18 per book total).**
For Multiple Books to the
same address enclose
$13.50 per book. Where tax
applies **add $1.11 sales tax for a
total of $14.61 per book.**

The Authoritative Kosher Dining Set
(1 New York City + 1 Mid Atlantic States)

Please send **$31.50 per set. If New York State Sales Tax applies
add $3.00 for a total of $34.50 per set.**

NAME:_____

ADDRESS:_____

CITY:_____STATE:_____ZIP:_____

TEL:_____AMT. ENCLOSED:_____

QUANTITIES: NYC_____   MAS_____   SETS_____

SEND CHECKS TO:
BELA FLOM. PO BOX 201, BROOKLYN, NY 11235-0201

Ackerman, Rabbi Pesach	see American Fed. of Retail Kosher Butchers
Adler, Rabbi Zecharye	see KEHILAH
Aicenman, Rabbi Avraham	see Rabbi Avraham Aicenman
Applebaum, Rabbi Sidney	see Vaad Harabbanim of Flatbush
Auman, Rabbi Kenneth	see KEHILAH
Babad, Rabbi Yechiel	see Rabbi Yechiel Babad
Beck, Rabbi Samuel David	see Rabbi Samuel David Beck
Ben Chaim, Rabbi Eliyahu	see Rabbinical Council of the Sephardic Community of Queens
Berman, Rabbi William	see Commack Jewish Center
Bronstein, Rabbi Leonard	see Rabbi Leonard Bronstein
Brook, Rabbi Yossi	see Bais Din of Crown Heights
Burg, Rabbi Melvin	see Vaad Harabbanim of Flatbush
Cohen, Rabbi David	see KEHILAH
Cohen, Rabbi Harry	see Orthodox Kashruth Supervision Services
Cohn, Rabbi Chaim	see "KOF-K" Kosher Supervision
Edelstein, Rabbi Moshe	see K'hal Adath Jeshurun
Eckstein, Rabbi Abraham, B.	see Rabbi Abraham B. Eckstein
Elbaz, Rabbi Hananiah	see Sephardic Rabbinical Council of America
Felder, Rabbi Aharon	see "KOF-K" Kosher Supervision
Fischer, Rabbi Menachem	see Adas Yereim of Vienner
Fishelis, Rabbi Avraham	see Torah Union Kashrus Agency
Fishelis, Rabbi Shmuel	see Rabbi Shmuel Fishelis
Flamer, Rabbi Reuven	see Golbel Kosher Food Consultants
Friedman, Rabbi David	see Rabbi David Friedman
Garelik, Rabbi Levi	see Organized Kashruth Laboratories
Gelley, Rabbi Zachariah	see K'hal Adath Jeshurun
Genack, Rabbi Menachem	see Union of Orthodox Jewish Cong.
Glick, Rabbi Yitzchok	see Beth Din Hameyuchad L'inyonei Kashrus of the Central Rabbinical Cong.
Gornish, RabbiYisroel	see Khal Chizuk Hadas of Flatbush
Gruber, Rabbi Binyamin	see Rabbi Binyamin Gruber
Gulevsky, Rabbi Chaim Dov-Ber	see Rabbi Chaim Dov-Ber Gulevsky
Hager, Rabbi Shraga Fievish	see Rabbi Shagra Fievish Hager
Hecht, Rabbi Abraham B.	see Sephardic Rabbinical Council of America
Heinemann, Rabbi Moshe	see "Star-K" Kosher Certification
Herskowitz, Rabbi William	see Vaad Harashrus of Westchester
Horowitz, Rabbi Pinchos D.	see Certified Kosher Underwriters
Josephy, Rabbi Nachum Zvi	see Menora-K & Vaad Hakashrus Le'Mehadrin
Juravel, Rabbi Avraham	see Organized Kashruth Laboratories

Katz, Rabbi Avrohom D. HaCohan	see Kosher "K" Mehadrin Supervision
Katz, Rabbi Dovid	see Rabbi Dovid Katz
Kaufman, Rabbi Eliyahu	see Vaad Harabonim of Staten Island
Kelemer, Rabbi Yehudah	see Young Israel of West Hempstead
Krauz, Rabbi Dovid Shmuel	see Rabbi Shmuel Dovid Krauz
Kohn, Rabbi Chaim	see K'hal Adath Jeshurun
Lax, Rabbi Harry	see Agudas Hamashgichim
Levertov, Rabbi Dov Ber	see Bais Din of Crown Heights
Lebowitz, Rabbi Chaim	see Globel Kosher Food Consultants
Levy, Rabbi Don Yoel	see Organized Kashruth Laboratories
Lichtenstein, Rabbi Aaron Hirsh	see "KOF-K" Kosher Supervision
Lieberman, Rabbi Zvulen	see Vaad Harabbanim of Flatbush
Mendelson, Rabbi Shlomo	see Rabbi Shlomo Mendelson
Nasirov, Rabbi Yachov	see Rabbi Yachov Nazirov
Neiman, Rabbi Yaakov	see Midtown Board of Kashrus
Polin, Rabbi Milton	see Vaad Harabbanim of Flatbush
Pollak, Dr.Avrom	see "Star-K" Kosher Supervision
Raskin, Rabbi Aharon Leib	see Rabbi Aharon Leib
Reisman, Rabbi Yaakov	see Association for Reliable Kashruth
Reitzes, Rabbi Mendel	see Organized Kashruth Laboratories
Rosenbaum, Rabbi Yehuda	see "KOF-K" Kosher Supervision
Rosenblatt, Rabbi J.	see Vaad of Riverdale
Roth, Rabbi Amrum	see Rabbi Amrum Roth
Saffra, Rabbi Rafael	see "Tablet K"
Sanderowitz, Rabbi	see Rabbi Sanderowitz
Scheinerman, Rabbi Moshe	see KEHILAH
Schulson, Rabbi Charles	see Rabbi Charles Schulson
Schwartz, Rabbi Alan	see Midtown Board of Kashrus
Seruyah, Rabbi Benjamin	see Sephardic Rabbinical Council of America
Shapiro, Mordechai	see Kay Kosher Supervision
Shapiro, Solomon	see Kay Kosher Supervision
Shuman, Rabbi Eliyahu	see "Star-K" Kosher Certification
Skaist, Rabbi Eli	see Vaad Harabbanim of Flatbush
Sladowsky, Rabbi Y.A.	see Vaad Harabonim of Queens
Spivak, Rabbi Yaakov	see United Kosher Supervision
Sommer, Rabbi Nesanel	see Association for Reliable Kashruth
Steinberg, Rabbi Israel Mayer	see Rabbi Israel Mayor Steinberg
Taub, Rabbi Binyomin	see "KOF-K" Kosher Supervision
Teitelbaum, Rabbi Leizer	see Organized Kashruth Laboratories
Tartikover Rav	see Yechiel Babad
Ullman, Rabbi Shlomo	see Association for Reliable Kashruth
Wagner, Rabbi Feivel	see Vaad Harabonim of Queens
Yakarov, Rabbi Chaim	see Rabbi Chaim Yakarov

Hashgacha Directory

Adas Yereim of Vienner
31 Blauvelt Road, Monsey, NY 10952
Phone: (914) 426-1046

Agudas Hamashgichim
Kashruth Supervisors Union, The
1310 East 18th St., Bklyn, NY 11230
Phone: (718) 336-7231

American Federation of
Retail Kosher Butchers
Phone: (718) 264-0922

Assoc. for Reliable Kashruth (ARK)
4705 16th Ave., Bklyn, N.Y 11204
Phone: (516) 239-5306

Bais Din of Crown Heights
512 Montgomery St. Bklyn, NY 11225
Phone: (718) 773-5446

Beth Din Hameyuchad L'inyonei
Kashrus of the Central Rabbinical
Congress aka. CRC
85 Division Ave., Bklyn, N.Y. 11211
Phone: (718) 384-6765

Certified Kosher Underwriters
(Chuster Rav)
1310 48th St., Bklyn, NY 11219
Phone: (718) 436-7373

Commack JCC
83 Shirley Court, Commack, NY 11725
Phone: (516) 543-3311

Globel Kosher Food Consultants
648 Central Pk Ave, Scars. NY 10583
Phone: (914) 426-0897

Kay Kosher Supervision
73-09 136th St.
Kew Gardens Hills, NY 11367
Phone: (718) 263-1574

KEHILAH (קהילה)
990 E. 31st St., Bklyn, N.Y. 11210
Phone: (718) 951-0481

Kahal Addas Vishnitz
186 Hooper St., Bklyn, N.Y. 11219
Phone: (718) 387-1871

K'hal Adath Jeshurun (Breuer's)
85-93 Bennett Ave., N.Y., N.Y. 10033
Phone: (212)923-3582/(914)425-9089

Khal Chizuk Hadas of Flatbush
(Rabbi Yisroel Gornish)
1421 Avenue O, Bklyn, NY 11230
Phone: (718) 376-3755

KOF-K Kosher Supervision
1444 Queen Anne Rd,
Teaneck, New Jersey, 07666
Phone: (201) 837-0500

Kosher "K" Mehadrin Supervision
1259 40th Street, Bklyn, NY 11218
Phone: (718) 435-9779

Kosher Overseers Assoc of America
Phone: (212) 724-8663

L. Badatz Kashrut Sepharadi
144-35 71st Road,
Kew Gardens Hills, NY 11367
Phone: (718) 793-2886

Menora-K
P.O. Box 190048 Bklyn, NY 11219
Phone: (718) 854-8047

Midtown Board of Kashrus
131 W. 86th St., NY, NY 10024
Phone: (212) 724-2700

(OK) Organized Kashruth Labs
1372 Carroll St., Bklyn, N.Y. 11213
Phone: (718) 756-7500

Orthodox Kashruth Superv. Serv.
165 West 91 St. #6D, NY, NY 10024
Phone: (212) 724-8663

Rabbi Dr. Abraham B. Eckstein
Phone: (718) 224-0404

Rabbi Aharon Leib Raskin
71 Pierrpont St., Bklyn, NY 11201-2427
Phone/Fax: (718)596-0069

Rabbi Amrum Roth
Phone: (718) 438-6418

Rabbi Avraham Aicenman
Beeper: (917) 245-6083

Rabbi Berman
Phone: (516) 543-3311

Rabbi Binyamin Gruber
10 Adar Ct., Monsey, NY 10952
Phone/Fax: (914) 425-7516

Rabbi Chaim Yakarov
Phone: (718) 853-0070

Rabbi Charles Schulson
Phone: (718) 896-1212

Rabbi David Friedman
Phone: (718) 436-4397

Rabbi Dovid Katz
918 Avenue O, Bklyn., N.Y. 11230
Beeper: (917) 429-6206

Rabbi Israel Mayer Steinberg
Phone: (718) 232-4275

Rabbi Leonard Bronstein
Phone: (914) 668-1952, 8782

Rabbi Samuel David Beck
Phone: (718) 692-1945

Rabbi Sanderowitz
Kahal Addas Vishnitz
186 Hooper St., Bklyn., N.Y. 11219
Phone: (718) 387-1871

Rabbi Shlomo Mendelson
Phone: (718) 853-0020

Rabbi Shmuel Fishelis
Phone: (212) 228-2429

Rabbi Shmuel Dovid Krauz
227 Rutledge St., Bklyn., N.Y. 11211
Phone: (718) 388-5355

Rabbi Shraga Fievish Hager
1248 53rd St., Bklyn., N. Y. 11219
Phone: (718) 851-2266

Rabbi Yechiel Babad
(Tartikover Rav)
5209 19th Ave., Bklyn, N.Y. 11204
Phone: (718) 951-0952

Rabbi Yachov Nasirov
Phone: (718) 217-2437

Rabbinical Council of the
Sephardic Community of Queens
77-55 Vleigh Place
Kew Garden Hills, N.Y. 11367
Phone: (718) 380-0808

Sephardic Rabbinical Council of
America (Cong. Shaare Zion)
30 Lancaster Ave., Bklyn., N.Y. 11223
Phone: (718) 743-3141

"Star-K" Kosher Certification
11 Warren Road, Baltimore, MD 21208
Phone: (401) 484-4110

"Tablet K" Religious and
Kosher Supervision
Phone /Fax: (516) 569-9081

Torah Union Kashrus Agency
575 Grand St., Suite 204
New York, N.Y. 10002
Phone: (212) 674-1502

(OU) Union of Orthodox
Jewish Congregations
333 Seventh Ave., N. Y., N.Y. 10001
Phone: (212) 563-4000

United Kosher Supervision
P.O. Box 317, Monsey, N. Y. 10952
Phone: (914) 352-1010

Vaad Hakashrus Le'Mehadrin
(Torah-K) PO Box 190048
Bklyn, NY 11219
Phone: (718) 854-8047

Vaad Hakashrus of Westchester
55 Rudolph Terrace West
Yonkers, NY 10701
Phone: (914) 423-0871

Vaad Harabbanim of Flatbush
1575 Coney Island Ave.
Bklyn, N. Y. 11230
Phone: (718) 951-8585

Vaad Harabonim of Queens
90-45 Myrtle Ave., Glendale, N.Y. 11385
Phone / Fax: (718) 847-9206

Vaad Harabonim/Hakashrus of S. I.
835 Forest Hill Rd., S.I., N. Y. 10314
Phone: (718) 494-6700

Vaad of Riverdale
3700 Independence Avenue
Bronx, New York 10463
Phone: (718) 548-1850

Restaurant Index